Contents at a Glance

Table of Contents

Introduction

Welcome to *Cloud Computing For Dummies,* 2nd Edition. The cloud — public, private, and hybrid — has emerged as the most important transformation in computing in decades. The cloud is changing how organizations are planning to deliver services to their customers, suppliers, and partners. They're using cloud services to increase the pace of business and to offer new and innovative services.

The first edition of this book was written more than ten years ago, and everything has changed . Therefore, it is important to understand these changes so that you can take full advantage of the ways that the cloud can make your business successful.

About This Book

This book is designed provide you with an understanding of the underlying technologies that are defining the new generation of cloud services. This book explains how you should approach these technology changes and how developing a cloud strategy can lead to success.

We wrote this book to help you understand the nuances of cloud services and how they can help you transform your organization. We think this book will give you the context to make informed decisions.

No matter your goal in reading this book, we address the following issues to help you understand the hybrid cloud environment and the impact it can have on your business:

>> How to determine what types of workloads and data should move to the cloud based on compliance and security

>> When it's a good idea to use a single public cloud service or you should select several

>> What critical standards and approaches enable portability of workloads and data

>> How your IT organization can become a service provider to the business

>> What cloud management means in a multicloud environment

>> What you need to know about the economics of the cloud

We wrote this book to help you understand the nuances of cloud services and how they can help you transform your organization. We think the book gives you the context you need to make informed decisions.

Foolish Assumptions

Try as we might to be all things to all people, when it came to writing this book, we had to pick who we thought would be most interested in cloud computing. Here's who we think you are:

>> **You're smart.** You're no dummy, yet the topic of the cloud gives you an uneasy feeling; you can't quite get your head around it; and if you're pressed for a definition, you might try to change the subject.

>> **You're a businessperson who wants little or nothing to do with technology.** But you live in the 21st century, so you can't escape it. Everybody's saying, "It's all about moving to the hybrid and multicloud," so you think you'd better find out what they're talking about.

>> **You're an IT person who knows a heck of a lot about technology.** But the underlying technology is changing, and you need to understand the impact of those changes on your business. Each vendor presents new offerings that sound compelling. You need to understand what's available today and what's coming, and you need to understand how these technologies will affect your organization.

Whoever you are, welcome. We're here to help.

Icons Used in This Book

What's a For Dummies book without icons pointing out useful tips, interesting facts, and potentially dangerous pitfalls? Familiarize yourself with these icons to ensure that you don't miss a thing:

WARNING

Pay attention. The bother you save may be your own.

REMEMBER

You may be sorry if this tidbit slips your mind.

TIP

With this icon, we mark particularly useful points to pay attention to.

TECHNICAL STUFF

This material is for the technically inclined.

Beyond the Book

In addition to what you're reading right now, this product also comes with a free access-anywhere Cheat Sheet that covers key characteristics of both public and private clouds and the role of emerging architectures. To get this Cheat Sheet, simply go to www.dummies.com and search for "Cloud Computing For Dummies Cheat Sheet" in the Search box.

Where to Go from Here

We've created an overview of the cloud and introduced you to all of its significant components. We recommend that you read the first six chapters to gain some context on what the cloud is about and see how it changes the way services will be delivered in the future. The next four chapters break down the different types of cloud models. The following three chapters give you an understanding of cloud management while the next four chapters give you guidance on developing and planning your cloud strategy.

You can read the book from cover to cover, but if you're not that kind of person, we've tried to adhere to the For Dummies style of keeping chapters self-contained, so you can go straight to the topics that interest you most. Wherever you start, we wish you well.

The cloud is a big focus for us at Hurwitz & Associates. We invite you to visit our site and read our blogs at https://hurwitz.com.

1

Understanding Cloud Concepts

Chapter **1**

Understanding the Cloud

There is no debate about it: The cloud is helping to change every business in every industry. The key attributes of the cloud — on-demand access to compute and storage, limitless scaling, and flexible pricing — have allowed startups to challenge well-established industry stalwarts. Likewise, the cloud has enabled established businesses to add new capabilities and transform business process at the speed of change.

The first phase of cloud adoption was mostly about cutting costs and changing technology spend from a capital expense to an operating expense. For many years, cloud vendors were focused on reducing costs for commodity compute and storage. While reducing costs is still a major driver of cloud adoption, companies are now leveraging cloud services to transform their businesses. Most companies have pragmatically adopted a hybrid cloud strategy. They're managing to use multiple public and private cloud services depending on the business requirements. IT leaders are maintaining key mission critical applications in their data centers while taking advantage of innovative Software as a Service (SaaS) applications and cloud infrastructure services. Increasingly, vendors are specializing so that they can provide differentiated value to customers. Some cloud providers offer machine learning services while others are providing governance cloud services. Other vendors are providing a variety of cloud storage services.

In this chapter, we provide an overview of cloud computing, including the basics you need to understand in order to move forward in the world of hybrid and multicloud environments.

Looking at the Ecosystem of Cloud Computing

It's important to understand that an ecosystem of participants define the market. This ecosystem consists of three categories of players:

>> **Consumers of services:** These are the end-users that use cloud services in their day-to-day business activities. They may have little understanding of where the service resides or how it is designed; they simply need the capabilities to get the job done.

>> **Provider of services:** These cloud providers offer a variety of functions ranging from infrastructure services to applications and tools.

>> **Designer of services:** These companies build applications and tools. Often services are intended to work within a specific cloud ecosystem or can augment a packaged cloud application.

Understanding Cloud Concepts

Cloud computing is a method of providing shared computing resources, including applications, computing, storage, networking, development, and deployment platforms as well as business processes. Cloud computing makes computing resources easier to use by providing standardization and automation.

Standardization is the implementation of services using a consistent approach supported by a set of consistent interfaces. Likewise, the cloud generally requires that processes be implemented through the use of automation.

Automation is a process that's triggered based on business rules, resource availability, and security demands. Automation is required to support a self-service provisioning model. To promote efficiency, automation can ensure that after a provisioned service is no longer needed, it is returned to the resource pool. This type of rules-based automation can help with capacity planning and overall workload management.

Most businesses today are already using some kind of cloud service — even if they don't think of it as a cloud. For example, any company that uses Microsoft 365, Slack, or DocuSign service is using a cloud-based service. A company may use online data backup or collaboration services in a commercial cloud. Your organization may also place advertisements or recruit new employees on an open community cloud like LinkedIn. If your company uses Google's Gmail service, it is using a cloud email service. Many companies are discovering that having Customer Relationship Management (CRM) available as a service is a better way to support the sales team than the traditional on-premises software options.

You should be getting the idea that cloud computing means that everything — from compute power to computing infrastructure and from applications and business processes to personal collaboration — can be delivered to you as a service. To be operational in the real world, the cloud must be implemented with common standardized processes and automation.

REMEMBER

Clouds come in different versions, depending on your needs. There are two primary deployment models of cloud: public and private. Most organizations will use a combination of private computing resources (data centers and private clouds) and public services, where some of the services existing in these environments interact with each other — which is what we call a *hybrid cloud environment*. In addition, many organizations use a variety of public cloud services to support different developer and business units – called a *multicloud environment*. Multicloud has grown in popularity because developers want access to the platform of their choice, and businesses want the flexibility to move between vendors.

The public cloud

The *public cloud* is a set of hardware, networking, storage, services, applications, and interfaces owned and operated by a third party for use by other companies or individuals. These commercial providers create a highly scalable data center that hides the details of the underlying infrastructure from the consumer. Public clouds are viable because they offer many options for computing, storage, and a rich set of other services. With many resources always available, public cloud consumers can quickly select, optimize, and use those resources that match the needs of the applications they will run in the public cloud. Most public cloud providers offer a wide variety of APIs and services, such as security, specialized infrastructure to support specific workloads like Graphic Processer Units (GPUs) for data science, application development pipelines, and other technologies to support customer needs. All of these cloud services are available in an on-demand manner.

TIP

Public cloud vendors are increasingly offering dedicated, non-multi-tenancy instances within their data center. In these instances, you are assigned your own machines and storage within the cloud vendor's data center. Although the workloads are physically isolated, at some point, you will share some networking with other cloud customers. Companies that take this dedicated instance approach typically have governance, compliance, or corporate rules that don't allow multi-tenancy. However, it is important to consider the fact that you will not have the same cost savings of a multi-tenancy approach.

The private cloud

A *private cloud* is a set of hardware, networking, storage, services, applications, and interfaces owned and operated by an organization for the use of its employees, partners, or customers. A private cloud can be created and managed by a third party for the exclusive use of one enterprise. The private cloud is a highly controlled environment not open for public consumption. Thus, a private cloud sits behind a firewall. The private cloud is highly automated with a focus on governance, security, and compliance. Automation replaces more manual processes of managing IT services to support customers. In this way, business rules and processes can be implemented inside software so that the environment becomes more predictable and manageable.

Increasingly, public cloud vendors are packaging their cloud services into appliances that can be installed within a customer's on-premises data center behind the firewall. The appliance typically contains access to all of the cloud services that the cloud vendor offers on the public cloud. The consumption models for these appliance based on premises public clouds can vary — the vendor may manage and own the appliance and bill the client in the same way that they bill public cloud use, or the customer may own and maintain the appliance. This model of public cloud capabilities behind the firewall is quickly gaining traction. In these cases, businesses get the scalability, ease of use, cost model and familiarity of a cloud environment while keeping data and workloads on premises.

The hybrid and multicloud model

A *hybrid cloud* is a combination of a private cloud combined with the use of public cloud services where the two cloud environments work together to solve business problems. The goal is to create a hybrid cloud environment that can combine services and data from a variety of cloud models to create a unified, automated, and well-managed computing environment. In a well-orchestrated hybrid cloud environment, end-users won't think about whether their using on premises or cloud services — it will all just be a technology service.

In addition to the hybrid cloud, *multicloud* is when two or more public cloud are being used within an organization. Many businesses initially found that they had a multicloud environment because different development teams or business units were choosing to use varying public clouds. As you can imagine, as businesses found themselves using multiple clouds, finance, operations, and IT teams needed a way to gain visibility, control, and choice between clouds. Therefore, multicloud management is emerging as an important consideration.

Combining multiple public services with private clouds and the data center is the definition of *corporate computing*. Not all companies that use some public and some private cloud services have a hybrid or multi cloud. Rather, a hybrid or multicloud environment is when multiple public and/or private services are used together to create value. In the following circumstances, a computing environment is not a hybrid or multicloud:

>> If a few developers in a company use a public cloud service to prototype a new application that is completely disconnected from the private cloud or the data center, the company does not have a hybrid environment.

>> If a company is using a SaaS application for a project but there is no movement of data from that application into the company's data center, the environment is not hybrid.

>> If different divisions within an enterprise are standardized on different public cloud infrastructures, but each division only utilizes and manages a single public cloud.

A cloud is hybrid or multi in the following situations:

>> If a company uses a public development platform that sends data to a private cloud or a data center–based application, the cloud is hybrid.

>> When a company leverages a number of SaaS applications and moves data between private or data center resources, the cloud is hybrid.

>> When a business process is designed as a service so that it can connect with environments as though they were a single environment, the cloud is hybrid.

>> When a SaaS analytics platform is used and data from multiple clouds sources is ingested.

>> When your organization can move workloads to different public clouds based on cost or performance concerns.

Cloud Computing Elements: Resource Pools/Cloud Models and Services

Now that you have a context for the types of cloud environments, it's important to understand the common elements required to make clouds functional. In this section, we give you the basics of what you need to know. Figure 1-1 illustrates the related elements that come together to create clouds. On the bottom of the diagram is a set of *resource pools* that feed a set of cloud delivery services. On the top of the diagram are the common service elements needed to support these delivery models.

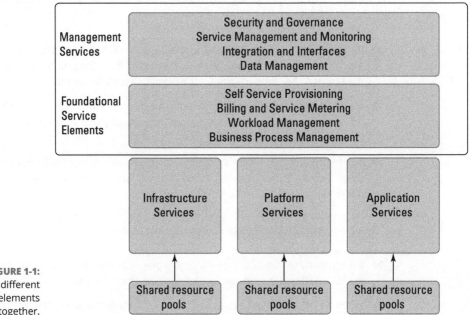

FIGURE 1-1:
How different cloud elements fit together.

So far we have been talking about resources that represent infrastructure technology like processors, storage, and networking. But resources also include software services like databases, identity management, and email servers. Those software services are also available in cloud environments, and they are typically constructed as a shared, *multi-tenant* service. Multi-tenancy is a computing architecture that allows customers to share computing resources in the cloud. Although customers are sharing resources, their individual configurations and data are isolated.

For example, say that you're a cloud provider. If each customer had their own dedicated server, storage device, and networking equipment, scaling your cloud business to support thousands of customers would be hugely expensive. In addition, you'd have to offer your cloud services at a very high cost. On the other hand, if the cloud vendor uses a multi-tenancy architecture, they can have multiple customers using shared infrastructure. Similarly, cloud software vendors use a multi-tenancy architecture so that they don't have to replicate their software for every single user. Your software data, settings, and preferences are all saved, but the underlying base software is shared in a multi-tenancy approach.

To make resource pooling work, each pooled element needs to be written with service-oriented constructs in mind. Consequently, each resource is written as an independent service without dependencies and with well-defined interfaces. For more details on cloud services, turn to Chapter 6.

Cloud delivery models

Understanding the foundations of cloud computing calls for an understanding of cloud delivery models. In this section, we focus on the models that represent computing environments:

>> Infrastructure as a Service

>> Platform as a Service

>> Software as a Service

Part 2 of this book has a chapter on each of these models, but here we cover the basics of the different cloud computing delivery models. These are illustrated as infrastructure services, platform services, and software services in Figure 1-1, earlier in this chapter.

Infrastructure as a Service

Infrastructure as a Service (IaaS) is the delivery of services, including an operating system, storage, networking, and various utility software elements, on a request basis. The easiest way to think of IaaS is that it provides a virtual server that is equivalent to a physical server — you have to select an operating system (for example, Linux, Windows, and so on), and everything "up the stack" to the applications that will run.

IaaS has both public and private versions. In the public IaaS, the public cloud provider creates the infrastructure and resources that consumer can use. The user simply needs a credit card to acquire these resources. When that user stops paying, the resource may disappear. In a private IaaS service, it is usually the IT organization or an integrator who creates an infrastructure and resources that internal users and sometimes business partners can use on demand. Whereas criteria for a public cloud are based primarily on the ability to pay for a service, a private service applies company policy to a service request. Some customers will bring their own tools and software to create applications. For more details on IaaS, turn to Chapter 8.

Platform as a Service

Platform as a Service (PaaS) is a mechanism for combining IaaS with an abstracted set of middleware services, software development, and deployment tools that allow the organization to have a consistent way to create and deploy applications on a cloud or on-premises environment. The easiest way to think about PaaS is that it's an IaaS, but the operating system and development tools are already in place. Because a PaaS environment is ready for development, productivity and time to value is greatly increased.

TIP

Many PaaS environments are anchored to software platforms. For example, Salesforce is a generalized Customer Relationship Management (CRM) to help companies manage their relationships and interactions with customers and prospective customers. Salesforce has a large PaaS platform so that partners with specific domain expertise can use the Salesforce PaaS platform to build industry specific CRMs specific industries, including pharmaceutical sales, education, retail clothing, and food sales.

A PaaS offers a consistent set of programming and middleware services that ensure developers have a well-tested and well-integrated way to create applications in a cloud environment. A PaaS environment brings development and deployment together to create a more manageable way to build and deploy applications. A PaaS requires an Infrastructure service. For more on PaaS, see Chapter 10.

Software as a Service

Software as a Service (SaaS) is a business application created and hosted by a provider in a multi-tenant model. Some of the most popular SaaS applications include Google's G Suite Apps, ServiceNow, Salesforce, Adobe Create Cloud, and Zendesk. Customers typically pay for the SaaS service per user on a monthly or yearly contract model. The SaaS application sits on top of both a Platform as a Service and foundational Infrastructure services. However, customers do not typically care about the underlying infrastructure and platform services. Instead, customers are concerned about the functionality, performance, and availability, and security of the applications. To read more details on SaaS, turn to Chapter 9.

The computing resources life cycle

A fundamental notion of the cloud, both public and private, is that consumers utilize computing resources only when they want to and are only charged for the resources they actually use, for the time they use those resources. In that sense, they rent resources for time periods they desire. Contrast that with the physical data center where computers, storage, and other resources are purchased and then used for the life of those resources.

To meet consumer needs, cloud service providers need to design their computing platforms to respond immediately to whatever consumers request. Since the providers don't know when consumers will make their requests, how many resources they will need, the size of those resources, and how long they will keep those resources, the design must keep many resources available for use at all times. Moreover, the cloud provider must track all resource usage down to fractions of a second so that consumers can be billed for exactly what they used on a pay-as-you-go basis. When consumers finish using resources, the cloud platform must return those resources to the set of available resources so that other consumers can use them.

In some situations, a service provider can't anticipate the needs of a customer. Therefore, it is common for a service provider to add capacity from a third-party service provider. Typically, consumers are unaware that they are dealing with an additional cloud service provider.

Understanding Self-Service Provisioning and Elasticity

Self-service provisioning is one of the most important capabilities of cloud computing. With self-service, cloud consumers can use a website in the cloud to select and purchase cloud services, configure them, launch them into the cloud environment, and start using them within minutes or perhaps even seconds. In the traditional data center model, that same consumer might have to file a request with IT operations for equipment or software, go through approval and payment processes, and then wait while IT procures the equipment, installs it, and configures it, and finally turns it over to the requesting consumer for use. The data center procurement process can take days, and often weeks.

For example, consider a developer with a new application that requires testing with a new server. The delay in waiting for the server not only holds up the development process, but delays the time to market for the application, costing the business for lost revenue and sometimes risking market share by not being a first mover. We go into more detail about how cloud computing helps with software development and operations in Chapter 11.

Closely related to self-service is the concept of *elasticity,* in which cloud resources can automatically change their own provisioned size. The basic meaning of elasticity is that many cloud resources can be selected at a specific size or quantity, but when usage of those resources starts to approach the original size, they automatically increase their own size.

For example, a cloud application that will store customer pictures can select an elastic file system to store the pictures. The application can specify a starting size of the filing system, but as more pictures are added and the total storage exceeds the originally configured size, the file system will automatically add more storage so there is again room for storing files. In this sense, the storage resource is elastic, growing to accommodate more files and, if files are removed, shrinking the storage as well. Because cloud consumers pay only for the resources they actually use, elasticity works to the consumer's financial, as well as technical, benefit by reducing costs.

Establishing a Dynamic Life Cycle across Workloads and Data

A cloud isn't a single unified environment; rather, it's a combination of resources that may be spread across systems and geographies. The cloud is a federated environment that brings together resources so that they can work together. To make this happen in an organized manner requires an organization of workloads. A *workload* is an independent service or collection of code that can be executed. So, you need to think about the cloud as a group of workloads that are managed as though they were a single cohesive environment.

It is important in a cloud environment that workloads be designed to support the right task with the right cloud services. For example, some workloads will need to be placed in a private cloud because they require fast transaction management with legacy systems that have not been moved to the cloud. Other workloads may not have legacy constraints and can be placed in a public cloud.

When organizations begin thinking about cloud computing as a strategy, they must do more than simply go to a public or private resource and leverage those services. Like any computing environment, cloud computing requires that workloads be balanced and managed. Today's reality includes many cloud providers and environments, and a strategy should include what is called multicloud — the strategic use of multiple cloud providers (we cover this topic in detail in Chapter 12). Within a well-designed cloud or multicloud environment, workloads and data can move across multiple cloud providers, geographic regions, or service levels. Because, in the real world, you will use a combination of services, it's important to think not just about an individual workload but also about a combination of workloads and how they interact with each other and with collaborators.

Other issues to consider include locating workloads and data in the same region as your primary customers to optimize performance, understanding the life cycle of your application and data to select optimizations based in increasing — or decreasing — demand, and even moving workloads to alternate cloud providers when the differential of costs, reliability, or features make it advantageous.

Management Services

Management services are mandatory for ensuring that the operation of your cloud workloads and resources meets constituent needs (whether they are customer, employee or partner) needs. This is the case regardless of the cloud deployment and delivery model. Some core services are illustrated at the top of Figure 1-1, which appears earlier in this chapter.

Network monitoring and management is critical because outages and slowdowns can have dramatic impact on the customer experience of cloud applications. Application and workload health monitoring can provide warnings of impending problems and can inform a support organization so they can provide the best service to customers. Security and governance are key services that ensure your applications and data are protected. Data management in a hybrid environment is also critical since data will be moving among cloud and physical environments.

Finally, since various services will need to be integrated in a hybrid or multicloud model, the interfaces between clouds are also important.

The Changing Role of the Data Center

What happens to the data center when companies begin to implement hybrid clouds? First, the data center does not go away. After all, almost all medium-size and large companies run their own data center — which is how many companies operate their systems of record, including accounting systems, inventory records, and line of business applications, to name a few. Many data centers have grown in an unplanned manner over many decades. The typical data center supports different hardware architectures, operating systems, applications, and hundreds, if not thousands, of different tools. To make matters worse, a lot of the money spent in supporting a data center is used for maintenance of existing systems, heating, air conditioning, floor space, and labor.

So, it's not surprising that many companies have taken the time to streamline their data centers through technologies, such as server virtualization. In essence, virtualization decouples the software from the hardware. In *decoupling*, the software is put into a virtual machine (much like in the cloud) so it's isolated from the underlying operating system. With the use of virtualization, data center management can more easily and efficiently manage the way applications are placed on servers.

However, even though IT has made the data center more efficient, cloud computing has made it apparent that more can be done to transform computing. Organizations are taking a hard look at what the centralized data center is well suited for in the light of what they have learned about cloud computing. A comprehensive strategy for managing workloads and data will consider the traditional data center as well as private, public, hybrid, and multicloud environments.

TIP

It wasn't long ago that the cloud was believed to be less secure than physical data centers. However, most commercial public clouds provide sophisticated levels of security. In a traditional data center, many attacks come from internal bad actors or employees who are well-meaning, but make mistakes that leave your company open to an intrusion.

REMEMBER

There are still good reasons to run certain workloads on premises — for example, legacy applications that are not prepared to take advantage of the scalability and elasticity of the cloud, or applications that have dependencies on external services or hardware that are not available in the cloud. In many cases, there many simply not be a reasonable business case to move an application to the cloud. Some data is also better kept in a physical data center, especially data which is subject to regulatory governance and compliance. Also, the growing issue of *data sovereignty* — the concept that information which is stored in digital form is subject to the laws of the country in which it is located — is a driver for keeping data in a physical data center.

Evolution of the data center into a private cloud

Just as businesses saw the value of virtualization in streamlining IT operations in the data center, the cloud is seen as the next step along that path.

IT organizations have discovered that it's much more efficient and effective to create private cloud services for developers to create new applications and services. Therefore, companies are setting up a highly automated computing environment enabled with a self-service portal. This portal is often designed with business process rules that dictate what services a developer or an authorized partner can use. For example, a developer beginning to develop a new application may be permitted to use the Java language with the Eclipse IDE, specific types of middleware, and a specified amount of computing capacity and storage. Once the project is completed, there may be a rule that automatically de-provisions the resources. The private cloud service is intended to support an organization's need for speed and agility based on fast-changing company requirements. Having a private cloud available for projects allows a company to easily experiment with new ideas and new applications without having to request funding for a project that might not become a reality.

Seeing how the public cloud fits

Some business initiatives are good matches for the public cloud. In the next section, we discuss situations that are more appropriate for a private cloud.

First, say that your company is a retailer with a vibrant and well-used SaaS portal for selling products online. The biggest event for the company is its yearly 50 percent–off sale. Although their public cloud has the elastic resources to scale up the portal to handle the increased demand during the sale, this year they plan to expand their sale to Europe and the Far East. Each of those regions has its own inventory to fulfill orders locally, but sales and inventory management is handled by the SaaS portal. Your company selected its cloud provider partly because they run worldwide cloud environments. The cloud provider makes it easy to replicate applications and data to different regions, so it was simple to set up the SaaS application in Europe and the Far East, ensuring that performance for customers in those regions is as good as in their home market. Furthermore, it was easy to take the SaaS application down in those other regions after the sale. Because your company can rely on its public cloud provider, it doesn't have to buy and install additional servers for the sale or have to remove them afterward, thus saving time and money.

Your company has selected two different software applications from service providers to replace existing on-premises applications. One application is a customer relationship management (CRM) that allows the sales force to easily get access to prospective and current customer information from a cloud-based public service. In addition, your company uses a human resources management platform as a service. The company has implemented integration software that allows data to be managed among their on-premises data center and the two cloud SaaS environments, forming a hybrid cloud. Both of these SaaS applications have enabled your company to avoid purchasing additional hardware and software that would require IT management. In addition, because the sales team can access their data much faster from any device they're using, from a business perspective, the sales team's performance is much more effective.

Your company is in a new market where getting a series of new services operational quickly has the potential to leapfrog the competition. Your company hasn't been in business very long. Because the company can use a public service, it can make services available before more established companies can act. At the same time, the company can use its on-premises data center in a hybrid cloud configuration to monitor the effectiveness of services, manage data privately, and combine with other services that aren't visible to customers. All the information collected in the on-premises data center is processed to create analytics that your company sees an opportunity to market and make available in the public cloud, further enhancing its revenue.

Knowing when the private cloud shines

In some situations, the private cloud is a better choice than a public cloud, for both applications and data.

Say that your financial services company's products and services are offered in a portal to your business partners. These products are key to a company's revenue. For example, your company might offer a key business service that is purchased by various banks around the globe. Because of the worldwide reach of your service, it makes sense for the company to establish its portal in a public cloud. However, your business service includes sensitive information that must, by some government's legal requirements, be stored in a physical data center. An architected private cloud that maintains the sensitive financial data is ideal for the financial services company. The resulting hybrid cloud connects the public cloud's portal with the private cloud financial data. The private cloud provides the scalability required for the quantity of data being managed, as well as meeting the legal obligations to store the regulated data in the country where the business is conducted.

A decade ago, your company's IT department realized that their physical data center was over-provisioning their hardware to meet growing computing demands, and decided to migrate their data center applications and data to a virtualized environment. At the time, it was a successful initiative, and they reduced costs by cutting back on over-provisioning and increasing their ability to manage their workloads and data. However, over time, the ease of creating new virtual machines (for example, when development would create new test and staging environments) led to "virtual machine sprawl" where management became impossible. Although their corporate goal became to move their applications to the public cloud, they realized that not only did they need to get control of their VM sprawl, some applications and systems were not cloud-ready. They decided to create a private cloud as a stepping stone to the public cloud. The private cloud allowed them to upgrade their applications to be cloud-native before putting them in the public cloud. It also provided a safe environment for getting control of their virtual machines. Using the private cloud as a testing and staging environment for the move to the public cloud minimized risks of failures in the public cloud and streamlined their management approaches. A further benefit was that after their applications were moved from the private to public cloud, they were left with a modern private cloud in their data center that already had the beginnings of a hybrid cloud configuration from their migration to the public cloud.

» Transforming your legacy

» Discovering the importance of multicloud in a flexible computing model

» Optimizing your business platform for modularity

» Rethinking the business of technology innovation

» Getting ready for the future

Chapter **2**

Embracing the Business Imperative

The cloud is the most disruptive computing revolution of our times; fostering dramatic changes in both the technology we live with every day and the way we use technology to transform business practices. As organizations are forced to deal with more innovative competitors, it is imperative that management can implement change fast. Cloud computing has become the engine of adaptive change.

If your business hasn't been on top of the technology curve and disrupting your competitors, your competitors are probably disrupting your business. Changes are affecting all businesses very quickly. Taxis have been disrupted by Lyft and Uber. Physical retail stores have been disrupted by Amazon and Wayfair. Many of these upstarts that are challenging industry stalwarts will likely be disrupted by even more agile startups or existing companies that can use their market power to reposition their businesses.

In this chapter, we explore how IT organizations can harness cloud services to simply and streamline operations and transform them for business disruption. We also discuss how businesses can rethink their business models to not only keep up, but to find and capitalize on new opportunities.

Understanding IT Transformation

With the rise of commercial cloud computing vendors and services, the role of IT is changing dramatically. While the IT organization in the past had total control of computing resources, now IT is tasked with providing oversight, management, and vetting of options. IT must be able provide the business with ways to integrate process and data across silos. The security organization is also responsible for ensuring security and compliance. IT now has to provide oversight and management of both cloud and on premises computing services. This means that IT needs to provide a transition plan for applications that no longer have the modularity to support business requirements. IT operations has to ensure that performance in a hybrid and multicloud world is consistent and predictable.

Unfortunately for many companies, their IT organizations were busy maintaining legacy applications in a data center that wasn't even ready for virtualization technology. It's hard to believe now, but two decades ago IT organizations spent up to 80 percent of their time just keeping workloads up and running in their data centers. Business leaders began losing patience with the slow pace of the IT organization to support new innovative initiatives. Some companies have invested in emerging cloud technologies and app modernization offerings that help them transform aging applications. The successful organizations are on a path toward transformation led by cloud and cloud services.

Escaping the IT Legacy Trap

Ironically, legacy applications are often core to managing core business processes, such as payment services and customer management. But the architectural foundation of these applications means that they're unable to be easily updated as business processes change. The applications themselves may be monolithic, complete with dependencies on other applications within the computing environment. Assuming that these applications can simply be lifted into a cloud platform is tempting. In reality, this approach is one of the most expensive and least productive ways of gaining productivity.

First, not only does the application itself need to be moved, but also all the related dependent applications. In addition, these applications were not efficiently developed because of the technical constraints of an older computing model. Moving these applications to the cloud will require a massive amount of compute and storage resources that will be expensive. Equally problematic is that you gain no strategic advantage of having these out-of-date applications live in the cloud. The code can't be easily modified to meet new business demands.

TIP

What is the solution? The applications have to be transformed and modernized, which means that dependencies are removed from the applications. The application is redesigned as a set of modular services. When possible, frequently used services are written once and reused. The bottom line is that it is imperative that these legacy applications are updated and modernized to gain the innovation benefits of the cloud.

Preparing for the Cloud

While focusing on the technical underpinnings of adopting a cloud strategy is necessary, you need to take a step back. Your journey needs to begin with the cultural changes that you'll have to embrace. While developers and business leaders may be excited about rushing to adopt cloud services from their favorite vendor, the IT organization may be resistant to change. Many organizations begin to use cloud services without a plan. For example, team leaders may want to rush to adopt cloud services without understanding the requirements for protecting sensitive data for compliance and security. This is asking for trouble.

WARNING

You have to make sure that everyone is educated about what the cloud can and can't do. Everyone should understand how the cloud would play a pivotal role in redefining the pace of business. It should be clear to everyone that adopting the cloud for the business is a team sport and requires that IT and business units collaborate. It also means that there needs to be a balance between total freedom to use whatever cloud or cloud services that seems useful and the need for management of computing. The more that everyone understands about responsibility and goals for the cloud, the more successful the company will be. Have a well-established set of guidelines that are agreed upon and well understood.

The adoption of cloud as a strategy and plan calls for new practices, skills, and roles. How do you go about modernizing existing applications? Are there Software as a Service (SaaS) applications that live in the cloud that are a better fit for the way business is being conducted today? If a SaaS application is the answer, you need to determine how and where it will be used. There may be a need for adding new business processes for that SaaS application. If enough departments are all using the same SaaS application, you should consider working with the selected vendor to create a licensing agreement that is beneficial to the business.

When building software is in the business interest of a company, the relatively new methodology and practice of *DevOps* (development combined with operations) is well suited to the cloud. DevOps and the agile approach for defining and developing software is a practice that may be new to your business.

REMEMBER

Most parts of a company will be affected by a move to the cloud and will also have to make adjustments in roles and skills. This degree of cultural change can be difficult to implement, and it will take time before staff are used to the new cloud ways of doing things. We recommend pilot projects, bringing in training from industry experts, and hiring people experienced with the cloud to take on important leadership roles.

After all that preparation, you'll be ready to deploy cloud technologies, in either a private, hybrid, public, or multicloud context. You will still learn more as you go and will have to make adjustments to your processes. Your staff will have an opportunity to upgrade their skills, which can lead to new opportunities. But if you've done a good job in cleaning up your legacy data center and creating a new cloud culture, your path forward will have a much better chance of success. Ultimately, what you have done is to create a new business agility and flexibility based on new practices and effective use of cloud technologies.

Building for Innovation

The cloud makes building connections between your employees, business partners, and customers easier. Innovative companies can no longer live with strict boundaries among business units, subsidiaries, partners, suppliers, and customers. These relationships are key to your company's success, and building better communications, feedback mechanisms, and transparency will benefit everyone. For example, supply chains benefit when both producers and consumers increase the transparency of their inventories, business plans, and customer needs.

REMEMBER

As IT transforms itself to help guide the cloud strategy, the organization can become an agent of change. With the use of well-defined cloud services supported by standard Application Programming Interfaces (APIs), it is possible to more quickly establish new innovative applications and services to support partners and suppliers. With the use of either public or private cloud services, a business can pilot new services with selected partners and iterate based on feedback. The ability to build quickly, test, change, and execute is the best way to experiment with new business models without requiring a massive capital investment.

As you move forward with connecting your ecosystem together more tightly, you'll find an increasing need to manage the myriad data sources your company and others maintain as though they were a single pool of information. It's a complex task that requires careful business and architectural planning. When these application, process, and data services are freed from their traditional constraints, the business benefits will be compelling.

In the previous generation of computing infrastructure, a business would have to create complex integration software to enable the ability to link customers and partners into the same set of services. This environment could take an enormous amount of time to architect and design. With the advent of the cloud, you can now create an environment where common APIs and cloud services can link an ecosystem together efficiently without having to build a separate computing environment. With the advent of agreed-upon cloud infrastructure standards, an ecosystem can be establish more quickly so that a business can transform business practices to increase revenue and satisfaction.

The Business Imperatives

There was a time when a business could design a set of applications and computing platform that could stand the test of time. The environment could take years to develop and could be in place for a decade or more.

Clearly, the competitive environment has changed, driven primarily from advances in cloud services. No longer does an emerging business have to spend millions of dollars on designing software and services from scratch. Now, a new company with an innovative idea can leverage inexpensive cloud services and build a new service; test it out with early adopters; and take over an established market, as shown in Figure 2-1. The advantage of these upstart companies is that they have no legacy, no installed base to protect, and can afford to take risks with new business models in the hope of up-ending an established and lucrative market. In that sense, bringing your IT organization up-to-date is table stakes — something that just must be done. The deeper advantage of modernizing IT comes from putting innovative concepts into action before an unknown competitor has a chance to lure your customers away.

By establishing a well-defined cloud strategy that is a collaboration between key constituents across your business, you will be in a good position to get started. You can begin the process of streamlining your IT organization by modernizing critical business applications and moving key workloads to the cloud. You'll be able to make well-informed decisions about which workloads should remain on premises and which services should reside in the cloud. Management as a team will decide which cloud services meet the company guidelines for security, governance, and stability. While most businesses will support multiple clouds, you can set guidelines to limit the number of vendors your IT team will need to work with and manage. With this preparation, you have set the stage for being ready to innovate to protect the relationship with your customers and partners. Setting a cloud strategy plan into action will help create an advantage for your company.

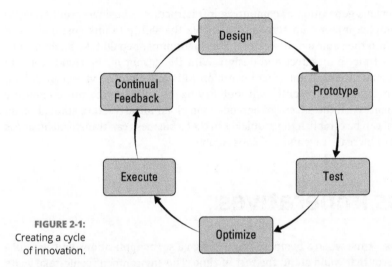

FIGURE 2-1:
Creating a cycle
of innovation.

Optimizing Your Existing Business

Before you rush to establish your cloud strategy, take a step back and think about how you interact with your customers. How do you reach your customers today? You'll discover that most of your customers are already consuming cloud services in many different ways. These customers will expect that you're using cloud services as a key business strategy. You want to be able to demonstrate that you can react to their needs for change without delay. Today's customers expect your applications and services to be able to transform in near real time. If you can't meet their expectations for rapid change, they'll find providers that are more responsive to their needs. The bottom line is that without the agility of the cloud platform, you can't quickly meet customer expectations.

Take the example of a furniture business that has served its community for more than a century. The company has strong ties to the local community and understands the taste of customers in the region. But the market is changing. New cloud-based online furniture companies are springing up everywhere. They have no relationships in the community, and they have a variety of products from many different suppliers. They don't have the solid reputation of the business that has been around for a long time. However, they have something that the established furniture business doesn't have: a wide selection of products that are not back-ordered. A customer simply goes onto their commerce site and finds the precise item, purchases it, and waits for two days before it shipped for free.

Can a physical furniture store hope to compete? There is no guarantee. However, a physical store can create a business model that is a hybrid between the physical store where a customer can see products they might want to buy, work with a designer, and create a trusting relationship. At the same time, the furniture company can create a companion cloud-based set of services where store-based offerings combined with third-party furniture and related items can be sold. Customers can order online and then come to the physical store to pick up items and potentially see them in the store after they're ordered. In addition, the store can begin to collect data about which customers are most likely to purchase and how tastes are changing. Innovative ideas, such as having local artisans custom build furniture and accessories based on buying patterns, can transform a traditional furniture store into a competitive business.

The furniture store has years of best practices experience that can be applied to the cloud model. With the cloud, the business can build out innovative services that leaders know are important to their customers and can experiment with new ideas that are managed in the cloud.

Modern Development and Deployment Strategies

How does an established business move to an innovative cloud strategy? How do applications get developed so that they're innovative and ready to support a multicloud environment? DevOps — a combination of modern application development and deployment techniques — are the requirement for building cloud-based innovation. With DevOps, developers employ an agile development approach that assumes an iterative development process. The focus of DevOps and agile development is to focus on customer needs and metrics that can predict success. How do customers use the new software? Is it intuitive? Does it encourage customers to stay on the site and purchase additional merchandise? Is the application modular and flexible enough to adopt as customers react to the environment? Is it easy to partner with businesses that offer complementary offerings? What is the performance like once the software is deployed across different cloud platforms and within an on premises environment?

In its ideal state, DevOps streamlines development and deployment processes so products can be deployed at any time, not just when a new "release" has been created. For example, say that your business has a custom suit tailoring SaaS application that your customers use successfully. However, your customers tell you that they need a feature where they can send a proposed suit design to someone who will sign off on the design before it goes into production. Before DevOps, the feature would get bundled with other features and eventually included in a product release, which might take months before it was released to customers. But with DevOps operating in a continuous development and continuous deployment model, the feature could be developed, tested, and then deployed in days or even less time. The deployment organization would update the SaaS application, and customers will see the new feature right away. Your customers will love your responsiveness and will stop asking you when features they have requested will finally be released.

Revisiting Your Business Model

One of the benefits of the cloud is that it makes it easier to adapt your business model or to experiment with new ideas that could transform your business.

In the past, businesses saw software services as a necessary part of their strategy but not a driver of growth. That has changed. You only have to analyze the success of companies like Uber, Airbnb, Netflix, and hundreds of other businesses that are challenging established businesses because of the cloud. In fact, the success of these types of companies is the fact that they have sophisticated cloud-based services where they can build and modify applications quickly and use data to understand customer expectations. The list of businesses with new business models is long and growing. The mindset in the software world is to find new ways to disrupt businesses — in other words, have a business model that is more compelling than what was previously used.

REMEMBER

So, if your business optimizes its data center, business relationships, and current business practices, you have probably increased your company's success. However, you must realize that the more successful you are, the more other businesses are looking at your business and trying to find weaknesses in your business model that they can take advantage of. Therefore, you have a responsibility to your business to reexamine your business model, and possibly change it, on a regular basis.

Transforming the Business Model

TIP

Smart businesses aren't afraid to break their business model and experiment with new approaches to satisfying customers. In fact, the cloud is also the perfect place to experiment with new ideas. All the agility and flexibility we discuss in this chapter can be applied to trying new things in the cloud. For example, it's relatively easy to create a new website that takes a different approach, like packaging your product as a service so that customers can begin by selecting one service and then adding other options over time. With the flexibility of cloud services, you can test these ideas with a set of willing customers to see what offerings and approaches have the best potential for success.

Business models are comprised of a set of characteristics of your business that can be adjusted to change how your company does business and how your customers and partners interact with you. Who are your partners today? What customers are you selling to today and can you expand your reach into new market segments? Is there a way to offer a subset of your products so that customers gain an appreciation of your offerings before they have to spend money? Offering compelling offerings that solve customer problems encourages them to buy once they get a taste of success. Being able to leverage the cloud to both offer and manage customer interaction transforms your ability to move quickly to increase your business.

To make such a significant business model change can be hard to do, but it is worth it if it gives your business a new life. The cloud can help you by making it easy to experiment with your business model via the agility and flexibility. Instead of changing your business completely overnight, you can set up a subsidiary division or even stand-alone business, perhaps with a different name and brand. Treat it as a real business, but limit the number of customers or services to keep it less complicated, and see whether you get the traction you need. If you do, you can grow the new business at your own rate. On the other hand, if you don't get the traction you need, you can close that experiment and try another until you find something that works for your business.

2

Examining Architectural Considerations

Chapter **3**

Architectural Considerations for the Cloud Environment

U nderstanding all the different models available for cloud deployments is important, but to be successful in the hybrid cloud world, you need to understand the architectural view. The architectural view includes both the underlying processes and computing elements combined with best practices needed to create a model that can stand the test of time. Start by asking these questions:

» Who are the constituents that will be served by the cloud?

» What functions are needed to meet your company's requirements?

» What's the nature of the workloads that you need to support in the cloud?

» What are the range of on-premises services that need to interact with your cloud services?

The reality is that cloud computing is part of your overall computing model. As with everything else in the world, nothing is black and white. There are tradeoffs to be made. However, at the end of the day, the way you plan and execute your computing environment will be tied directly to your optimal customer experience. In this chapter, we discuss the open issues and considerations in planning an environment that serve the best interest of your internal and external customers.

Rethinking the Type of Constituents Your Cloud Serves

Two constituents that are part of the cloud ecosystem determine how you view the cloud architecture:

>> **Cloud consumers:** The individuals and groups within your business unit that use different types of cloud services to get a task accomplished. A cloud consumer could be a developer using compute services from a public cloud.

>> **Direct customers:** Users who often take advantage of services that your business has created within a cloud environment. End users of your service have no idea that you're using a public or private cloud. As far as the users are concerned, they're interacting directly with your services and value.

>> **Cloud service provider:** Commercial vendors or companies that create their own capabilities. The commercial vendors sell their services to cloud consumers. In contrast, a company might decide to become an internal cloud service provider to its own employees, partners, and customers — either as an internal service or as a profit center. These providers also create applications or services for these environments.

What your organization does will set the requirements for how you plan your cloud architecture. If you're a cloud consumer, you have the responsibility to select the right set of services based on your business requirements. You don't need to think about how to necessarily architect each element; instead, think about how to link elements together that you'll use. A cloud consumer has to be careful not to create a set of disconnected silos that can't be managed. This is one of the benefits of the increasingly wide adoption of containerization and microservices that help organizations abstract the content from the underlying platform.

WARNING

In contrast, if your organization is a cloud service provider, you'll spend a lot more time architecting the elements. You also need to understand how to build applications and business services that are optimized for this environment. These service creators need to be concerned with consistency of the services that they're building so that they can support their customers — both short term and for the long run.

A cloud service provider can be a commercial vendor selling services, or it could be a private cloud designed for the use of employees and partners. The cloud service provider has to create an entire environment that can easily connect with an ecosystem of partners.

Putting the Pieces Together

How do all the components of a cloud model fit together from an architectural perspective? The National Institute of Standards and Technology Cloud Reference Model (www.nist.gov/index.html), shown in Figure 3-1, depicts how the various cloud services are related to support the needs of businesses. On the left side Figure 3-1, the cloud service consumer represents the types of uses of cloud services. No matter what the requirements of the particular constituent, it is critical to bring together the right type of services that can support both internal and external users. Management of these consumers must be able to make services easily available to support changing business needs. Within this category are the applications, middleware, infrastructure, and services that are built based on on-premises computing models. In addition, this model depicts the role of the cloud auditor. This organization provides the oversight either by an internal or an external group that makes sure that the consumer group meets its obligations.

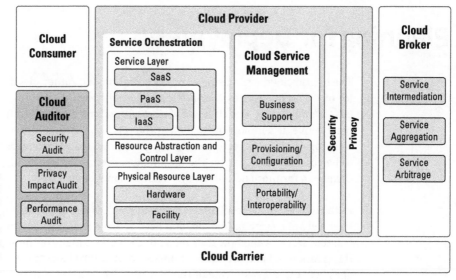

FIGURE 3-1: The NIST Cloud Reference Model provides a depiction of the various services needed to operate in cloud.

Cloud service providers (see the center of Figure 3-1) represent all the models of cloud services that we discuss in Chapters 8, 9, and 10. A cloud service provider might be a commercial company or a corporation that decides to become its own cloud service operator. Cloud providers may provide the underlying physical and virtualized resources needed to run various cloud services. They also may create the actual applications and business services that operate in these environments.

These various cloud models don't exist in isolation — they're all related to each other. In addition, there's an entire ecosystem of partners that support various vendors with offerings. The cloud service provider provides a unified architecture to support and manage these services in a consistent manner. Managing these services is a major requirement for any cloud service provider. These management platforms have to provide both support for the operation of the various services as well as manage the way they perform to support business requirements.

The cloud provider has to support all the important cloud models that we discuss in Chapters 8 through 10. In addition to supporting the physical and virtual environment, it is important to remember that all these cloud models and the supporting environment have to be linked together in the form of service orchestration. Without service orchestration, each service would become an independent silo.

Clearly, all the components in the cloud provider model must be managed. There have to be services to support the business, manage configurations, and provision the right resources on demand. Management services must also support interoperability and service portability. For more details on cloud management, take a look at Chapter 4.

Planning for Deployment

The hybrid cloud isn't a single architectural model; rather, it's a combination of a lot of different services that are located on different platforms. Therefore, there isn't a simple way to define a hybrid architecture. Instead, from an architecture perspective, it's important to look at the relationship among the services that are used together. To be effective, the usage of cloud management technologies needs to be considered as part of the architectural framework of the hybrid cloud. (See Chapter 4 for more details on multicloud management.)

In the hybrid cloud, you'll never bring all services and elements together as though they were one system. Instead, you need to have a clear understanding of the distributed services and how they relate to each other. Many of the approaches require the creation of best-practices templates that can be used to create the right linkages between services. One of the best practices needed is to be able to keep track of what task a specific service executes, the rules for how it can be used, as well as definitions and dependencies. But the issues don't stop with dependency. In a world where you're going to leverage services based on different physical and virtual environments, you need to think about how the entire environment behaves under different circumstances. A well-designed hybrid cloud environment has to be built to support change. Change can be the addition of another cloud service, such as a SaaS application, or a new business partner and its set of services. In essence, hybrid models have four primary architectural considerations:

» Latency and performance

» Security

» Governance

» Reliability in the context of change

We discuss each one throughout this section.

Latency: Performance matters

When planning your hybrid model, you need to consider the overall performance of your platform, which means that you have to monitor and measure your entire environment. *Latency*, or slow response or performance, is a constant concern for customers. For example, say that a critical issue for your business is the speed at which customers' orders are confirmed. If you don't handle this issue efficiently, customers won't be happy and may move to another supplier. So, you may want to keep transaction management running within a private cloud or data center environment. If you were to use a public cloud transaction management service, the latency involved in moving data between networks would cause service delays. In addition, some applications require regular access to and manipulation of complex data. If this were to happen on a regular basis, you may not be able to perform as customers expect. In this situation, stick with either your current on-premises solution or a well-architected private cloud environment. On the other hand, you may discover that for other applications, such as customer management or human resource management workloads, a SaaS application provides acceptable latency to meet the needs of your constituents.

In addition to the performance of a specific cloud service, you need to consider the location of a service. A service in a public cloud may be fine for one type of use but may have unacceptable latency when several services need to exchange data very rapidly. Therefore, part of the hybrid architecture requires that you understand what role each service plays and how those services need to interact with each other.

Determining when to use a public versus private service depends on the context of what service is being delivered to the customer. The choices you make will depend on the task being executed. Therefore, you need to build flexibility into the way you plan for latency in a hybrid cloud environment. For example, if you're setting up a collaborative workspace with three partners, a public cloud environment will be cost-effective. Depending on the type of collaboration, this environment may perform well based on the type of collaboration being conducted.

However, if you have set up a mission-critical, high-volume transaction management platform, performance must be optimized. In contrast, if customers are looking up information occasionally or if data can be easily distributed, latency will not be an overarching problem. Many services have low volumes of data, in which case the system won't constantly reach for massive amounts of data from on-premises data sources. These environments are practical for a public cloud platform environment.

Although people typically think of individual models and services, it's worth looking at the issue of latency differently. Instead of assuming that each service runs as a stand-alone service, imagine that you combine a number of services to create a composite service. For example, say that you have a service where latency must be very low, but you want to take advantage of an inexpensive public commodity service in combination with a secure private cloud and some on-premises services. In this situation, you must determine which components of the environment will benefit from the public cloud services so that they match the overall service level requirement. As the needs of the organization change, it will be important to be able to change the location of a service if a different level of performance is required. There are situations where the volume of data that a customer needs to access has expanded so much that a different configuration will be needed.

CAN MICROSERVICES AND CONTAINERS REDUCE LATENCY?

In a service-based approach to computing, you can tightly couple a set of services that must execute with low latency. Pioneers in the services-based approaches to software development and deployment learned the hard way that loosely coupling (or connecting) business services doesn't always provide the level of performance an organization needs. After learning this lesson, companies began tightly coupling services that needed faster performance. You can apply these same techniques to a cloud environment.

Placing microservices into containers supported by orchestration services and well-defined APIs is transforming the way businesses gain control over performance in complex computing environments. If you have a dependency to an outside service running outside that environment, you need to make sure that you leverage APIs that provide techniques such as caching so that a service can connect to the right data without causing latency problems. At the end of the day, having a well-architected hybrid cloud environment will work well if it's based on best practices and good engineering principles.

Security: Planning in context

When planning your hybrid environment, at the outset, you need to think about the security requirements for customers. What type of environment are you providing for your customers? Are you creating an informational resource that might be tied to a set of product data sheets? However, if you've created a platform that manages private health data, you must ensure that you've created the level of protection and privacy your customers demand. (Check Chapter 15 for more details about security and governance.) You need to understand these considerations before you begin your design. So, make sure your cloud providers can match your requirements.

Governance: Getting the right balance

Like security, governance requirements will determine how you plan and architect your hybrid cloud environment. Many industries have rules of engagement that are considered best practices. If you're part of an industry that's required to meet sophisticated governance requirements, it's important to select partners that meet your needs. You may discover that you can't use a third party for this part of your environment.

Likewise, many countries have strict guidelines and requirements for how private data must be handled. In some countries, for example, an individual's data must be stored physically within that country. These types of governance requirements demand that IT organizations plan their platform with this in mind. This means including process management services that determine where data must be stored — which means that, in some countries, data is stored in a single physical data center. In other countries, data may be highly distributed across geographies without violating rules. Some cloud providers can implement automated policies that ensure that certain services run based on these rules.

Again, it's critical to validate that your cloud vendors can meet your business requirements. For example, you must make sure that you can deploy your application and data in a specific country or region if necessary. The bottom line is that you have to match your architectural plan with the governance requirements in both your company and the industry.

Managing colocation

In the real world, compromise is a requirement for making computing perform well at an affordable price. In a perfect world, cost would never be an issue, but in complicated environments, compromise is a reality. The trick is to be able to manage across a hybrid environment that creates an architecturally balanced approach. So, when planning your hybrid cloud environment, you need to first select applications that fit well into the benefits and limitations of the cloud. Applications that do not match well for such a public cloud environment may need to stay on-premises, either on a traditional middleware deployment or in a private cloud environment. When companies or cloud creators have carefully architected their applications or services, they will be well positioned to support a hybrid cloud environment.

Creating flexibility in the model

Companies looking at cloud computing typically assume that it's an all-or-nothing model. However, cloud computing is simply part of an overall distributed architectural plan. Within an architectural framework, determining business, performance, and customer goals is important, and to do so, you must take into account all aspects of computing.

You need to consider the issue of latency of overall performance and latency of managing data. (See the section "Latency: Performance matters," earlier in this chapter.) If applications and services being offered to customers are based on a tightly coupled set of services with many dependencies, a public cloud service will cause serious problems with performance. However, if the organization is creating and leveraging a platform of well-defined and loosely coupled services that are designed to be easily linked together at run time, a public cloud service is ideal.

Most organizations have a combination of these two scenarios; thus, architecturally, you need to think of your platform as a combination of data center, private cloud, and public cloud services. When you approach architectural considerations from this holistic perspective, the customer is well served and protected.

Some vendors will actually help you by providing several deployment options (public, private, data center) from the same platform, making it easier for your company to have a unified platform that can adapt to a wide number of use cases and constraints.

Setting the Right Policies and Business Rules

Companies generally think about policy and business rules from an overall governance perspective. On the contrary, making policies and rules operational in a hybrid cloud environment means that these dictates must be integrated from an architectural perspective. Building a policy or rule into the actual application may be straightforward in an on-premises environment. In a hybrid environment, however, you must make sure those policy requirements can be applied across components. For example, if a policy requires that personal data about French customers is stored in a physical server in France, this policy must be designed as a middleware service that controls the movement of data based on rules and conditions. It's not practical to try to implement each rule and policy inside each component of the hybrid environment.

Navigating the Choices in a Hybrid World

The great thing about a hybrid cloud is that the environment allows you to select the right service for the right task. But, you might ask, how do you select the right balance of services from an architectural perspective? Think about the collection of requirements from a business perspective and match that perspective to an architectural approach.

In general, you want the platforms you select to be appropriate for the service level requirements of the business. If a portion of your environment requires real-time performance and guaranteed uptime, you'll choose a public service with a sophisticated Quality of Service (QoS) or a completely private service that your company controls. For services such as customer relationship management, where availability and manageability are the most important business concerns, a SaaS environment makes business sense. From both an architectural and a business process perspective, you must decide which services need to interact with each other and which ones are, in essence, stand-alone services. In the end, you want to end up with a highly optimized environment that matches the needs of the customers that you need to support.

Optimizing for Workloads

Being able to optimize workloads across environments is one of the fundamental architectural principles of hybrid cloud computing. (For more on workload management, see Chapter 12.) Unless workload optimization and balancing are one of the starting points, satisfying customer requirements will be difficult. One way to allow interoperability across workloads is through federation. *Federation* is a technique for linking together different environments at the interface level. Common interfaces across different public and private cloud services are needed. Even if various services aren't federated, consumers of cloud services must at least have an uncomplicated way to access data or business services across different environments and networks.

Keep in mind, however, that the creation of true portability and interoperability of workloads across hybrid cloud environments is at an early stage.

Supporting a Dynamic Life Cycle

The life cycle of cloud computing is different in many ways from the life cycle of a traditional computing environment. The architecture of the cloud environment is predicated on the ability to abstract the details away from users based on a services-oriented architecture. As a result of the cloud, you must think about the term *life cycle* in a new way. Now the focus isn't on disconnected tools and capabilities; instead, the cloud begins to enforce a discipline that has been missing in traditional computing environments. One of the benefits of a cloud environment is that it is designed to support change. To support changing numbers of users, applications, and workloads requires an environment that is architected for change. Therefore, the life cycle of working with the architecture has to expect changes. One day you might be support-ing 100 developers who are working on a new experimental application that will be gone in a month. The architecture has to expect shifts in workloads.

Your business will gain real benefits by approaching cloud computing as a dynamic architectural model that speeds the development and deployment of applications and that makes linking services together easier. For example, you might find that by tying together development and deployment in the cloud environment that there are fewer misunderstandings between those developing applications and those deploying those applications. In addition, when a company adds new employees through an acquisition, it will be straightforward to provision addi-tional capacity or to add more users to a SaaS application. Because security becomes a service within the cloud environment, it is much easier to update and change security requirements.

As you start thinking about supporting a dynamic life cycle to support a hybrid cloud environment, consider the following:

» Think about an overall services-based model that breaks down traditional disconnected silos of applications, processes, and services.

» Think about creating an environment with fewer dependencies so that when you add new cloud services, you'll have the flexibility to advance as the industry advances.

» Think about the performance requirements that will give your customers excellent experiences.

» Think about creating a predictable, safe, and well-governed environment that will support business operations in the long run.

Chapter **4**

Managing a Hybrid and Multicloud Environment

anagement of a hybrid and multicloud environment is a complex topic as it spans computing activities in on-premises data centers, private and hybrid clouds, and numerous public cloud environments. In the past, computing resources were physical and highly siloed. Therefore, managing individual systems combined with their workloads made sense.

But times have changed with the advent of cloud computing. In this distributed work, many applications are independent of their underlying infrastructure. Organizations no longer look at individual computing resources as stand-alone systems. Rather the combination of the data center, private and public cloud, and Software as a Service (SaaS) applications now define computing. The users of computing services within your business no longer distinguish between a workload running in a data center and a service running in a public cloud. Users simply want everything to work predictably. In this chapter, we discuss what it means to manage computing in the era of the hybrid cloud.

What Are You Managing?

So, what are you actually managing in a multicloud environment? What are the considerations? Not only do you have to ensure that a service is up and running, but you have to make sure that you address the diversity of goals, roles, resources, and other issues that must be supported and addressed. Take a step back and look at the type of services you need to manage in this world of hybrid computing. We have divided the capabilities that you'll need to manage into five categories:

>> SaaS applications

>> External cloud resources

>> Internal cloud resources

>> External cloud resources

>> Managing external services

Managing SaaS Applications

Increasingly businesses are turning to SaaS applications that are owned and operated by third-party vendors. It's not uncommon for a single business to support hundreds of SaaS applications. However, businesses are beginning to bring some level of control to the use of SaaS applications. IT management have to contend with several key problems in managing SaaS applications.

Anyone with access to a browser can access and sign up for a license and start using a SaaS application. For example, to exchange large files, it's not uncommon for well-meaning employees to use a file-sharing application like Box or Dropbox to circumvent email attachment limits. With the growing popularity of SaaS applications, a business can quickly lose control.

REMEMBER

All SaaS applications are not equal. Some well-designed SaaS applications provide value to the business along with governance and auditability for administrators. On the other hand, other SaaS applications are designed for consumers and do not have the visibility that businesses require. Additionally, the application may not have well-defined interfaces so that it can easily connect to other corporate applications. Furthermore, applications that are not there may have vulnerabilities in the application that can put the business at risk.

Needless to say, these and other reasons are why a business needs to have oversight into the use of SaaS applications. Many corporate IT organizations have long battled with business units for control of computing resources. Often called *shadow IT,* business units use a variety of SaaS applications and tolls without the knowledge of IT. The cloud has accelerated this process.

Smart IT organizations have learned how to collaborate with business units so that business management can use the tools that are best suited for their task while protecting the business from risk. These organizations often will set up a working group consisting of IT leaders and business leaders to set parameters for what is acceptable. For example, everyone can agree on a set of SaaS applications that both meet their day-to-day needs and are fully vetted for security and reliability. One of the benefits is that IT or the procurement organization can negotiate for both price and support.

TIP

But a better solution is for IT to proactively research and approve a full set of tools that the company will use and create a library of easily findable and usable tools in a convenient place. This solution allows employees to self-serve only approved items from the SaaS application library. IT should go further still, to encourage employees to engage with the team when they have a problem that isn't met by the standard tools. Rather than push back or delay, IT would be more successful by offering a bonus for finding unmet needs and then providing a commitment to solve the problem quickly. (We talk about service level agreements in the section later in this chapter.)

Generally, SaaS applications are managed by the organizations that created them, so IT is probably not responsible for managing external SaaS applications. However, IT isn't off the hook. The users of the SaaS application have little interest in excuses. Users simply want to know that an application is operational at all times. When IT operations explains that the SaaS vendor is responsible for the management of that application, the user is rarely satisfied. They won't make a distinction between an application that resides in the data center or a private cloud and a third-party application managed in a public cloud.

For example, a great SaaS application is hosted in a public cloud, such as Amazon or Google. The public cloud experiences an outage that lasts for several hours. Once users begin calling IT to complain, IT contacts the SaaS vendor who explains that the problem is with the cloud provider. The problem, of course, is that the SaaS application user will have no sympathy and will demand action.

Optimizing SaaS Management

Once a business has set the ground rules for using SaaS within the organization and educated users on the best practices of using public SaaS applications, it can take additional steps to improve costs, productivity, and security.

As use of SaaS applications expands through an enterprise, IT and security teams should review use of SaaS applications. Security should examine actual use to understand whether any practices are risking loss of the business's intellectual property (IP), opening up connections that hackers can exploit or where other insecure activities can occur.

A SaaS CAUTIONARY TALE

As a business modernized itself with a cloud-based office productivity suite for creating marketing content, employees were thrilled with the ability to create and edit content at any time, whether in the home office or on the road. Their organization was widely distributed physically, and having their documents in the cloud allowed sharing and reviews from many divisions of the business, regardless of where they were located. Users quickly became used to the SaaS application and became dependent on its powerful features.

Then, one day, the SaaS service experienced an outage of the. The outage's impact on the company was massive because nearly every employee had transitioned over to the new offering. Employees were furious with IT, which had researched, selected, and deployed the application. However, at this point, IT was not involved with assuring that the SaaS application met specific SLAs — the responsibility was on the vendor. The vendor had specified SLAs for the application's availability, but any downtime had an impact on the company.

Further complicating the problem, the outage may have been caused by a variety of points between the SaaS offering's cloud and the company. For example, the SaaS application may be running fine, but a networking switch may be disrupting communication. In this instance, the SaaS application itself was not functioning properly, and IT had to just wait for the vendor to fix the software problem.

Unfortunately, this situation isn't uncommon. Arguably, IT did not meet all of its responsibilities for ensuring that the company had continuous access to the tools employees require to do their jobs. IT must prepare for outages and have failover solutions ready to fill in on a literal moment's notice. Those stand-by, fill-in solutions may be from another vendor (assuming the vendor has a compatible product), or perhaps the original vendor can provide a better SLA for a higher price or offer a failover to a different region that would provide the same service (at perhaps greater latency).

Cloud Access Management (CAM) is a form of identity management that is specifically targeted to cloud service. Using CAM, users can be explicitly given rights to specific SaaS applications (and not to others), and governance specified for what information they can access. Security can use CAM to formalize which company personnel can access which SaaS applications and the rights they can exercise within SaaS applications. For example, HR employees may have the right to update all employees' job performance ratings, while people outside of HR may be granted the rights to see only their own information.

IT will be interested in how many employees are using each SaaS application, and what they use the application for. As more people use a SaaS application, IT may be able to use that information to negotiate better terms for using the SaaS application from its vendor. For example, if multiple business units have purchased the same SaaS application, your business can receive a more favorable licensing agreement if you combine the management and purchasing of the application. From observing patterns of application use, IT may also see opportunities for purchasing other tools that can improve the operation of the business. Or, the need to integrate one SaaS application with others may become apparent.

Managing External Cloud Resources

Businesses use many types of external or public cloud resources that require management. Resources may be virtual machines that developers use, storage for backups or disaster recovery, databases for big data activities, and the list goes on.

Cloud resources are the building blocks used create applications. These infrastructure services are designed as a layer below SaaS applications and therefore are the responsibility of software developers.

Understanding who is using cloud services is important because that's where management should be focused. Management of cloud services is typically practiced in IT and software development organizations.

Visibility and control of external resources

As with SaaS applications, simply grabbing a cloud resource to execute a task is often too easy. To be successful, you need to have the ability to apply controls so that you can gain visibility into the cloud applications and services.

The biggest management challenges of external cloud resources are identifying the most appropriate services to use, verifying their characteristics (performance, security, cost, and so on), and making sure that these services are used exclusively. The rationale for using these resources to the exclusion of other resources is that after a service has been selected, investments in training, testing, and building infrastructure software will occur to make the service work effectively. You should avoid selecting and using a different service that has the same functionality, as it can double the costs of using the functionality.

Because using resources and building applications are fundamentally technical activities, the development organization or IT (if software is being developed for internal company use) should drive their management. Development has knowledge of the functionality of the resources required for the product(s) they're developing, how a service will integrate into the product framework, and the long-term technical goals of the business.

TIP

The general cycle for approval, use, and eventual reuse of cloud services is:

1. **Identify and define the functional requirements of the software being developed.**

2. **Research resources available from the cloud providers that are already used by the business to find a good match.**

   Extend the search to other cloud providers if adequate solutions aren't found or if additional cloud providers should be nurtured in the spirit of multicloud.

3. **Perform tests in a pilot project to verify the resource(s) found in Step 2 meet the functional requirements.**

4. **If the testing is successful, form a business relationship with the service vendor and get access to the production version of the resource.**

TIP

   The vendor may be a cloud provider or a third party who makes its software available in a cloud platform. If the testing is not successful, go back to Step 2 or consider building the resource internally.

5. **Document the new service and its availability to the full development organization.**

6. **On a regular basis, perhaps yearly, revisit existing resources (internally developed as well as external resources), the requirements they need to meet, and their operational history and issues.**

   If requirements or the resource have changed, consider restarting this process at Step 2 to see whether a new resource may be a better fit.

The importance of self-service

The idea of creating a catalog of approved computing resources that consumers may select from is critical to being able to manage in a consistent and predictable way. It's a simple idea, but a very important one.

Cloud providers make it as easy as possible for consumers to find and use their services. At the low pay-as-you-go prices of most cloud resources, it's a very compelling bargain. However, the company should limit employee choices of computing resources to approved resources.

REMEMBER

The challenge is to make it easier for employees to use the company's catalog to select what they want rather than go to the cloud themselves. To do so, the company must get ahead of the curve to understand the requirements and needs of development organizations. If the work of looking for, testing, and approving resources can be completed before the needs of the development organization become critical, then the catalog can include what the development organization needs. That proactivity will allow the easiest choice to be the right choice.

Service level agreements (SLAs)

Every cloud resource comes with a contractual agreement, known as a *service level agreement* (SLA), that outlines what the provider is delivering, along with the customer's responsibilities. The agreement should outline characteristics like availability, accuracy, response time, throughput, and security. These important traits are critical for selecting resources that will meet the performance requirements of the services or applications that will use them.

WARNING

Many public cloud services are quite clear that the vendor accepts responsibility in only a limited set of situations for a problem. For example, if someone in the organization misconfigures a service and it's out of commission, the vendor accepts responsibility. If the vendor is directly responsible for a security breach, the responsibility is clear. However, there are many gray areas. For example, what happens if a flood in the region knocks out service or destroys data? What if third-party networking services that link a customer and the cloud are down? The vendor didn't create the flood or outage. Therefore, the disruption may not be covered by the SLA. What does it mean if the problem is the vendor's responsibility? Will the vendor be liable for your lost business when the service is down, or will it simply refund the money you were charged during the outage? In many cases, end-user businesses have complex insurance policies to cover these types of technology outages that lead to business disruptions.

Performance claims also constitute SLAs, which are formal commitments for performance of the resource in actual use. In many cases, cloud vendors battle each other and on-premises technologies in terms of uptime. One vendor may claim 99.99 percent uptime while another might claim 99.999 percent uptime. Although the difference may seem negligible, an extra nine is equivalent to approximately 47 more minutes of uptime a year. Forty-seven minutes may sound like a small disruption or a catastrophe, depending on the workload — for example, a test environment versus a retailer's transactional system. Table 4-1 shows the approximate amount of downtime per a year based on system availability.

TABLE 4-1   **Downtime Based on System Availability**

Availability as a percentage	Downtime per year
90% known as "one nine"	36.53 days
99% "two nines"	3.65 days
99.9% "three nines"	8.77 hours
99.99% "four nines"	52.60 hours
99.999% "five nines"	5.26 minutes
99.9999% "six nines"	31.56 seconds

Of course, as you get more nines, the cost of the service will increase. A cloud that claims five nines will be more expensive than a less predictable offering that has two nines Claims are routinely verified by consumers and third-party auditors, either through test harnesses or within operation of the completed application or service. But SLAs go further: Failure of a computing resource to meet SLAs can and should be grounds for canceling contracts.

Addressing Poor Cloud and Computing Behaviors

Cloud providers routinely seek to make their computing environments secure and robust, but users of those environments can still engage in risky behaviors. We've all heard about people choosing passwords that are easy to guess, possibly leading to unauthorized theft of information or damage to software and systems. That's just one example of a dangerous behavior that companies work hard to prevent.

WARNING

Many corporate users bring their own devices to the workplace or use them when they're working remotely. The IT organization is responsible for making sure that the right software and the right best practices are in place to ensure safety and security. IT organizations can take steps to avoid these dangerous behaviors, starting with employee education about the dangers of poor security practices. Many companies implement governance strategies that explicitly control which systems employees can access and the data they're qualified to read or modify. Often, governance is based on the specific job the employee is performing with *role-based access control* (RBAC).

One more example of a security risk that is particularly relevant to today's employees is the use of social media. In previous generations, knowledge of company policies and information was understood to be proprietary to the company and employees helped each other learn and follow safe practices. However, a new generation has grown up with social media and uses it to share information, answer questions, and generally extend the user's community outside the company's boundaries. Many social media users do understand the risks, but some don't and may not recognize the danger in sharing corporate information or business practices outside the company.

Managing Internal Cloud Resources

As the cloud becomes ubiquitous as a way to deliver services to customers, the management of those resources can make the difference between success and failure. Because the business is serving cloud resources to its own employees and perhaps its business partners, it's not a public cloud provider, but will deliver cloud resources via private or hybrid clouds. If it's using a hybrid cloud, the business may well pass public cloud resources to its internal customers, making the business both a public cloud consumer as well as a private cloud provider.

Not surprisingly, many of the issues regarding the consumption of cloud services are still relevant if your business provides cloud resources to customers, employees, and/or partners. The biggest difference is that the consumers of public cloud providers are much more diverse than the consumers within a single business, so it's normal for a private or hybrid cloud to offer only resources and services that are specific to that business.

REMEMBER

Regardless of the scope of offerings, issues like self-service, SLAs, and approved resources are just as critical, if not more so, to consumers of private and hybrid clouds.

Managing a hybrid cloud environment

Businesses are increasingly leveraging a combination of public and private clouds. The combination of these resources provides the benefits of scalability, flexibility, and performance to their internal computing consumers. Nowadays, with public clouds offering a high degree of security to match its broad catalog of services and resources, companies who still use private or hybrid clouds may have even more stringent requirements than before. As cloud computing matures and becomes core to the business strategy, the organization will likely select well vetted applications and resources, with more thorough security. In a private or hybrid cloud context, the approval process will be more important than ever.

REMEMBER

Carefully curated cloud resources offered for use in private or hybrid clouds are perfect for self-service. Not only will the carefully selected resources have been preapproved by the business with licensing or purchase already completed, but the resources will be specifically what the company requires to enable and secure critical in-house applications. In a mature self-service hybrid cloud, all the available resources and applications will be well architected to be the building blocks of a productive and safe data center.

Understanding the role of internal SLAs

When a company is a private or hybrid cloud provider to its internal consumers, the company should define SLAs for the resources and services provided. Doing so will formalize the operational requirements for those services and increase the chances that consumers will be pleased with the internal services. SLAs provide objective targets for performance and other operational characteristics, such as meantime between failures, and therefore are important for determining whether performance problems with applications are due to problems with the application or problems with the resources and services that the application uses.

In the public cloud, management of resources and services is the responsibility of the public cloud vendor or the third party who provides the software. A responsible organization should continually monitor the software operation to ensure that SLAs are being met. In the private cloud environment, it's usually the responsibility of IT operations to monitor the software for deviations from SLA commitments.

While public cloud providers have the responsibility to watch SLAs, they have many customers and may not always respond immediately. On the other hand, a company running its own private cloud has one customer (itself) and is equally responsible for ensuring that all applications, services, and resources are always working effectively. In some organizations, executives will be watching whether SLAs are being met because problems can affect the company's bottom line.

Managing Internal Services

As more businesses rely on cloud computing, they're creating internal services that are delivered to consumers within a company via a private or public cloud or a hybrid of both. These consumers are likely to be spread across all divisions of a company and have differing levels of technical expertise. They may not be aware of differences between applications running in private, hybrid, or public cloud contexts. But regardless of where applications are served from, internal consumers of cloud services expect professional applications to be operating with reliability and security and be backed by professional support. This situation is not very different from applications provided from a precloud data center or running on a desktop workstation.

Support for internal applications may come from IT or from a call center — both managed within the company providing the private or hybrid cloud. It's important that the company handling the support have first-hand access to the computing environment so that it can determine the causes of problems that consumers run into, or better, see and resolve problems before consumers call with a problem.

Supporting cloud customers

Providing call centers and support for internal consumers of private/hybrid cloud applications is an essential part of managing a private or hybrid cloud. When customers run into problems with an application, they expect quick help. For third-party applications, comprehensive support will usually come from those third parties although internal support should be aware of the common issues consumers may encounter. But if applications are developed or maintained in-house by internal development teams or by IT acting as a development organization, then development has a role to play with support.

For their part, support organizations pride and measure themselves on delivering quality and timely support. In fact, support organizations increasingly see a reduction of support calls as a goal. Reducing the number of calls can be accomplished by making the software more robust and more intuitive, but support organizations have little control over the software features being developed. Hence, development and support need to work closely together to provide world-class support.

Monitoring internal and external systems

High quality support requires knowledge of the systems being supported and their operational status. Customer problems may be due to misunderstandings or lack of knowledge of how an application works or how to use it to get a specific result.

In these cases, support needs to understand the application in depth so that it can guide the customer in the right direction. Of course, hopefully the customer has been trained to use the application, but once the customer calls, support must address the issues.

Imagine that a customer calls with a problem regarding a specific feature of an application. When support receives the call, the first step will likely be to ask the customer what application they were using and what they were doing. This type of call probably happens every day, perhaps all day long. Remember that support is being measured on how quickly they can help customers, so how can they streamline this process? One answer is that the application should be tracking each user's activities and saving the information in a location that is accessible to support. Then, when a customer calls, support can look up the customer's recent activities and quickly know exactly what they were doing when they called support. When the process is fully automated, the phone system can recognize the caller, find the username, and present the support staff with the customer's latest activities.

Rather than asking the caller for what application they were using, the support staff can answer the call with "I see you were using our CRM application and just got an error message when you tried to look up a business by its nickname. Is that what you're calling about?" The time saved on each call, multiplied by all the calls, will be a big success for the support organization, the customer, and the company.

This example is just one of many that shows how monitoring applications improves the management of those applications. The following sections look at a few more examples.

Monitoring resources imported from the public cloud

In a hybrid cloud context, you rely on public cloud resources to augment the services used in the private cloud portion of the hybrid environment. To verify that those resources are operating with sufficient performance and meeting SLAs, you have a few choices:

>> **Set up test software in the public cloud to sample performance of the resources.** On the positive side, by testing the resource outside of your computing stack, you'll avoid affecting your application's performance. On the negative side, you may be testing resources that are so independent of your application that the testing results aren't applicable to your application's performance.

>> **Set up that same test software in the hybrid cloud.** The results are more likely to be consistent with what your application is experiencing, but the downside is that the testing will have a greater impact on the performance of your infrastructure because that's where the testing is operating.

>> **Look to see whether the resources you're testing have a dashboard or other operational information available to you.** If so, it may provide the performance information you're looking for.

>> **Instrument the application running in the hybrid environment to log the actual performance of the resources as delivered to the application.** If done carefully, it will have little impact on the application's performance. This approach, which is perhaps the best solution, is desirable as it will be the most accurate way to monitor the resources' behavior, and the results can be integrated with all the other issues being monitored by the application.

Regardless of which path you follow, the testing and reporting of resource performance should be automated (so humans don't have to keep watching), and a notification system should be used to send serious failure information to support teams.

Monitoring the cloud infrastructure

Public cloud vendors provide information about the operational status of major subsystems and services within their cloud environments. The same type of information should be maintained for private and hybrid clouds. Although this information is usually high level, ensuring that basic services are working properly should be the first thing that support people look to verify.

Monitoring applications and services

Applications can report on the actions of application users to help support personnel provide advice to users who call with troubles. That same information about what users are doing is also very useful for developers and IT. User experience experts can look at how users work with the application to see problems in the user interface, opportunities for streamlining the user's experience, and bugs in the application. Product managers use the information to verify that features are being used as intended and to explore how new features can improve the application.

Applications routinely generate *logs*, or records of exactly what the application has done. Developers examine logs after applications crash to help figure out why the crash occurred. With the use of log analysis tools, logs can reveal operational patterns that may suggest ways to improve the application.

Applications can also be instrumented to provide other useful information to the business, including Key Performance Indicators (KPIs) that, when designed properly, can disclose whether applications are meeting the goals they were designed to achieve.

TIP

Increasingly, artificial intelligence and machine learning are being applied to old operational data to discover the patterns associated with problems so that current performance can be quickly assessed for recurring problems or the symptoms of problems that can then be evaluated by other tools.

Constructing dashboards

A wealth of data and information comes from a busy cloud environment, and many employees can use that information to solve their daily challenges. No one can process all that information in its raw state; there are just too many details.

Harnessing this information into a form that is useful requires at least two parts:

» Analysis software that processes and reduces the data to a manageable form

» A visualization technique that makes the information easy for people to recognize

Dashboards are often the best tool for presenting operational information to various audiences. With flexibility in how dashboards are constructed, different views with different focuses can be designed for different audiences. Support needs information to help users with problems, developers need to see performance data and information about what customers are doing, product managers need to see KPI and other usability information, and executives need to see high-level status and data on customer acceptance.

Managing External Services

One characteristic of a hybrid cloud environment is that an organization will have a variety of services that need to be managed. Some will be straightforward services, such as the ability to store data that is rarely used but must be kept. In other situations, businesses are developing their own applications that will operate in the public cloud. To be successful, visibility and control over external and internal resources is critical.

DevOps and deployment to public clouds

Nowadays, best practices for developing software for the cloud are based on DevOps practices. *DevOps* combines Development with Operations and enables continuous development and deployment of software. (See Chapter 11 for a more in-depth discussion of DevOps.) DevOps streamlines the management of application and service life cycles by eliminating handoffs between development and operations and makes the software more robust because developers are now paying more attention to operational issues.

After an application is deployed to the cloud, DevOps engineers continue to watch the software while it's running. If operational issues come up, the engineers responsible for the software are immediately involved and can either solve problems tactically in the cloud or, if necessary, make changes to the application and redeploy it with fixes as quickly as the code can be changed and tested.

External system monitoring

With applications and services used by customers in other companies, it's even more important that system monitoring gather application and service usage than it was within a single company. After all, companies have many more opportunities to quiz their own employees about how well systems work than quizzing employees of other companies.

Similarly, pushing product and operational status to external customers becomes more important because the customers will have less awareness of those issues and less loyalty to the software than internal customers.

Application and service life cycles

In the public cloud, there is less tolerance for problems, outages, and frustrations. Applications and services in the public cloud must be as robust as possible. Consider these issues for making applications and services fit the "always on and always available" expectations of the public cloud:

>> DevOps's goal for continuous development and deployment is to release new features as soon as they're ready. But while it was once okay to take the application down while it was being upgraded, it isn't acceptable in the cloud. Applications and services must be able to be upgraded without disturbing customers who are using the application.

>> Application and server failures are always bad, but they're probably worse in the cloud (if only because there may be many more users). Designing in failover capabilities so that a failure causes only a momentary pause is much more desirable than having the application be completely unavailable, or perhaps worse, cause user data loss.

The Future of Multicloud Management

Many different services and deployment models are emerging as part of the hybrid cloud fabric. We're at the stage where it's becoming more and more important to be able to bring together the management of all the internal and external cloud and data center services necessary to manage a well-run operation.

Not only are businesses leveraging a public cloud, they often will be using several different public cloud services across departments. When you combine that with all the private and third-party services being deployed and operated, there is escalating complexity as you scale. You should begin asking some key questions:

>> What are all the services being used, and which ones do you anticipate adding?

>> Why is a service being used? Does it fulfill the business requirement?

>> Do the services provide the level of security and governance demanded by management?

>> Is the data that the application generates stored in the appropriate geography?

>> Is the latency of the overall environment acceptable to all service consumers?

You have to deal with a lot of issues as you begin to put together your multicloud management strategy. You can't think of your services as separate islands of computing, applications, or storage. Rather you need to put in place an infrastructure and approach that provides a seamless interface across all of your services so that you can provide consistency and predictability across all of your services.

Chapter **5**

Standards in a Multicloud World

As the cloud market matures, standards are becoming more important than ever. Very few companies are using a single cloud or computing platform to meet all their needs. Therefore, it is critical that there are consistent and predictable ways to collaborate across computing services. A variety of standards are important for cloud computing. In this chapter, we discuss the standards that are becoming imperative to the wide adoption of cloud computing.

What Are Standards?

Standards are established common and repeatable practices that have been agreed to by a business or group. An *open standard* is one that is publicly and freely available, one that has been developed in a public context where anyone who is affected by the standard can contribute. An open standard assumes that experienced developers will contribute to the viability of the offering. Typically, different vendors, groups, and end users collaborate to develop standards based on the broad expertise of a large number of stakeholders. Organizations can leverage these standards as a common foundation and build on top of them.

Broad adoption of open standards throughout an industry or other groups is critical in order to yield the benefits. Building software that complies with standards allows systems to work together, reduces costs by allowing competition between different implementations of a standard, and gives consumers more choices while ensuring compatibility. Without broadly adopted open standards for the models, formats, and conventions for interacting with cloud capabilities, multicloud environments would present many different interfaces for the same services, causing much greater complexity and incompatibilities.

Simply put, without standards or agreed upon approaches, moving your infrastructure or applications from one cloud provider to another or from on-premises to a public or private cloud is a difficult prospect that can slow an organization's development. Integrating your on-premises data center in a multicloud model would be difficult without open source standards. Standards also help ensure security and prevent vendor lock-in. All these issues are key to establishing a hybrid and multicloud environment.

Evolution of Standards

Standards have generally been established in four ways:

>> **Multinational bodies:** Treaties or other similar international legal agreements typically govern these bodies. These groups generally have long procedures and red tape before agreement is reached. Members may be diplomats instead of technical experts. The International Organization for Standards (ISO) is one such group and is comprised of representatives from countries all over the world. ISO has developed more than 17,500 standards covering many subject areas, and new standards are developed every year.

>> **Industry consortiums:** A *consortium* is typically an organized group dedicated to developing standards for a specific industry requirement. Even though the members may be competitors, they know that coming together will help everyone. These groups are often more streamlined and agile than international bodies and often directly engage technical experts in the process. The Apache Group, The Open Group, World Wide Web Consortium, and OASIS are some examples of industry consortiums.

>> **An ad hoc group:** *Ad hoc groups* are self-organized and governed. These groups are often built around open-source initiatives. They can be a loose body that discusses their matters through an Internet message board, or they may be more formally organized. These groups have even fewer processes than industry consortiums and are therefore able to quickly adapt and change as technology moves. A downside to the lower process overhead is that when difficult decisions need to be made or problems arise, getting to the correct solution and reaching a consensus may be difficult or impossible.

>> **De facto standards:** A *de facto standard* emerges when an approach or product is used so extensively used that it becomes a standard. The important distinction is that a de facto standard is not created by a specific body or organization, but instead develops through practice. Often, de facto standards emerge when industry best practices converge.

According to the National Institute of Standards and Technology (NIST), standards can be categorized based on their level of maturity:

>> None

>> Under development

>> Approved

>> A reference

>> Market accepted (in widespread use)

>> Retired

Some standards organizations require at least two implementations of a standard before it can be accepted, which, needless to say, takes time and accounts for why de facto standards often become standards.

On the other hand, multiple implementations is how customers get the benefit of choice. In new technology environments, the philosophy is often to innovate now and standardize later. In fast-paced IT environments, developers may implement nonstandard features to get a job done quickly. They leave the problems of implementing standard components for another day or let somebody else deal with them.

Categories of Cloud-Related Standards

Most standards continue to evolve over time. Given the relative youth of the cloud, it's not surprising that cloud standards are still in the process of being developed and implemented. For example, Kubernetes, which has grown into a well-accepted standard for container orchestration, did not exist a few years ago.

Following the development of these standards can be frustrating to vendor and consumers who are anxious to develop new software. Sometimes a software platform is created by a single vendor that provides that software freely to the industry. In some situations, a vendor with a product that can't gain acceptance in the market will give away its product in hopes of gaining traction.

For a standard to truly succeed, it needs to be

>> Broadly recognized and adopted by vendors

>> Broadly adopted and demanded by consumers

>> Open source

If these criteria aren't met, a "standard" is far from standard and is instead just a document.

Regardless, establishing cloud standards is important because standards help improve choice, reduce cost, and improve quality. While standards are being developed in many specific areas, areas where standards are being broadly developed include the following:

>> Interoperability

>> Portability

>> Security

Interoperability

Interoperability is the ability for independent systems to work together and/or share information. One of the most important aspects of interoperability is the ability to enable applications to exchange data in a multicloud or on-premises data center. It also includes independent cloud deployments working together, such as public clouds from different vendors or interoperability between a private cloud and an external public cloud. This goal is most easily achieved when one vendor offers cloud products for different contexts: public, private, and hybrid clouds.

Interoperability is especially important in a multicloud environment because the goal of being able to easily move workloads among multiple clouds requires some means of achieving interoperability; without it, the separate clouds will require much more effort to support your goals.

To reach the goal of interoperability, standardized interfaces are required. For example, typically, cloud providers will develop an Application Programming Interface (API) that describes how your resources communicate with their resources.

WARNING

APIs are important, but problems can arise. If every cloud provider develops a different API, you run into the problem of *API proliferation,* a situation where there are so many APIs that organizations have difficulty managing and using them all. Having proprietary APIs leads to vendor lock-in, which means that once you start using a particular vendor, you're committed to it. All of these situations can also lead to portability issues.

One of the most important emerging standards for cloud interoperability and orchestration is Kubernetes. *Kubernetes* provides an open-source container orchestration platform that can automate the tasks of creating modern applications. Applications can either be encapsulated, as they exist today, or rewritten as a series of native microservices. Kubernetes has emerged as an important open-source standard that is being widely adopted. For more details about Kubernetes, see Chapter 6.

Several emerging open-source standards are critical for interoperability that are related to Kubernetes. These standards include

>> **Istio,** a service mesh that is designed to enable services to connect to each other in a secure and controlled manner

>> **Calico,** another open-source standard that allows networking and network policy within a Kubernetes cluster across clouds

>> **Helm,** an open-source platform, a package manager for Kubernetes that enables developers to package, configure, and deploy applications and services onto a Kubernetes cluster

The benefit of the combination of Kubernetes with services such as Istio, Calico, and Helm is that it permits developers to write services once and deploy them on any cloud. With a Kubernetes and microservices approach, developers can push code out to any deployment model without changing the entire app. This capability allows an increased ability to respond to customer feedback, competition, and potential security issues. With Kubernetes in place, the same infrastructure can exist on any public cloud or private cloud without any change.

Knative is a pure Kubernetes universal resource model that provides a consistent API-based wrapper service for legacy workloads. Knative can work with a variety of models, including Cloud Foundry, OpenShift, and serverless frameworks, such as Apache OpenWhisk and Fission, which are both built on top of Kubernetes and Istio in order to support serverless event driven functions.

Another player in the interoperability space is the Open Services for Lifecycle Collaboration (OSLC). The OSLC is working on the specifications for linked data to be used to federate information and capabilities across cloud services and systems.

NIST has also cataloged existing standards. According to NIST, many existing IT standards can contribute to interoperability among cloud consumer applications and among cloud services themselves. The following two interoperability standards were developed and accepted specifically for the cloud:

>> **Open Cloud Computing Interface (OCCI):** A set of standards developed by the Open Grid Forum, OCCI is a protocol and API for all kinds of management tasks and utilizes the REST (Representational State Transfer) approach for interaction. It began its life as a management API for IaaS services. It now supports PaaS and SaaS deployments.

>> **The Cloud Data Management Interface (CDMI):** Developed by the Storage Networking Industry Association (SNIA), it defines the functional interface that applications should use to create, retrieve, update, and delete data elements from the cloud. It also utilizes a RESTful approach.

Portability

Portability enables you to take applications, data, or instances running on one vendor's system and deploy it on another vendor's implementation. For example, you may want to move your data or application from one cloud environment to another. Or you may want to use IaaS services to gain additional compute power from a variety of public cloud during peak demand times or when on-premises resources are otherwise tied up. An example is when you need extra capacity to meet peak demands, so you share the load with external cloud providers. Or you may want to move your virtual server from one environment to another.

The goal of portability is to allow your components (such as an application or data) to be moved between different contexts without modification. At one time, this would have required each context to provide the same APIs and a set of reusable services to execute consistently. However, new approaches allow portability between contexts regardless of the platform, operating system, location, storage, or anything else in a provider's environment — much as how the Java programming language achieves portability by providing a common operating environment in each context.

REMEMBER

Portability of workloads from one cloud to another is a key requirement for mature hybrid computing environments. It is only through standards that portability will happen.

In addition to Kubernetes, a number of important standards are key. For example, the Open Virtualization Format (OVF) developed by the Distributed Management Task Force (DMTF) focuses on portability and interoperability for virtual machines.

On the data side, if the data is being moved from one application to a different application, then standard formats and protocols are needed for data to be moved between one environment and another. Most experts believe that this kind of data portability is more difficult than application portability because there are different kinds of data, with different volumes, and that ultimately the control of that data belongs to the data's owner.

The CDMI standard has been approved to help in data portability. Another standard currently under development by the IEEE is IEEE P2301, Draft Guide for Cloud Portability and Interoperability Profiles (CPIP).

Security

Cloud security is such a big concern that we devote Chapter 15 to it. You need to make sure that the right controls, procedures, and technology are in place to protect your corporate assets. Your organization has invested a great deal internally to protect your assets, and it's reasonable to assume that your cloud provider will do the same. A sound security strategy is especially true in a hybrid environment where your private cloud or data center has touchpoints with public cloud services.

Cloud security standards are a set of processes, policies, and best practices that ensure the proper controls are placed over an environment to prevent application, information, identity, and access issues (to name a few).

Numerous standards have already been approved and are currently used widely in the area of security, including standards for the following:

>> **Authentication and authorization:** Several standards are in use to verify the identity of a person or computer, including standards associated with the following keys:

- IETF RFC 3820: X.509 Public Key Infrastructure (PKI) Proxy Certificate Profile

- IETF RFC5280: Internet X.509 Public Key Infrastructure Certificate and Certificate Revocation List (CRL) Profile

- ITU-T X.509 | ISO/IEC 9594-8 — The Directory: Public Key and attribute certificate frameworks: Information technology — open systems interconnection

See Chapter 15 for more on keys and encryption.

>> **Security monitoring and incident response:** Some standards have been approved to handle security monitoring and incident response, including the best practices developed by NIST in the NIST SP 800-61Rev. 2 Computer Security Incident Handling Guide.

>> **Confidentiality, integrity, and availability of data:** We address data issues more fully in Chapter 14. However, a number of standards that have been on the market for some time deal with encryption of data, keys, and data transport. These standards include the Key Management Interoperability Protocol (KMIP), developed by OASIS, and FIPS 186-3 Digital Signature Standard (DSS), developed by NIST.

>> **Security policy management:** These standards set forth best practices and procedures for implementing policies around security. FIPS 200: Minimum Security Requirements for Federal Information and Information Systems developed by NIST is an example of this kind of standard.

For a complete list of these standards and gaps in security standards, we encourage you to get a copy of the NIST Cloud Computing Standards Roadmap at https://nvlpubs.nist.gov/nistpubs/SpecialPublications/NIST.SP.500-291r2.pdf.

Organizations Building Momentum around Standards

Several organizations and informal groups are addressing standards issues in the cloud environment. Some of these organizations have been around for years; others are relatively new.

Note: Some of these standards bodies aren't necessarily looking to create new standards. Instead, they're looking to leverage existing best practices and standards, such as those used in implementing the web.

Cloud Security Alliance

We talk a lot about the Cloud Security Alliance (CSA) (www.cloudsecurity.org) in Chapter 15. The CSA formed in late 2008 when cloud security became important in users' minds. Its founding members include Dell, PGP, QualSys, Ascaler, and the Information Systems Audit and Control Association (ISACA). The CSA's goal is to promote best practices to provide security assurance in cloud computing and to provide education.

REMEMBER

CSA itself isn't a formal standards body. However, its objectives include promoting understanding between users and providers of cloud computing regarding security requirements and researching best practices for cloud security.

The CSA offers training in three areas:

>> Governance, Risk Management, and Compliance (GRC)

>> Payment Card Industry Data Security Standard (PCI DSS) controls in the cloud

>> Cloud Computing Security Knowledge (CCSK)

The CSA also provides a certificate in CCSK via a 50-question timed online test. According to the CSA, the CCSK is meant to augment, not replace, certifications in information security, audit, and governance. In 2012, the CSA rolled out its Security, Trust & Assurance Registry (STAR), a free, publicly accessible registry that documents the security controls provided by cloud vendors. The registry is a form of self-regulation by cloud providers and is meant to help ensure that CSA best practices become de facto standards.

Recent reports produced by the CSA include version 3 of its Security Guidance for Critical Areas of Focus in Cloud Computing (https://cloudsecurityalliance. org/research/security-guidance/), which we talk more about in Chapter 15.

Distributed Management Task Force (DMTF)

The DMTF (www.dmtf.org) has been around for nearly 30 years and may best be known for its *common information model,* which is a common view of IT equipment. Its goal is to bring the IT industry together to collaborate on systems management standards.

The DTMF formed the Cloud Management Initiative to advance standards and technologies across the various DMTF working groups, including the Cloud Management Working Group (CMWG), the Cloud Auditing Data Federation Working Group (CADF), the Software Entitlement Working Group (SEWG), and the Open Virtualization Working Group (OVF).

National Institute of Standards and Technology (NIST)

NIST (www.nist.gov) has been in existence since 1901. It's a nonregulatory federal agency that is part of the U.S. Department of Commerce. Its goal is to promote innovation and U.S. competitiveness by advancing standards, measurement science, and technology. NIST has its hands in all kinds of standards, from fire-related standards for your mattress to the auto emissions your car must (not) pass on the road.

NIST formed its cloud computing group to help federal agencies understand cloud computing. However, its reach has gone much further than the federal government. For example, its definition of cloud computing models are widely used across all industries (refer to the NIST special publication 800-545, September 2011).

NIST completed its Cloud Computing Standards Roadmap Version 2 (NIST special publication 500-291, July 2013, https://nvlpubs.nist.gov/nistpubs/SpecialPublications/NIST.SP.500-291r2.pdf). The document's purpose is to assess the state of standards in cloud computing and advance the U.S. federal government's secure adoption of cloud computing. In doing so, it works closely with public and private organizations, including U.S. industry. The document contains an inventory of standards that currently exist to support cloud computing in the areas of security, interoperability, and portability. It also identifies some of the gaps. We discuss this document in the previous section of this chapter.

Cloud Standards Customer Council (CSCC)

The OMG (Object Management Group; www.omg.org) was formed in 1989 and is an international group focused on developing enterprise integration standards for a wide range of industries, including government, life sciences, and health care. The OMG creates many working groups that focus on issues important to both vendors and customers. One important group within the OMG is called the Cloud Standards Customer Council (CSCC).

The CSCC (www.cloud-council.org) provides modeling standards for software and other processes and has brought together many of the most influential companies in cloud computing. IBM, Computer Associates, Kaavo, Software AG, and Rackspace are the groups founding sponsors. The goal of the CSCC is to establish a set of customer-driven/end-user requirements to ensure cloud users have the same flexibility and openness that they have with traditional IT environments. CSCC will prioritize key interoperability issues in reference architecture, security and compliance, cloud management, and hybrid clouds.

OPEN COMMONS CONSORTIUM (OCC)

The OCC (www.occ-data.org), previously the Open Cloud Consortium, was formed in 2008. One of its goals is to support the development of standards for cloud computing and frameworks for interoperability among clouds. In fact, it operates cloud infrastructure. It also manages cloud computing infrastructure to support scientific research. Members include Cisco and Yahoo! as well as a number of universities including Johns Hopkins University.

The OCC has a number of working groups. One in particular deals with standards — Malstone is a reference benchmark and standard for dealing with data-intensive computing in the cloud.

The idea is that this group will work with most of the standards bodies listed in the following sections to bring the end-user perspective more fully into the standards discussion.

The Open Group

The Open Group (http://www.opengroup.org/) is a global consortium with more than 400 member organizations that focuses on achieving business objectives through standards. Its goal is to lead the development of vendor-neutral IT standards and certifications.

In the cloud, the Open Group Cloud Work Group is looking to create a common understanding among various groups about ensuring safe and secure architectures. The group is working with organizations such as the Cloud Security Alliance to make this happen.

Storage Networking Industry Association (SNIA)

The SNIA (www.snia.org) has focused for more than 20 years on developing storage solution specifications and technologies, global standards, and storage education. This organization's mission is to "lead the storage industry worldwide in developing and promoting vendor-neutral architectures, standards, and educational services that facilitate the efficient management, movement, and security of information."

The SNIA is responsible for the Cloud Data Management Interface. Applications can use this functional interface "to create, retrieve, update and delete data elements from the Cloud." Clearly, this standard is important for hybrid cloud environments that deal with data between on-premises and public cloud deployments.

Vertical groups

In addition to the preceding standards groups and discussion groups, vertical industry groups — groups comprised of members from a particular industry such as technology and retail — are also beginning to look at cloud standards. Here are two examples:

» **TeleManagement Forum (TM Forum):** This large group consists of service providers, cable and network operators, software suppliers, equipment suppliers, and systems integrators. It has provided a standardized operational framework for the creation, delivery, and monetization of digital services. It recently launched its TM Forum Cloud & New Services Initiative that focuses on leveraging these standards into the cloud marketplace. To learn more about the group, visit www.tmforum.org.

» **Association for Retail Technology Standards (ARTS):** The goal of this group is to create an open environment where retailers and technology vendors can work together to create international retail technology standards. To read more about ARTS, you can visit https://nrf.com/.

The Impact of Standards on the Multicloud

Standards, whether developed by SDOs or through the de facto method, play an important role in cloud computing and in a multicloud model. In a multicloud world, many interfaces are between those that exist at your cloud provider and your applications, data, servers, and so on. This state of affairs means that security is a risk in many places. These risks can include areas where it's costly to interoperate and where you can get bogged down and limit your options in terms of cloud providers. Standards let you do the following:

» **Move your infrastructure or applications from one cloud provider to another.** With cloud standards across clouds, you don't have to rewrite code. In a multicloud world, where you may have part of the resources associated with an application on your own premises and part with a cloud provider, this capability is important because it enables your organization to be more flexible about where your resources may be located.

» **Prevent vendor lock-in.** Lock-in occurs when you're so entrenched with a particular provider and its interfaces that moving to another provider is too costly. Removing barriers to lock-in increases your choices.

» **Integrate applications more easily between your on-premises data center and private and public cloud environments.** Face it; integrating your assets across multiple environments can be time-consuming and costly if every cloud provider has a proprietary model. Standards help to make integration easier and eliminate many common barriers.

> » **Defining and understanding microservices**

> » **Making sense of containers**

> » **Realizing the critical need for cloud native services**

> » **Discovering why APIs are growing in importance**

Chapter **6**

A Closer Look at Cloud Services

One of the most important benefits businesses gain from cloud computing is the ability to modularize application services so that they can be linked together to create a cohesive environment. The new generation of agile application development and deployment means software services can be developed and deployed virtually anywhere.

In this chapter, we discuss what it means to transform your computing environment into independent services that are supported by containers and container orchestration. The techniques needed to create these new services are defined in a new generation of software development and deployment — Platform as a Service (PaaS). (For more details on PaaS, refer to Chapter 10.) The combination of microservices, containers, container management, and PaaS provides the agility and flexibility to turn cloud computing into a platform for the future.

The Importance of Modularity

To gain the benefit of cloud computing, you must understand the importance of modularity. Typical users of computing services do not care where a service is running — they only care about availability and performance of that service. This requirement is changing everything from development of software to how those software services are deployed and managed. Therefore, code needs to be designed as lightweight code without dependencies. Each service can be developed and deployed by small independent teams. This flexibility provides greater benefits in terms of performance, cost and scalability. This approach of building services, packaging them together and managing them consistently and predictably, demands a new approach to software development and deployment.

Fundamentally, services encapsulate business functions needed by software and provide those functions in an easily accessible way. In fact, software developers have been creating services as long as programs have used subroutines, an early model for delivering a computing service. In other words, some forms of services have been around for a very long time. However, the practice of designing services has matured and services are more important than ever, particularly in cloud environments.

The movement toward a service orientation mindset is still relevant for organizations who want to build robust and flexible systems, achieve quicker time-to-market, and enhance workload portability. This containerization is becoming the means of deploying workloads into PaaS (Platform as a Service) cloud environments where an application's only connection to the environment is through services. Application containerization has brought about new management frameworks that simplify and streamline service and other workloads. This requires a more sophisticated approach to managing APIs (Application Programming Interfaces) as a fundamental means defining services and providing access to applications and other users of services.

Discovering Why Services Matter in the Cloud

The idea of creating services supported by Application Programming Interfaces (APIs) has been around for decades. In the early days of software development, subroutine libraries provided a shortcut for developers to execute a task quickly. Today services have been reimaged so that they're the actual building blocks of reusable services. In many instances, today's development teams are assembling applications from prebuilt services rather than coding applications from scratch.

TECHNICAL STUFF

The original concept that developed in the early 2000s was the *Service Oriented Architecture* (SOA). The concept was correct. Rather than build monolithic applications full of dependencies, SOA was intended to create smaller modular services that could be reused. The SOA concept preceded the wide adoption of cloud services. Therefore, SOA was intended as a way to make on-premises applications development and deployment more agile.

Once cloud services began to explode, it became clear that this new distributed model of computing required an even more comprehensive and sophisticated way of developing, deploying, and managing services. These services had to be able to work independently of each other but be able to be integrated together to create value.

These services also had to be designed to operate on different public and private clouds, which meant that there needed to be standardization.

Another key requirement is to be able to create application services that are designed and architected for the cloud — what is commonly called *cloud native*. The idea of cloud native is that these services take advantage of the underlying distributed nature of the cloud to improve agility, flexibility, and modularity.

Explaining Microservices

A cloud environment requires that you think differently about what an application is and how it operates in this highly distributed environment. Cloud-enabled applications are designed to be modular, distributed, deployed, and managed in an automated way. These characteristics require technologies that go beyond what was typical for the development of traditional software.

WARNING

It is common to think that you can simply take an existing monolithic application and simply move it to the cloud. While it is physically possible to place an aging application into a cloud, you gain no advantage in terms of costs or flexibility. The most practical way to gain value from the cloud is to think modular, which is why microservices are so important for cloud computing.

Microservices is a process of developing applications that consist of code that is independent of each other and of the underlying developing platform. Once created, each microservice runs a unique process and communicates through well-defined and standardized APIs. These services are defined in a catalog so that developers can more easily locate the right service and understand the governance rules for usage.

The future of cloud applications will be designed to support a cloud native approach (as we discuss later in this chapter in the "Defining Cloud Native Applications" section). Cloud native applications are built as a collection of multiple, independent microservices. Each of these microservices is designed to support one discrete, bounded piece of application functionality. Although these microservices are independent, they can be linked together in a coordinated fashion to provide all the functionality the application is intended to deliver.

Why are microservices so important for a true cloud environment? Consider these four key benefits:

>> Application development is simplified because each microservice is built to serve a specific and limited purpose. Small development teams can focus on writing code for narrowly defined and more easily understood functions.

>> Code changes will be smaller and less complex than with a complex integrated application, making it easier and faster to make changes, whether to fix a problem or to upgrade a service with new requirements.

>> Scalability — both up and down — makes it simpler to deploy an additional instance of a service or change that service as needs evolve.

>> Microservices are fully tested and validated. When new applications leverage existing microservices, developers can assume the integrity of the new application without the need for continual testing.

The imperative to manage microservices

Microservices can help organizations fully exploit the advantages of the cloud. Microservices are designed to be packaged within containers. *Containers* provide a technique for packaging applications so that they are abstracted from their runtime environments. Containers are then managed through orchestration services. These orchestration services are needed to manage both process and logic as well as data services. *Orchestration services* are designed to determine how and where the logic is deployed and how it is managed without worrying about version numbers and application-specific configuration issues.

In effect, it's a game of numbers; often many microservices and many instances of microservices are distributed over many systems. Combining microservices with Kubernetes creates a compelling way for organizations to optimize their environment for the cloud. For more on Kubernetes, see the section "Kubernetes and container orchestration," later in this chapter.

Containers

Docker, CRI-O, Containerd, and frakti are four of the most common container run times. You can think of a *container* as packaged up software code along with all of its dependencies so that it can run consistently across clouds and on premises. This packaging up of code is often call *encapsulation*. Encapsulating code is significant for developers because they don't have to develop code based on each individual environment. Developers don't have to worry about version numbers and platform-specific configuration issues. With containerization, a developer can transfer code from a desktop to a virtual machine (VM) or from a Windows operating system to Linux running on a public cloud, with the confidence that the code will execute in a predictable way. The single container package eliminates the complexities of bundling the application code together with the related configuration files, libraries, and dependencies required for it to run. The developer can simply focus on the application logic and any services required to support that application logic.

Containers bring virtualization abstraction to the next level

Containers build on the virtualization concept. Traditional applications ran on physical servers and utilized the compute resources of that infrastructure. To ensure that applications would run predictability, businesses placed each application on its own server. If multiple applications were placed on the same server, there was the chance that one application would monopolize all of the hardware resources, causing the other application to fail. If, for example, you had two applications on a server, there was no way of telling the server to prioritize one application over another. The operating system treated each application equally.

Many businesses have hundreds, if not thousands, of applications. Purchasing more and more servers for each application and each new prototype is clearly expensive, difficult to manage, and cannot scale as a business grow.

Virtualization dramatically changed the way businesses approached application deployment. In essence, virtualization "tricks" the hardware into thinking there are multiple servers. So, for example, if you run two virtual machines (VMs) on a single a server, the underlying hardware acts as if there are two separate servers. Your operations team can dedicate 75 percent of the hardware resources to one application and the remaining resources to the other application. The VM allows companies to abstract servers from the underlying hardware. Each VM runs its own operating system and can be completely isolated from other VMs running on the same hardware. From a cost perspective, VMs, of course, make sense; you no longer need to purchase more and more hardware to support new projects. In addition, IT departments could become much more efficient. Rather than operating servers at 10 or 20 percent of capacity, hardware could run at close to full capacity with multiple VMs running on top. In addition, it is easy to "spin up" a VM or delete one. So if a team wanted to experiment with a new project, they can quickly create a VM rather than needing to procure hardware. Likewise, if they decide to move on from the project or bring it to the next level, the VM can be easily destroyed.

Containerization technology brings the abstraction layer to the next level: Containers abstract the operating system. Therefore, a container or cluster of containers can run directly on top of the operating system kernel. Containers eliminate the need for each application to have its own operating system. This advancement means that containers are dramatically smaller than virtual machines and can be spun up more quickly and more easily moved between on-premises and the cloud and between cloud environments. Containers are highly portable between environments because they carry with them all of their dependencies.

Companies, such as Facebook, Netflix, and Uber, must constantly change their platforms to adapt to changing user expectations. All these companies take advantage of continuous integration and continuous delivery (CI/CD), containerization, and microservices to help quickly respond to customer demands and market conditions. Companies must be prepared for surges in demand as well as unpredictable competitive threats. The sense of urgency is palpable: Adapt quickly or die.

Container orchestration

As you begin to containerize applications and microservices, you need a way to manage your containers. A single application can be made up of hundreds or even thousands of containers. Containers orchestration platforms help to streamline processes like the installation, scaling, and management of containerized applications.

The platform also automates the management of a container environment. Scaling containerized applications for higher demand, updating applications, controlling the versioning of containers, and providing monitoring, logging, and debugging of containers are all processes that are assisted by the orchestration platform. Kubernetes is the most popular container orchestration platform.

Kubernetes

Kubernetes (often called "k8s" or "kube" by developers) is an open-source platform for managing containerized workloads and services. The technology was created by engineers at Google and later open sourced by the company in 2014. It's worth noting that Kubernetes is Greek for helmsman or captain, hence the logo contains a helm and many of the ancillary Kubernetes technologies have nautical names, such as Helm, Rudr, Harbor, and others. Like a larger ship loading, safeguarding, transporting, and delivering real life containers, Kubernetes controls software containers.

TIP

One way to think about Kubernetes is to understand its relationship to other services. For example, think of microservices as the content of the service and containers as the wrapper. Now, think of Kubernetes as the way that the microservices managed within containers are brought together based on the defined workflow.

Kubernetes is not the only container orchestration platform. Other platforms, including open-source projects like Docker, Swarm, and Apache Mesos along with platforms tied to a specific cloud, like Amazon Elastic Container Service (Amazon ECS), emerged early on and continue to have users. However, Kubernetes has become the dominant choice for developers. The market has coalesced around Kubernetes because of its functionality, large and growing ecosystem, and portability between on premises, multiple public cloud environments, and private clouds.

Kubernetes has become a de facto standard across many businesses and clouds. In fact, Kubernetes has matured into a computing platform and ecosystem that helps organizations develop cloud native applications that can span multiple public and private clouds as well as on-premises architecture. (We discuss cloud native applications in the upcoming "Defining Cloud Native Applications" section.) Nearly every cloud vendor supports Kubernetes, and some are offering managed Kubernetes environments.

One of the important benefits of Kubernetes is that it standardizes the orchestration of container services. The technology is designed to support both stateful and stateless applications. Kubernetes abstracts each individual infrastructure platform and supports cluster federation and auto-balancing across hybrid clouds.

REMEMBER

Because Kubernetes has such a large open-source contributing community, the platforms support a large and rapidly growing ecosystem of tools and services, including Prometheus (an open-source tool for monitoring), Istio (an open-source service meshes), Kaniko (an open-source tool for building containers), and Open Tracing (an open-source tool for distributed tracing).

Kubernetes provides a platform for automating the development, scaling, and operation of systems across a cluster of hosts. In addition, some of the primary benefits of Kubernetes include

>> A standardized way to build, package, deploy, and run applications of any language

>> Portability across multiple cloud providers and the ability to avoid vendor lock-in

>> Horizontal auto-scaling so that additional pods are created as application demand increases

>> High availability through continual health checks to ensure that nodes and containers are operating as expected

>> Automated rollouts to updated applications or its configurations without causing downtime

Kubernetes provides tools for application deployment, service discovery, scheduling, updating, maintenance, and scaling. Kubernetes is extensible so that it can support a variety of use cases across many different implementations. Therefore, Kubernetes is architected to sit on top of the physical infrastructure.

Like most platforms, Kubernetes has a built-in set of rudimentary tools that allow you to monitor your servers. Given the extensible nature of Kubernetes, it's possible to add components to gain visibility into Kubernetes. For example, Custom Resource Definitions (CRD) are the way to extend Kubernetes and still leverage capabilities from the platform. CRD extends the API so that additional services can be added to the cluster.

Cataloging services

When you move to a microservices approach, you need to be able to keep track of each service as well as understand everything about that service.

First and foremost, you have to know that the service has been fully vetted. Is the service tested and approved for use? Who is able to make changes to the service? Under what conditions is it approved for use?

A microservice can contain a variety of capabilities, such as application services, networking services, and data services. Because a cloud needs to be able to use a service that may originate from many different places, a catalog is essential in both locating a service and understanding its characteristics.

Defining Cloud Native Applications

In the early days of computing, applications were constrained by the limitations of the expense of the hardware platforms and the limitations of memory and storage. Software had to be built in the most efficient way possible, even if that meant that the systems were inefficient and difficult to modernize.

The cloud model has changed these restrictions. As the cloud continues to mature, the way application services are designed has evolved. The solution is a cloud native application approach. *Cloud native* is a software framework designed with microservices, containers, and dynamic orchestration as well as continuous delivery of software. Every part of the cloud native application is housed within its own container and dynamically orchestrated with other containers to optimize the way resources are utilized.

The idea of cloud native was codified by The Cloud Native Computing Foundation (CNCF), an organization founded in 2015 under the auspices of the Linux Foundation. According to the foundation's documentation, "The Cloud Native Computing Foundation states that they builds sustainable ecosystems and fosters a community around a constellation of high-quality projects that orchestrate containers as part of a microservices architecture." The founding members of CNCF are some of the most important companies in the public and private cloud market and include Google, Twitter, Huawei, Intel, Cisco, IBM, Docker, Univa, and VMware.

The Cloud Native Computing Foundation offers a clear definition of cloud native:

>> **Container packaged:** A standard way to package applications that is resource efficient. More applications can be densely packed using a standard container format.

>> **Dynamically managed:** A standard way to discover, deploy, and scale up and down containerized applications.

>> **Microservices oriented:** A method to decompose the application into modular, independent services that interact through well-defined service contracts.

Moving from virtual machines to cloud native

Cloud computing has evolved significantly over the past decade making it easier for developers to quickly gain access to compute and storage capabilities and create a platform for applications creation and deployment.

Traditionally, developers have relied on virtual machines as a technique to create cloud services. In essence, *virtual machine software* makes a single system act as though it were a discrete collection of independent services. However, virtual machines sit on a layer of software, including the operating system, middleware, and tools, which makes the VM more complex and slows down the process of continuous integration and rapid applications development.

While virtual machines will continue to be an important software layer for many years to come, containers and container orchestration will become increasingly important. With the growth of cloud native applications, the requirement for containers will expand dramatically.

Creating innovation

Optimizing business value means that applications can take advantage of the distributed, scalable architecture the cloud platform provides in order to offer the highest levels of flexibility, scalability, and reusability. For a cloud native application, this is where true innovation lies today.

REMEMBER

A cloud native application fully exploits the benefits of cloud technology. It is important to recognize that a cloud native application is not defined by where it is running, but rather how it is built. Because a cloud native environment is based on containerization, it is not physically tied to a specific hardware or operating system. Therefore, cloud native applications are designed to work on a variety of cloud environment.

Differentiating cloud native applications

Traditionally, many organizations considered the cloud because of lower costs — a valid reason, but a limited one. Prior to being able to build cloud native applications, cost savings was often the main driver. Cloud native applications enable businesses to shift from focusing exclusively on cost savings to being able to quickly build applications that bring a competitive advantage. In a highly fluid business environment, adding differentiation and value is critical for success.

Cloud native applications are built to run on hardware that is modular and automated, allowing them to become both resilient and predictable. Performance and scalability become important benefits, resulting from the ability to flexibly deploy workloads wherever they need to be. Traditional applications simply do not offer those benefits.

The technologies used to create and deploy cloud-enabled applications (covered in more detail in the next section of this chapter) provide an abstraction layer away from the underlying software and hardware infrastructures, including the operating system. Developers can focus exclusively on building their applications without the need to deal with dependencies of the underlying infrastructure. By creating applications that do not rely on the underlying infrastructure, development and deployment teams can deploy applications on the most pragmatic platform.

Well-designed cloud native applications automatically provision and configure tasks and can dynamically allocate resources based on application requirements. This automation is one way that scalability can be achieved and how applications can balance themselves to prevent failures.

While DevOps methodologies aren't unique to cloud native application development, DevOps is a necessary component of cloud native applications. The collaboration associated with a DevOps approach involves the integration of processes, tools, and, of course, developers. DevOps creates an environment where software can be written, tested, and released quickly and as often as needed with minimum disruption. DevOps can be the enabler of an organization's CI/CD goals because the software modules created for a cloud native application can be released continuously and in an automated fashion.

Communicating Using APIs

Of course, in a highly distributed environment composed of microservices, the ability to communicate between services is critical if the benefits of the cloud are to be fully realized. Application programming interfaces (APIs) serve this purpose and have special applicability to the cloud. In fact, they're the mode of communication among microservices and containers using interprocess communication mechanisms.

TECHNICAL
STUFF

APIs have been used extensively in the past for communicating with and connecting various IT assets. They're an important connectivity mechanism for the way services are combined to create an application. In addition, at the Infrastructure as a Service (IaaS) level, APIs are used to provide control and distribution mechanisms for resources, such as provisioning. At the application level, Software as a Service (SaaS) APIs furnish the ability to connect applications with the underlying infrastructure and, when applicable, cloud resources.

APIs become even more critical when one or more cloud providers are involved. In these multicloud cases, your API strategy needs to consider the APIs provided by the cloud providers themselves to allow connectivity and communication with their clouds. Many cloud providers are offering more generic (for example, HTTP) integration capabilities to make it easy for their customers to integrate and access resources.

With microservices typically deployed in the form of containers, the interprocess communication mechanisms used with microservices are different from traditional applications. Because the microservices are more granular, so, too, are the APIs. Client data requests may span a number of microservices, requiring the request to follow a one-to-many form of interaction.

A number of API platforms, including API management platforms, are available today that address a variety of needs in the cloud. Choosing the right API platform involves a careful assessment of the application environment.

Setting the Stage for Cloud-Enabled Applications

For many organizations, enabling applications for the cloud is a journey, which in many cases begins with the obvious step of setting a vision and goals. Establishing business objectives is an important first step because there is a tendency to look at exciting technologies before figuring out direction and what specific business goals need to be achieved. Additionally, planning should involve all stakeholders — corporate management, IT, partners, and even customers.

REMEMBER

Once goals are set, a team of development, security, and operations personnel needs to be created that can take the cloud application implementation to the next level using a DevSecOps approach. One of the first decisions this team will face is which workloads represent the highest priority in terms of cloud-enablement — and this holds true for both legacy and new, more modern applications, some of which need to be created. The team will need to consider several factors, including business criticality and technical complexity and difficulty. Overall, workloads need to be assessed and prioritized based on business requirements and financial return on investment considerations.

Business services will then need to be defined based on the required application functionality. Decomposing an application into a set of microservices follows no set rules. In general, however, examining the specific services and how they interact outward (to customers and other stakeholders) and inward (with internal and back office services), and dividing functionality will be based on the most efficient way to orchestrate these interactions. Interacting with back-end systems is particularly important because in some cases, containerization may not be a viable option.

A variety of container platforms are available in the marketplace, and some are open source. In addition, some container platforms are offered by vendors who add value in terms of ease of use and scalability. The careful examination of current and future needs will play into determining the right platform to use.

Finally, the role of operations will change where cloud-enabled applications prevail. Cloud enablement can add complexity and pose management challenges, but also create great opportunity to exploit the cloud. Kubernetes as a management and orchestration system for cloud native applications built with containers is a way to effectively get the most out of a distributed, modularized application implementation.

3

Understanding Cloud Models

Chapter **7**

Introducing All Types of Clouds

A s cloud technologies have evolved, many different cloud models have emerged to solve specific business challenges. This evolution isn't surprising since more and more businesses are viewing the cloud as the future of their computing environment. Although these different computing models make the world of the cloud more complicated, it has given rise to cloud solutions that incorporate all the capabilities needed to efficiently and effective solve specific problems. But having more types of clouds doesn't mean that they're in conflict — quite the opposite. When a business builds a technical strategy for using many of these different cloud environments in a harmonized and coordinated way, it is called a multicloud.

Understanding Public Clouds

Public clouds are probably the most well-known type of cloud, particularly because they were the first viable cloud computing environments for consumers. Because of the various classes of users, public clouds offer a broad selection of computing services. From SaaS applications to the infrastructure services used to build applications, public clouds must be prepared for their users to use or build any kind of applications.

All major public clouds offer IaaS capabilities where users can select an operating system and deploy applications. Many public clouds also offer Platform as a Service (PaaS) capabilities where the operating system is hidden and deployed applications use only PaaS services. Some PaaS services now offer serverless environments where the cloud takes on even more responsibility for the underlying services used by applications.

The following sections look at three types of public clouds:

» Commercial public clouds

» Open community clouds

» Public clouds that have been designed for use by the U.S. government

Commercial public clouds

Commercial public clouds are primarily intended for professional and business use, although they're available to anyone with a web browser. These public clouds offer services that provide value to businesses, such as SaaS applications, or infrastructure services, such as databases and scalable storage. Because a professional service is being offered, commercial public clouds provide a high level of security and protection.

You can typically access a public cloud to deploy software or use computing or storage services via a portal on the web. Using SaaS applications on a public cloud is even easier; just go to the application's address on the web.

Commercial public clouds offer a service level agreement (SLA) — an agreement outlining the performance and operational obligations of the cloud provider to the consumer of a service. An SLA is typically designed to protect the vendor rather than the customer. However, these vendors have an unwritten commitment to maintain the level of security and service required to protect their business relationships.

SLAs address issues such as

» Meantime between failures (MTBF) and meantime to repair (MTTR)

» Service availability

- » Performance and response time

- » Security commitments

- » Data protection commitments

- » Customer notification method in the event of an outage

- » Exit strategies that ensure a smooth transition if the customer must terminate service

Although the SLA may appear to give customers a great deal of comfort and knowledge regarding the services that they'll receive, as with any contract, the fine print matters. SLAs describe situations where the cloud provider isn't responsible for an outage. For example, many wide-ranging cloud outages have not triggered SLA clauses because the outage was caused by networking problems or other issues that the agreement specifically identified.

A pay-as-you-use cost model is fairly standard for cloud infrastructure and storage. As you scale up and need to support more users and large applications, your costs will increase. Likewise, this metering cost model will help you save money if you design your environment to scale down during lower usage times. Billing is typically on a monthly basis.

On the other hand, SaaS applications have their own pricing models that are defined by the SaaS vendor. For example, if you want to use a customer relationship management (CRM) SaaS application, such as Salesforce, you'll have to sign a contract under its terms of service. The term may be as short as a month or, more typically, a year or longer. In some cases, you're able to transfer an on-premises license that you already hold for usage in the cloud. With other SaaS applications, such as PayPal, you sign a contract, even though you pay only when you use the service. Sometimes a SaaS application is available for free, but with limited functionality.

When SaaS applications aren't purchased with a long-term commitment, users can drop their use of the application whenever they want. This freedom is especially relevant during the early stage of the relationship. Often, a customer will sign on for a month-long trial subscription to a service. If service is poor or not a good match for the user's needs, the customer will inevitably look elsewhere for another service. Of course, the ability to easily sever a relationship will also depend on how much integration and customization the customer has done.

SaaS applications also typically manage customer data, which adds to the level of responsibility that the SaaS vendor must provide for securing and protecting information.

WARNING

Although the SaaS vendor manages the data, the data should be owned by the customer. Likewise, customers who build software in a SaaS or PaaS environment should own the software intellectual property they've created. Therefore, it is important that customers maintain a copy of their proprietary business logic as well as their own data. Be sure to read the fine print; there are environments where vendors claim the rights to customers' data or intellectual property.

Open social community clouds

The most open type of cloud environment is an open community cloud, a cloud environment that doesn't require any criteria for joining other than signing up and creating a password. You can even create an account under an alias. The word open alludes to a cloud that isn't commercial and also often refers to open source — the nonproprietary software based upon which most major clouds are built.

Open social community clouds come in two primary types:

>> **Commercial sites with a strong advertising model:** These clouds may be private or publicly owned and include social networking connections, such as Facebook, LinkedIn, and Twitter. These sites rarely charge a fee to users and use the size and scope of their user base to sell advertising. Some sites, such as LinkedIn, have professional, fee-based services that offer access to more in-depth services and information. Although these sites do not have an explicit guarantee of service to users, they do have an obligation to advertisers.

WARNING

Keep in mind that these sites view advertisers, not individual users, as their clients, so you shouldn't rely on these companies to completely safeguard your data. In addition, they may sell some of your data (anonymized or not) to various other companies for the purpose of displaying highly targeted advertising.

>> **Open community sites with a compelling focus that enables individuals with common interests to participate in online discussions:** A community of professionals in a certain industry, such as manufacturing or retail, may want to share ideas. Many communities are based on individuals who share a passion for a hobby, such as biking or chess. There is typically very little security and no guarantee that the site will remain active over time. Open community sites can disappear when the most active members move on.

All these community sites have some characteristics in common, including the following:

>> **A relatively simple sign-up process:** All you need is a login name, password, and an email account.

>> **Requests for additional information:** More sophisticated sites may ask you to provide information about yourself, whereas others don't ask users for any information at all.

>> **Low-level security:** The level of security is very low for these sites. With little effort, someone without authorization to do so could gain access to an account. Nowadays, all these sites include disclaimers about how they will or will not use customer data. They explain their responsibilities in managing the site and warn users not to use copyrighted material and the like.

>> **No service-level guarantee to the individual user:** The lack of a guarantee doesn't mean that these community sites perform poorly. How well they perform is based on their underlying technology and how important that site is to those managing the site. For example, it is critical to Facebook's business that its site is always available and viewable for mobile and web users. On the other hand, a niche site for a specific hobby or an industry trade group may experience outages from time to time because it's using the least expensive hosting services available.

REMEMBER

If the company changes its business focus or determines the community is no longer worth the expense, it can shut down the community at will. No guarantees are made to users that the content generated and stored on the community cloud will be accessible for any specific amount of time. In such a case, the community members who have become dependent on the site can do nothing.

Abandoned community sites are a common occurrence with open community clouds. For example, Google and LinkedIn both allow users to create their own online communities on any topic on the planet. Some of these sites are well moderated and well managed and therefore have hundreds or thousands of visitors. Others become phantom sites and disappear.

WARNING

Keep in mind that these open social community clouds do not have SLAs. Both individuals and small and medium businesses may upload important information on these community cloud without understanding the potential risk. For example, if photos, videos, or documents are deleted or otherwise lost, you will have no recourse. In fact, in many cases, even reaching a live person for help will be difficult.

Some community sites are very sophisticated. Sites with a strong revenue model based on selling advertising to users have a compelling incentive to ensure a minimum amount of downtime because it will have an impact on revenue. Some of these communities may actually be private clouds that are open only to qualified customers.

TECHNICAL
STUFF

One last note about open community clouds: When you use one of these sites, you may find it hard to tell whether you're using a cloud site or just a regular website. If the site offers a way for users to construct applications using configurable computing resources, then you can be sure you're using a community cloud. There's nothing wrong with websites, but they typically offer users less ability to perform processing on their data and other functionality than community clouds.

Open technical community clouds

There is another type of open community cloud — a technical incubator cloud that serves as a platform for joint development of, mainly, open-source systems. Being based on open source helps these types of cloud stay nonproprietary and noncommercial.

One well-known example is GitHub, a web-based hosting service for version control of software systems. Used for a very broad range of software development projects, GitHub is used by software developers around the world.

Another example is the Mass Open Cloud (Mass is short for Massachusetts, where it is located). This cloud was built using donations from software and hardware vendors and nurtured by a variety of nonprofit and educational institutions. The goal of this cloud is to serve as a self-sustaining, at-scale, public cloud used by researchers and industry to innovate important new technologies and involve the public in its innovations.

Government clouds

You may have read about clouds created specifically for use by the United States government. Unless you work for the government, you'll probably never have access to these clouds, so we don't discuss this form of cloud in great detail.

Not surprisingly, the U.S. government needs the power and flexibility of the cloud for the many computing systems it uses and develops. The public cloud has many of the kinds of services that the government needs. Like businesses, government organizations need to share information between different groups. Likewise, big data and data science is critical for certain governmental organizations. In particular, many law enforcement agencies, such as the FBI and CIA, utilize the cloud because of the cloud's ability to provide a big data and analytics platform. However, as you can imagine, the government has special needs that aren't served by public clouds. For example, although public clouds have excellent security characteristics and services, the government has more stringent security requirements than the public sector.

Although private companies can face massive fines, embarrassment, and loss of trust from a data breach, a governmental breach can lead to an international incident. One of the government's security requirements is that they may not share any infrastructure with the public, including servers, storage, networking, and power. Many government organizations require that their data never travel through any shared infrastructure.

Government clouds are generally created by public cloud providers who set up segregated versions of their public clouds. Many of the services found in public cloud can be found in the government version of the cloud, but some services may be excluded. Moreover, public clouds generally include marketplaces where third parties make their applications and services available. Third-party software is not made available in a government cloud without passing rigorous reviews to ensure that the software is safe for use in the government cloud.

Looking at Private Clouds

In some situations, a company will want to create a cloud environment that sits behind an on-premises firewall. Unlike a data center, a private cloud is a pool of common resources optimized for the use of the IT organization. When an organization regularly builds and deploys complex applications, creating a highly automated private cloud that supports internal needs is practical. Unlike a public cloud, a private cloud adheres to the company's security, governance, and compliance requirements. Whatever service level is required for the company applies to the private cloud.

There are three different types of private clouds:

>> A private cloud owned and managed by a company for benefit of its employees and partners

>> An appliance that is based on the services offered in the public cloud and managed by a cloud vendor but behind a client's firewall

>> A commercial private cloud operated by a vendor to support a company that doesn't want to build or operate its own private cloud

Privately owned and managed clouds

Organizations with a business model that requires the company to provide commercial technology services within a business ecosystem often will build a private partner cloud, in which case these companies effectively become a cloud provider. Instead of hiring a public cloud vendor to take full responsibility for creating, managing, monitoring, and updating the software, the private cloud provider assumes those responsibilities.

Like commercial public cloud providers, a private partner cloud provider creates an optimized environment to support the workloads used by its customers. The main difference is that in a private partner cloud scenario, the company isn't hiring a third party to operate the cloud. For example, a financial services company that provides individual banks with payment services can create a sophisticated service that is automated and streamlined to support its customers.

TIP

Because of the security and compliance demands of its customers, the private cloud provided by the financial services company is based on a stringent SLA and even indemnifies customers against lawsuits. Likewise, because the financial services company already acts like an IT vendor to its customers, it has the economies of scale to make creating and managing such a service cost-effective.

Appliances based on public cloud offerings

An emerging approach to create an on-premises private cloud is to use an appliance that is custom built to re-create the functionality of a public cloud. The benefit of this approach is that technical teams will be able to develop, deploy, and maintain applications on the environment that they're familiar with while at the same time keeping certain workloads behind the firewall. Many businesses are choosing to keep certain workloads and data on premises and behind the firewall because of security, compliance, and regulatory concerns.

In some instances, these custom built and integrated hardware offerings are fully installed, maintained, and upgraded by a public cloud vendor. One example is AWS's Outpost offering. Outpost will offer customers AWS compute and storage hardware on premises.

An alternative approach is for public cloud vendors to partner with hardware vendors. For example, Google Cloud Platform (GCP) is partnering with hardware vendors like HPE to offer on premises instances of Google Cloud.

In these cases, public cloud customers choose their own hardware vendor and can negotiate the maintenance and licensing contracts. Other cloud providers, such as Microsoft, are also offering on-premises versions of their cloud services.

Commercial private cloud

Although many companies see the benefits of creating their own private clouds, others want to have the security and governance of a private cloud but want to obtain that service from a third party. Therefore, vendors have created private clouds that are based on a contracted service model.

Unlike a commercial public cloud where anyone with a credit card can sign up, a private customer contractual cloud requires that customers sign a formal contract with the vendor. In exchange, the vendor will provide strict governance and security capabilities and even indemnify customers from lawsuits related to the use of the service. In addition, vendors of commercial open clouds often offer customers private cloud options, including virtual private networks and mirrored sites so that if one data center is offline, a second data center can support customers. As a result of these types of offerings, customers receive a more explicit SLA. This service is different from hosting because, in the private contractual cloud, the service is designed with a self-service portal interface so that customers can add and subtract services based on demand.

When private clouds first emerged, they required experts to deploy and configure. Since then, private clouds have matured, and deployment has become largely automated. Increasingly, public cloud companies have seen an opportunity to create physical cloud computing appliances that can be plugged into the data center infrastructure and start working quickly. Sometimes referred to as *Cloud in a Box*, these private clouds inherit the services and applications available in the vendor's public cloud, meaning that applications, services, and practices can be moved seamlessly between a vendor's public cloud and its private cloud appliance.

Exploring Hybrid Clouds

A public cloud environment is open to anyone with an Internet connection. In contrast, a private cloud environment is available only to the owners of that service environment and other entities they choose to share it with, such as business partners or customers. A *hybrid cloud,* on the other hand, offers the ability to integrate and connect to services across public and private clouds and data centers to create a virtual computing environment — a fluid mix of on-premises physical infrastructure and virtualized infrastructure that may be located on- or off-premises. However, before we get into more detail about how this environment actually works, you need to understand the continuum from public to private clouds.

Obviously, all cloud environments are different. In fact, because the computing needs of a business aren't static and change frequently, the best way to determine the type of environment that meets your needs is to think of clouds as a continuum. Although public and private clouds share many characteristics, they have important differences. For example, a public cloud service may be available only to customers who sign a long-term agreement, or a public SaaS service may offer a private version of the same application. You may have a private cloud that is part of a company's on-premises data center. Public clouds may offer a greater variety of SaaS products and other services, while a private cloud will probably offer only applications and services specifically approved by the company.

Understanding the Continuum of the Cloud

The continuum of services, which is depicted in Figure 7-1, encompasses a variety of different types of public services that serve different needs within organizations. Open public clouds are often great resources for sharing ideas, while commercial public clouds are more tuned to the needs of businesses in terms of providing oversight and accountability. On the other hand, companies are increasingly using private clouds for their own internal uses. Some companies with sophisticated IT organizations may build and manage their own private clouds for employees and partners. These companies may actually become service providers in their own right. Other companies who need a private cloud for security and governance requirements may decide to have a third party manage a private cloud on their behalf.

Model	Open Community	Controlled Open Mode	Contractual Open	Public/Private Hybrid	Private Closed
Characteristics	No SLA	Simple SLA	SLA with no indemnification	SLA guaranteeing uptime	Explicit SLA Capital expense with ongoing maintenance
	No Contract Simple Password Protection No governance model	Transactional pricing More Security No explicit governance	Contract High security provided Governance in place	Contract Highest level of security Explicit governance	Secure platform Explicit governance

FIGURE 7-1: The continuum of public and private cloud resources.

REMEMBER

Nearly every business will use a variety of cloud models to meet their needs. For example, a business will likely share information about recruiting on open community clouds like LinkedIn. At the same time, for internal corporate use, the business will want to use a cloud with outlined SLAs, security, and governance.

REMEMBER

The bottom line is this: Meeting the needs of a business requires that IT provide different types of cloud services. Understanding the characteristics of a continuum of cloud services will help you understand what's required to meet your specific business goals. Ultimately, you need to select the type of cloud service that will use the right resources at the right time with the right level of security and governance.

Selecting Multicloud for Choice, Efficiency, and Performance

Multicloud is the synthesis of specific types of cloud — public clouds, private clouds, and hybrid clouds — into a seamless and comprehensive computing environment that provides more power and flexibility than what has come before.

To be clear, multicloud is not a type of cloud; it is the concept of using more than one cloud within a business's overall computing architecture. Whereas our exploration of cloud types was focused on matching specific business needs with specific cloud types, multicloud is more about recognizing that cloud technologies and cloud providers are still evolving. As such, developing relationships with multiple clouds is a sound business practice for many reasons.

From a pragmatic perspective, even after you've found your ideal cloud provider for your existing needs, things may change. Cloud providers may change their focus, prices, or practices. Rising costs or too many outages or security problems may cause you to seek other providers. Your own requirements may change, perhaps from evolving business needs or regulatory requirements. If one of these changes forces you to find a new cloud provider, having one already vetted will save you significant time and minimize the time back to market.

REMEMBER

From another perspective, developing your cloud management practices to include multiple cloud providers will improve your management approach and will keep your business more in touch with the evolution of the cloud. Staying ahead of your competition in the cloud will position your business to be a first mover with new cloud capabilities. Multicloud management will also streamline your management approach and tools, speeding your time to deployment and reducing costs by prioritizing the use of the best cloud environments in your cloud ecosystem.

THE FUTURE OF MULTICLOUD

Multicloud computing is the practice of using multiple cloud computing and storage services within your company's technology architecture. There are many reasons to be using multiple cloud providers at the same time. You may have exploratory projects with different cloud providers to decide which is the best for your business. You may have workloads that need special features of more than one cloud provider. You may be in the midst of moving from one cloud provider to another. Or, your company may have acquired other companies, and you've ended up with different business divisions working with different cloud providers.

Those are good reasons to use multiple cloud environments, but that's not the ultimate vision of multicloud. In Chapter 12, we discuss workload portability as a means of moving applications and services between cloud environments. Today, moving a workload between different cloud providers is possible with some effort — that is, as long as your workloads have been coded for portability and your use of cloud services isn't too incompatible between cloud providers (or you've built a portability layer that hides service incompatibilities between different clouds).

The ultimate vision of multicloud is the ability to move workloads and services between cloud environments with automation and almost instantaneously. Although some management solutions can provide that functionality for a limited number of clouds, they're not yet comprehensive and mature. The ability to deploy a workload to different cloud environments is being addressed successfully with container technologies, but the ability to move workloads between environments — while those workloads are still running and serving customers — is still in the future.

Now, consider the opportunities that multicloud will offer when management solutions can quickly move running workloads between different environments.

First, businesses that are cost sensitive will be able to define policies where, for example, if a different cloud environment is lower priced than your own, the multicloud management system will be able to automatically move your workloads to save money.

Second, if your cloud provider is having service problems (for example, networking problems), you'll be able to simply move your workloads to a different cloud provider.

Third, as advanced multicloud management services mature, they will have the effect of commoditizing cloud services, which should reduce cloud computing costs.

Importantly, multicloud management solutions will do a better job solving the challenges of developing software that can be moved between cloud environments easily, making it much easier for businesses to deploy their software to any cloud computing environment. Adopting a multicloud approach will decrease the costs of developing software and maximize revenue when that software is deployed to any and every cloud computing environment.

The companies that have reached maturity with their cloud practices will be the first to reap the advantage of multicloud and will extend their business lead over their competition.

In day-to-day practice, an increasingly wide variety of choice exists in the cloud market. For example, some vendors are completely focused on providing the most inexpensive possible service. Others specialize in high-performance computing, extending to vast scales. Other vendors may offer specialty offerings, such as HIPAA compliant cloud or environments that are tuned for data science. We are in a period of innovation and rapid growth of cloud technologies, so it is important to understand your breadth of choices before committing to one or more specific cloud platforms for your business. In this chapter, we help you learn about your computing choices so that you can meet your business needs.

Thinking about the Integration Imperative

After you have a sense of the different types of cloud environments and services that are available, you can think about how you can bring these clouds and services together to form a computing ecosystem that meets your needs. Generally, clouds and services have been developed to provide their individual capabilities, but they may not have been designed to work together. If you use only one cloud, this won't be much of a problem as services within a single cloud platform have typically been developed together. But if, as we advise, you're using multiple clouds in either a hybrid or multicloud configuration, then integration will become more of a challenge.

TIP

Before you make your selections of cloud platforms and services, make sure that you understand the needs of the workloads you plan on deploying to your upcoming cloud ecosystem. Each cloud platform has different strengths and weaknesses, and finding good matches for your workloads will maximize your success.

REMEMBER

As time goes by and you have new workloads to deploy to your cloud ecosystem, you should repeat the process of checking your workload against the resources of your cloud ecosystem. Don't be afraid to make changes as constant re-examination of the efficacy of your computing resources will drive any changes required to keep your cloud ecosystem well-tuned and serving your needs. If you've gone the extra mile to develop a multicloud strategy and portfolio, you're likely to find you already have experience with a cloud provider that is ideal for that new workload.

Once you understand your workloads' needs and have matched them to cloud platforms and services, you'll be ready to assemble those clouds and services into your cloud ecosystem. The challenge then is to integrate your cloud resources together and to integrate your workloads with the cloud resources.

Types of integration

Three types of integration are relevant to assembling systems of applications and services:

>> **Integration at the service level:** A multicloud ecosystem will probably have services in multiple cloud environments that address the same resources (in other words, each cloud environment will have a storage service). The organization responsible for managing the cloud ecosystem will need to either select specific services for specific uses, let applications use the services available in their native cloud environment, or require all applications to use a service in one specific environment.

>> **Integration at the data level:** Organizations need access to business information stored in different applications, databases, and other information sources. The business information will need to be accessed in an integrated and standardized form. In addition, data will be labeled differently (one data set may label states as "St" while others label them as "States," for example). Having a common data glossary and definitions across the environment will help you achieve consistency.

>> **Integration at the application level:** Application integration is needed in all computing environments, but is particularly important and more challenging when applications run in different cloud environments. Integration will conveniently increase the functionality of cooperating applications, improve workload portability, and further support data integration.

All three types of integration benefit from APIs and standards as they often represent the points of integration between services, applications, and systems. Although the innovative and quickly changing world of the cloud means that APIs and standards often change with those new innovations, vendors and developers focus on creating clear interfaces and try to protect the APIs from change. Cloud vendors take particular care in defining stable APIs for the services they provide, but applications themselves tend to define their own APIs without attempting to be consistent with their competition.

The evolution of APIs and well-defined computing interfaces has definitely made perform some types of integration easier, but difficult challenges still remain, particularly when the systems being integrated have different data models, business flows, or sophistication of APIs.

Responsibility for integrations

The need to integrate is a business requirement, but integrations are implemented at different business and technical levels by different types of worker. For example, service level integrations are typically performed by cloud engineers who understand the nature of cloud services. They can judge which services are the best for specific workloads or whether independent services can be integrated together to create a new hybrid service.

REMEMBER

Data level integrations require domain experts to understand the structure and meaning of the data that must be integrated. For example, if an application being integrated is a banking application, the team performing the integration will need to understand banking rules. Once the nature of the data is understood, it often falls to software engineers to implement the integration with data connectors, data transforms, mapping tables, encryption of sensitive data, and the other piece-parts of the data integration trade. Then, database administrators will create the schemas, tables, import functions, and other parts of organizing the integrated data into a form that applications can used.

Finally, application level integration is a quintessentially technical activity, calling for software engineers to look for appropriate application APIs and perhaps build connectors or adapters when suitable APIs are not found. Granted, the need for application integration usually comes from business requirements. For example, the use of a big data application will likely need cooperating visualization applications to help interpret the results of big data analysis. Also, because multicloud environments may include different versions of the same application running in different contexts, integrating the different versions may be easy, but may still require transformations or other processing to make the different versions work together seamlessly.

As you can see, many of these integrations will be performed by software developers who will know the best technical means of solving those integration problems.

Integration at the service level

Services come in many forms and roles, so it's hard to generalize which service integration challenges you will run into in your cloud ecosystem. However, the following examples may be helpful:

>> **Storage service integration:** Each cloud provider in your computing ecosystem will offer a storage service for your applications. In addition, many cloud providers offer multiple tiers of storage. You may want to use a cloud's flash storage for fast processing, while using cold (and much less expensive) storage for data that is just being held for compliance reasons. Each application will

have good performance if you always use the native storage server available in the same cloud environment as your application.

On the other hand, if an application uses storage in a different cloud environment, there will be higher latency for the storage access, and it's likely to seriously degrade the application's performance. However, if you have another application that is integrating data from both applications and the performance of that process is a high priority, you may want to consider designating only one cloud's storage service for use by both applications. That will slow down at least one of those applications (the one in a different cloud from the storage), but it will optimize your data integration application.

>> **Identity management integration:** Say that you have an enterprise application that serves company employees in the cloud. You'll need access to the enterprise's identity management system to authenticate those employees, but that Active Directory or Lightweight Directory Access Protocol (LDAP) identity system probably resides in the enterprise's corporate data center. If that data center is part of a hybrid cloud, your application may be able to use the on-premises identity management system directly. Otherwise, you may need to find a complementary identity management service in one of the clouds in your ecosystem that can run as a remote version of the on-premises identity system.

>> **Disaster recovery (DR) service integration:** When you set up DR services for your cloud ecosystem, you'll probably want to have all of your replicated data stored in one place. If you use the DR services provided by each cloud of your ecosystem, their default action will be to store your data in their own designated locations. At the least, you'll need to configure them, if possible, to store data in the same location. Otherwise, you may need to designate one cloud's DR service to handle all application data, assuming that is possible. If neither of those scenarios is possible, it may force you to find an independent DR solution or build other integration solutions.

Integration at the data level

Data integration is probably the integration you're most likely to require. Businesses need access to all their data in a consistent, easy, and integrated way, even when managed by separate applications. Chapter 14 discusses this challenge in depth. Here are some of the common data challenges:

>> Data tied to different applications becomes attached to those applications. These segregated pockets of data are often called *silos*.

>> Creating a consistent and comprehensive view of data maintained in silos requires access to each application's data, transformations to make it

consistent, and a way of storing the integrated data so that other applications can use it.

» Generally, you'll not be able to stop applications while you access and transform their data, and applications will continue to change their data while you're accessing it.

» All critical data must have a single source of truth. In other words, integrating data must not obscure the primary location and accuracy of data.

As you can see, integrating data across a broad set of applications and their databases can be a challenge.

Integration at the application level

Application integration is a long-practiced discipline with lots of technical experience available. Techniques are the same whether the context is a physical data center or a cloud environment. The difference here is the potential number of environments that are involved. If a company has created a multicloud ecosystem, applications that need to be integrated may be running on premises, in a hybrid-cloud context, and in multiple public clouds.

Many application integrations seek to extend or modify business processes. For example, consider a retail business that extends credit to its customers, but the initial implementation didn't include a step where the application would check to verify the customer's credit rating is in a good shape before extending the credit. The application needs to be integrated with a credit agency to provide that credit rating check. This step changes the credit business process. Applications that use business process rules to guide the steps of a business process will adapt those rules as part of the integration. However, whether the application uses formal business process rules or not, the credit rating service will have to be integrated with the retail application.

Companies that embrace a multicloud ecosystem are likely to have made a significant commitment to running their business in the cloud. That means the company probably manages many applications in the cloud, likely organized in independent computing environments, to suit the needs of specific independent business divisions. For example, finance, HR, sales, and marketing probably all have dedicated computing environments, and each will have its own needs for application integration. Some of these divisions may be running their workloads in a hybrid context, perhaps with processing in the cloud, but data storage on premises to meet regulatory and auditing requirements.

This diversity of environments and applications creates some challenges not found in single environment computing contexts. For example, in setting up a hybrid context, a company may replace its legacy on-premises application with the SaaS version of the same application, but the APIs may differ between the on-premises and SaaS versions. Previous integrations involving the on-premises application may not work with the SaaS version, and even if they do, the integration may need to work between the SaaS application and other on-premises applications, requiring networking and perhaps new governance controls as the SaaS may be running with a different identity than the on-premises version.

Other issues may arise in a multicloud context if independent clouds run the same application. A business may set up a configuration like this if they're comparing performance between clouds or are developing portability controls so that the application can be easily moved between different clouds. If the application being moved must integrate with other applications in different cloud contexts, but those other applications have different versions in other contexts, additional work will be required to ensure the integration works in all contexts.

» Discovering resource pools/cloud models and services

» Evaluating the role of the data center

» Finding out how the public cloud fits and when the private cloud shines

Chapter **8**

Using Infrastructure as a Service

nfrastructure as a Service (IaaS) is the best known of the cloud computing environments available for deploying service and software. IaaS is the virtual delivery of computing capacity, storage, and networking services. On top of these computing resources, customers can install operating systems, create DevOps environments, and build applications. In essence, rather than buying and installing hardware in your own data center, IaaS allows companies to rent computing resources on an as-needed basis.

In this chapter, we provide an overview of IaaS, its capabilities, and different approaches that are emerging to support changing customer needs.

Understanding IaaS

As its name implies, *Infrastructure as a Service* (IaaS) is the foundational infrastructure cloud service. IaaS provisions compute, storage, and networking services through either a virtualized image, a container or directly on the computer systems (also known as "bare metal). Organizations that purchase IaaS typically agree to a pay-as-you-go agreement for compute, network, and storage resources.

The advantage of IaaS is that a business can scale resources up and down depending on demand. The scalability of IaaS differs from the typical upfront capital expenditures for on-premises infrastructure. In addition, IaaS gives companies the flexibility to experiment with new proofs of concepts without length and expensive procurement processes.

An IaaS service is designed as a self-service environment. A customer can simply use a credit card to purchase cloud infrastructure, such as compute or storage. Consumers are typically charged based on the amount of resources they consume and how long they want to use those services. A consumer can have a reserved instance of a service or simply use an instance on demand. When a consumer stops paying for the service, the customer loses access to the resources. In a private IaaS, the environment is controlled directly by a company's IT organization. The IT organization will have direct control over things like security and who has access to what resources. As IaaS becomes commoditized, many businesses are focused on purchasing blocks of compute resources at a corporate rate.

Access to IaaS is typically gained through Application Programming Interfaces (APIs) that abstract the underlying physical computing resources. These physical compute resources include details like where those resources are located, the underlying operating system and tools, scaling, security, and orchestration. With IaaS, you typically create a virtual machine that works collaboratively with services, such as self-service provisioning, billing, and management. A variety of implementations have evolved to support IaaS. For example, your cloud provider may use a hypervisor or a container to create isolation within a physical environment.

A variety of vendors offer many different options for IaaS, and they're not all the same. You might, for example, be experimenting with developing a new application that currently has no strategic value. In that case, you might select a simple inexpensive IaaS with little security, support, or management. On the other hand, your organization may be managing private client medical information that requires a high level of security and governance. Likewise, if a team is running data-intensive analytics workloads, the infrastructure has to support high availability.

If a business prefers, rather than purchase a virtual machine, it can procure "bare metal" IaaS services. Bare metal cloud services are physical, dedicated servers that are provisioned to individual customers. Users are given access to the entire server along with storage, networking, and other physical resources. Bare metal IaaS does not include *multi-tenancy* (the sharing of underlying infrastructure), and entire servers are provisioned to customers rather than virtual machines. The advantage of bare metal is that the customer can control the entire server, meaning that performance and security can be enhanced. Of course, having this level of control comes at an increased cost.

IaaS is the cloud version of a hardware server, providing a platform that runs a complete software stack, including an operating system, services, and applications.

Upon introduction, cloud IaaS was immediately seen as a direct alternative to physical servers, much as virtualization and virtual machines (VMs) were perceived before introduction of cloud technologies. However, IaaS offers significant advantages over hardware servers, including ease of deployment, dramatically shortened deployment time, and replacement of capital expenditures with operational costs. Further, IaaS was essentially a drop-in replacement for the standard hardware servers being used at the time. In the next two chapters, we discuss how other cloud computing environments, such as Software as a Service (SaaS) and Platform as a Service (PaaS), provide alternatives that go beyond IaaS.

In this chapter, we describe the relationship between physical computing resources and IaaS in more detail, cover scalability and other cloud capabilities of IaaS platforms, and discuss the financial models you'll encounter when working with IaaS. We also provide an overview of the major IaaS cloud providers.

Exploring the Key Components of Public Cloud IaaS

Public IaaS services are very well known thanks to the pioneering work done by Amazon with its Amazon Web Services (AWS) business. In its early days, Amazon had created more capacity than it needed and found that developers began asking if it would be possible to "rent" some capacity. Amazon recognized the potential and the opportunity and created a commercial IaaS service that launched the cloud services commercial market. AWS was the first commercial public cloud. Before AWS was made available to the public, Amazon used it to run its own online business. By the time the public started using AWS, it had been hardened by Amazon's internal use of the service.

When AWS was made generally available, business users were impressed by the ability to get access to the same computing facilities used by Amazon itself. By purchasing IaaS virtual servers, or VMs, with a credit card, customers could immediately get access to a virtual server and run their favorite applications or build new software systems. Before AWS, business users were accustomed to purchasing and provisioning physical servers via their IT organization, which could take weeks or longer depending on IT's backlog, approvals, room in the data center, and all the other overhead associated with using physical computing resources. With AWS, the time required for physical machine procurement and deployment was compressed down to minutes.

Quickly innovating, improving services and offering addition, businesses quickly saw ways to leverage cloud providers to improve and accelerate their IT and development practices. With the new cloud capabilities, businesses took some of the following steps:

>> Retail websites moved to the cloud so that they could provision more capacity as needed during busy seasons without having to purchase additional hardware that would sit idle during quiet times. Think about the compute power needed to meet the demands of Black Friday and Cyber Monday compared to normal periods.

>> IaaS has become the backbone for many different cloud use cases ranging from software development to the foundational layer for SaaS applications. In many situations, modern applications are being designed to be cloud native so that they take advantage of all the built-in capabilities of IaaS.

>> Development activities were moved to the cloud where development, test, and staging environments could be quickly created, provisioned, and used and then equally quickly removed. (Previously, additional hardware would have to be purchased and used and probably still shared between development teams because of cost management.)

>> Born on the web, mobile app companies have emerged as important tools for consumers and business users alike. These new, mobile app developers could have never afforded the physical infrastructure required to handle their rapidly expanding user bases.

In the early days of cloud and IaaS, vendors chiefly competed on price. One cloud vendor might offer an hour of compute for $0.20, and a competitor would undercut them with an offer of $0.185. As the cloud market has matured, vendors are more focused on value-add capabilities. While pricing is still important, differentiations based on artificial intelligence and data, security, and industry-specific capabilities are now important. In addition, pricing models have evolved. While many business are still billed on a monthly consumption basis for IaaS, vendors now offer multiyear contracts with fixed pricing.

The hardware architecture of public clouds

Perhaps the foremost characteristic of the cloud is its virtual and highly distributed nature; cloud providers stress how public clouds are different than physical computing resources. While clouds do offer different experiences than physical data centers, cloud technologies also rely on their underlying hardware to provide their resources and services to customers. For example, each virtual machine you use in the cloud actually runs on a physical server in some data center managed by the cloud provider. When you scale your virtual machine to have greater storage, additional physical storage is made available to the physical machine that hosts your virtual machine.

Every cloud provider depends on a physical data center to run the physical computing infrastructure that, in its virtualized form, becomes a cloud. These cloud provider data centers are enormous so that they can provide the vast and scalable computing resources used by their many customers. Just as traditional physical data centers are overprovisioned to make sure enough resources are available when users need them, cloud data centers must also be overprovisioned to meet the needs of their customers. While overprovisioning always implies some amount of unused hardware, the virtualization used in cloud data centers keeps overprovisioning to a minimum.

When a customer selects a virtual machine to use, they typically choose the type of processor and its capacities (for example, storage, networking, and so on). In response, the cloud provider selects a physical computer in the cloud data center that matches those characteristics and hosts the customer's virtual machine on that hardware. The physical characteristics don't have to match the physical characteristics exactly as the virtualization process can mask some of the physical components. For example, one might select a virtual machine with an x86 CPU architecture, 8GB of RAM, and one network connection. In response, the cloud provider might select a machine with 16GB of RAM and two network connections, but hide the extra RAM and network connection. This machine meets the customer's specification and provides some additional resources in case the customer needs to scale up their RAM or network connections. On the other hand, the cloud provider will almost certainly select a physical x86 machine to back the virtual machine as processor performance must match the customer's request exactly.

Cloud vendors are increasingly offering specialized hardware for specific workloads. For example, Graphics Processing Units (GPUs) are often used to efficiently execute machine learning and artificial intelligence (AI) workloads. Organizations that want to perform AI often seek out cloud options that are designed for AI-heavy activities. Likewise, IBM has made the mainframe available in the cloud for large-scale transactional workloads that require high security. A cloud provider's data centers are a super-sized version of traditional physical data centers with many more types and sizes of hardware to meet the combined needs of the diverse set of cloud consumers. Add in virtualization on top of all computing resources, and you can see the tremendous size and power of cloud computing environments.

Virtualization

In an IaaS cloud computing environment, the fundamental computing resource that customers use is a virtual machine; just as in a traditional physical data center, the fundamental computing resource is a physical server. Of course, networking, storage resources, and other components are also present in physical and cloud environments.

Just as a hardware server needs an operating system at the foundation of its software stack, so does a virtual machine. (A *software stack* refers to the layers of software from the level just above the hardware up to and including the application.) Just as in the physical world, operating systems in the cloud include Microsoft Windows, various releases of Linux (such as Red Hat Enterprise Linux, SUSE, and Ubuntu), and other operating systems, such as specialized operating systems, like the mainframe's z/OS. The fact that on-premises operating systems are available on the cloud is not a coincidence; businesses want the same operating system to run on physical hardware as well as virtual and cloud hardware. Having the same operating system work in different contexts allows applications to be moved between those environments — one of the promises of the cloud. The rest of the software stack includes middleware software, applications, and all the other software components found on servers in physical data centers.

When a cloud consumer selects a virtual machine from a cloud provider, they typically specify the server characteristics they need. This task is very much like detailing the characteristics of a physical server. Most important are the processor (CPU) type and machine size. Because cloud virtual machines are run by physical processors, choice of virtual machine processors is generally the same as when choosing a physical server. However, cloud providers don't always document exactly which physical machine is used to implement each virtual machine they offer.

In fact, the trend seems to be that cloud providers increasingly characterize virtual machines not by physical brand and CPU names, but by the workloads that are best handled by the virtual machines. Typical VM designations include types like general purpose, compute optimized, memory optimized, database optimized, storage optimized, and graphics optimized (based on physical GPUs). Moreover, instead of referring to CPUs, often the term vCPU is used to emphasize that the CPU is virtual and therefore more general than a physical CPU.

REMEMBER

Cloud providers use general terms to describe their VMs for good reasons. For one thing, physical machines evolve in the marketplace quickly, and frequently updating the description of the VM type can be confusing to users. Frequent updates also force users to research new CPU architectures. More importantly, users are usually more interested in finding VMs that meet the needs of the software the users will run on the VM, so characterizing VMs by the workloads they handle well is what many users want. Having said that, characterizing VMs by workload type is more likely to occur with smaller and entry-level VMs, while expensive VMs are more likely to have their brand and model name stated as users are investing more in their cloud services and want to be assured they're getting exactly what they want. And in some cases, cloud providers want to advertise how they offer the latest and greatest underlying physical hardware.

THE BENEFIT OF SERVERLESS

Serverless computing is a technique offered by cloud providers that enables code to be executed by dynamically allocating resources. Instead of having the developer select the specific resources needed, the code runs in a *stateless* (no hard connection to a specific physical resource) container. This container service is activated by events, such as a database event, file uploads, or the request to schedule an event.

Cloud providers, including Amazon AWS (Lamda), Microsoft Azure (Azure Functions), and Google Cloud (Cloud Functions), all use serverless functions to support developers. Therefore, serverless is often called *function as a service.*

One of the benefits of serverless is that the developer does not have to anticipate the infrastructure services needed. The functional service calculates precisely what services are being used and only charges for those cloud services. Serverless is most beneficial when used in conjunction with microservices. (For more details on microservices, take a look at Chapter 3.)

After a user has selected a VM by workload or physical type, they typically also need to specify the size of the VM. VM sizes are often described with words like micro, small, large, and extra large. The differences between the sizes are based on features such as the amount of RAM, number of cores in the processor, quantity of dedicated storage, and sometimes memory and storage technology — for example, spinning hard disk drives (HDDs) versus solid state drives (SSDs). Of course, more expensive processors and larger VM sizes will cost more.

Elastic resources and services

Although cloud virtual machines are implemented on physical machines, cloud resources like VMs have capabilities that go well beyond physical resources. The ability to provide elasticity by scaling, automatically or on demand, to larger or smaller performance and storage capacities is a standard capability for most cloud vendors. Cloud elasticity is one of the most compelling reasons to use the cloud. Elasticity provides dynamic scaling of processing power, memory, storage, and other scalable computing resources so that workloads can automatically handle higher or lower computing demands.

It's the cloud's virtualization capabilities that add the ability to scale to virtual cloud resources. Sometimes virtualization hides the underlying physical hardware's capabilities until there's a need to scale them. Virtualization then exposes the hidden resources, causing the capacity to appear to grow. Other times, virtualization may deliver scaling by moving a workload from one set of physical resources to a larger or smaller set of physical resources. Often, moving workloads can happen very quickly and does not degrade the performance experienced by users.

By skillfully combining use of scalable cloud resources and services, cloud SaaS applications can handle very large loads with excellent performance. Amazon and Google are great examples.

Self-service provisioning

Before the cloud, when employees of a company needed computing resources for running applications, developing software, or some other task, they would request the hardware from their IT department. The request might include configuration requirements of the hardware, but IT would be responsible for procuring, configuring, and deploying the hardware.

That made sense when purchasing and deploying hardware was a completely different activity than using the hardware. However, acquiring virtual hardware from the cloud is less complicated than making a hardware request of IT. SaaS applications are easily accessed from the cloud, and developers know more about the hardware they need than IT does. So, now IT usually doesn't need to be the gatekeeper for acquiring cloud applications.

With the cloud, companies can now streamline procurement of their computing resources. Employees can be empowered to work directly with cloud providers to select the SaaS applications they need, and developers can procure the computing resources that will drive their DevOps and develop-test-deploy activities. IT and technology management still have a role to play in selecting the cloud providers who will provide the services most suited to the company's needs and in building templates and standards for computing best practices. Before the emergence of the cloud, IT was often thought of as a bottleneck. However, with the cloud's self-service model, IT can pre-vet services and then allow teams access to the tools they need. Of course, some IT organizations are still seen at bottlenecks. These slower to react IT organizations are often in a reactionary posture rather than working with the business to help understand team needs before employees require specific cloud technologies.

REMEMBER

For example, a company can and should create a set of business rules for employees to follow, including which cloud providers can be used, selection of best-of-breed SaaS applications viable for the company, virtual machine profiles that have been determined to be the best for software development, and so on. These business rules should be made with user involvement to ensure the results will be beneficial to everyone. If these technology decisions are made ahead of time with the right services and resources, selecting the right technology at the right time will be easier. In this way, everyone is satisfied. The business can control expenses and reduce capital expenditures, and business units have the freedom to avoid time-consuming processes that slow down the ability to get the job done.

Service level agreements (SLA)

When you select computing resources for use with a cloud provider, you're entering a contract to pay for the use of the computing resources you've selected. In return, the cloud provider is committing to provide the resources, and the cloud provider generally backs that commitment with a service level agreement (SLA).

The SLA can take different forms and make various levels of guarantee. At the low end, cloud providers might simply state that they will do their best to provide good service. If consumers are willing to pay a premium price, they may be able to leverage a mirrored service to minimize the chance of service interruptions.

A typical service level agreement states what the provider has agreed to deliver in terms of availability and response to demand. The service level might, for example, specify that the resources will be available 99.999 percent of the time and that more resources will be provided dynamically if greater than 80 percent of any given resource is being used.

If consumers find that they're not receiving the level of performance or availability that they've been promised, then the SLA will be of value in working with the cloud provider to rectify the situation and perhaps receive some form of compensation.

WARNING

SLAs are also valuable to consumers who are using IaaS resources to build software that will run in the cloud. Software design must consider the achievable performance, reliability of the cloud, and other resources that will be used, and SLAs can provide that information. If the cloud resources don't meet the required level of performance, the software design or the choice of resources may need to be changed. And if the Mean Time Between Failures (MTBF) of cloud resources isn't adequate for the business obligations of the software, then something will definitely have to be changed in the software design. Remember, software being built for the cloud should itself define SLAs for its consumers.

Metering, billing, and licensing

Obviously, consumers generally have to pay for the cloud computing resources they use, and there are different models for how the use of cloud resources are measured and how consumers pay. In the following sections, we discuss the pay-as-you-go model, the licensing model, SaaS models, subscription models, and even free models. These models aren't defined in stone, and new models can emerge, so we discuss how each generally works.

As with any financial matter, you should familiarize yourself with the service and its financial model, and make sure you read the fine print.

Pay-as-you-go models

Pay-as-you-go is the traditional cloud computing billing model. You select a cloud resource and pay for your actual use. The cloud provider measures the time you're actually using the resource and calculates which optional features or configured characteristics should contribute to the cost.

For example, you may have selected a VM at one price level, but scaled up the memory to a higher cost level. Depending on the type of cloud resource you're consuming, the vendor may count your usage by the hour, minute, or, in some cases, by the second. Then, you're typically billed on a monthly basis for all the resources used during the previous month.

This model may also have other features within it. For example, if you know you'll be using a cloud resource for a long time, check to see whether the cloud provider offers that resource at a lower cost if you're willing to guarantee you'll be using the resource for that longer period of time, which is sometimes called *reserved pricing.* Alternately, a cloud provider may drop the price of a resource automatically if you use it long enough to qualify.

Licensing model

The *licensing model* for software used in an on-premises traditional data center is well understood. You purchase a license for using the software for some pre-defined period, typically at least a year. Cloud providers generally don't offer licensing plans for cloud resources. The pay-as-you-go service would presumably cost less if you didn't use the resource for a full year.

However, if you've purchased a license for using software in your physical data center, but then decide you want to use the cloud version of that software, some vendors will allow you to transfer the license from the physical version to the cloud version. If you're currently not in the cloud, but planning to be, it may be worthwhile to examine the software you're currently using to see whether the vendor's license allows moving your license to the cloud.

SaaS models

SaaS models are a bit different than the other pricing models we discuss in this chapter. For one thing, SaaS products may not be owned by the cloud provider that is selling them and may be completely separate from the cloud provider's pricing and billing scheme.

For example, you can think of your cloud provider like a mobile phone offered through a cellphone provider. You pay a monthly fee for voice, data, and messaging. In addition, your credit card may get separately billed for apps that you download or subscribe to. Like a cloud vendor, your cellphone provider is not responsible for the way in which each app chooses to price its services.

Likewise, SaaS vendors have great latitude in the pricing of their software. They may provide a pay-as-you-go model, but they may use a yearly licensing or subscription model. You have to look into the pricing model of any SaaS application you're thinking of using. Don't assume it is the same as other cloud resources.

Subscription models

Subscription models sometimes apply to SaaS application and on-premises applications that have been moved to the cloud. Subscriptions have also been used in the cloud for cloud services — for example, when long-term use qualifies the consumer for a lower price than the prevailing pay-as-you-go price.

Subscriptions are popular with open-source software (many open-source licenses prohibit open-source applications from being sold) as a means of bundling training or support with the software to provide revenue to the vendor. In addition, vendors are increasingly looking for ways to create annual recurring revenue where they can receive yearly revenue from each customer, and subscriptions are a means of doing that.

Subscriptions are not common in the cloud, but they do exist, and there are reasons that they may become more popular.

Free models

Free models may seem unlikely in the cloud because at a minimum, any cloud service requires the use of various cloud compute resources. However, free is always a big motivator, and some vendors offer free introductory or trial use of products, especially if the products are new and haven't yet gained significant market share. Even powerful business and enterprises cloud resources are often offered for free.

WARNING

Don't be surprised if free usage is accompanied by limitations. Common limitations on free use include a reduced feature set, the lack of ability to save your work, or a strictly limited duration for the free use.

Costs

In the fast-moving world of the cloud, prices can change quickly. Because of that, any specifics that we would mention may be obsolete by the time this book is published. However, we can make some general points about costs here.

The cloud infrastructure market is very competitive. To succeed in this market, cloud providers have to offer better features, higher performance, targeting of specific markets, and / or lower pricing. Over time, there will be new pricing models and new services optimized for specific requirements, such as governance, security, or data.

Also, *Moore's Law* originally observed that the density of transistors (a building block of computer circuitry) doubled in density and decreased in cost by half every 18 months. Since then, that elapsed time grew from 18 months to 24 months, and it is not certain whether this pace will be maintained in the future. Regardless, so far Moore's Law has correctly predicted the continuing increase in computing power and drop in prices of computing technology, including the cloud. No one can be positive about future trends, but so far cloud technologies have reduced the price of computing for cloud consumers.

Getting to Know Prominent IaaS Cloud Providers

The following quick thumbnail of the current important IaaS cloud providers gives you an awareness of prominent IaaS cloud vendors and their focuses:

» **Amazon AWS:** This all-purpose cloud provider offers IaaS and a vast number of other services. With the largest current IaaS market share, Amazon provides worldwide cloud services and a broad set of resources, services, and SaaS products.

» **Microsoft Azure:** Microsoft offers a consistent platform across both its public and private cloud services. It has a growing acceptance in the enterprise market.

» **Google Cloud Platform:** Google's cloud, like Amazon's, runs Google's own software products and supports many key emerging standards, such as Kubernetes, which it developed and put into the open-source community. The company is gaining traction in the enterprise market.

» **IBM Cloud:** A stalwart of enterprise computing, IBM's cloud provides the same computing infrastructure services on both its public and private clouds as well as supporting bare metal computing services. IBM has standardized on Red Hat's OpenShift as its Kubernetes orchestration layer.

» **Alibaba Cloud:** A subsidiary of Chinese e-commerce platform, Alibaba offers a suite of cloud services with an initial focus on the Asian market.

» **Oracle Cloud:** This all-purpose cloud is focused on enterprise clients in both the data center and in the public cloud.

Discovering the Key Components of Private Cloud IaaS

The private cloud is becoming increasingly important to organizations that want the elasticity, self-service provisioning, and manageability of the public cloud but want those services behind the firewall.

The cloud is changing and becoming a core to the business computing strategy. It is therefore not surprising that one size does not fit all. Depending on workloads and circumstances, companies are looking to transform their internal computing resources so that they are as flexible as the public cloud.

In the earlier days of private cloud, it was common to simply add capabilities like self-service provisioning as a service within their data center. You could add more automation that made computing easier to manage. However, at this early stage, the private cloud did not resemble the flexibility of the public cloud. That is beginning to change. The advent of standard infrastructure, including Kubernetes, Istio, and standardized APIs, is changing the nature of the cloud (see Chapter 6). Increasingly, vendors are leveraging the same technology services that are ubiquitous in the public cloud and making them available in the private cloud. This is happening in two ways:

» Public cloud vendors are creating the identical cloud environment to support a private cloud within a customer's data center. In addition, these vendors are offering these services as a hosted option.

» Public cloud vendors are offering a closed server implementation of the public cloud that resides within the data center. In this situation, the vendor implements all the cloud services within the server and controls and manages the environment on a day-to-day basis. If an update is needed, the vendor takes care of that change. In addition, the vendor charges customers at the same rate as though they were using a public cloud service.

Customers are interested in a combination of public and private cloud services for two key reasons. First, senior management, aware of their governance responsibility, wants to ensure that certain workloads are stored behind the firewall. Second, many businesses are not ready to embrace the public cloud either because of cultural issues or simply because of the lack of trust.

Using IaaS in Multicloud

As we move to a technical architectural foundation based on common standards for cloud native and Kubernetes, you can now use a variety of clouds across the business. The adoption of different clouds in different business units has been the norm for a decade. Renegades within the business defied IT and bought their own public cloud services, and IT had no way to force compliance with their preferred computing methods.

At this point, IT management understands that it is better to collaborate with business units and provide oversight and management across multiple public and private clouds. This transition has accelerated with the wide adoption of cloud standards, common services, and APIs.

The value of multicloud is clear:

>> The potential to move workloads from one cloud platform to another

>> The desire to place workloads based on corporate requirements or preferences

>> The need to control costs

Chapter **9**

Using Software as a Service

While software developers are familiar with using IaaS (see Chapter 8), end users are much more familiar with Software as a Service (SaaS). Software as a Service is the way many business users are first introduced to the cloud. For example, common consumer and business applications like Slack, Google's Gmail, and Office 365 are SaaS applications. Many SaaS applications are designed to implement a specific business process — ranging from accounting to customer relationship management (CRM), collaboration, and human resource management. Business users have increasingly found that SaaS applications represent a more manageable, flexible, and secure alternative to traditional on-premises applications. At the same time, managers are also surprised at the monthly costs to support a growing base of users for a SaaS application. Therefore, it's important to consider costs as the number of users expands.

In this chapter, we take a look at the world of SaaS applications and how they work in a multicloud world.

Understanding the Characteristics of SaaS

Many companies have discovered that they can realize important organizational and economic benefits by using SaaS applications. Well-designed SaaS applications provide the opportunity to have a third-party organization handle all the details that go into keeping complex applications running. SaaS applications are typically not used in isolation. Rather, these applications and services are frequently used in combination with lots of other cloud and on-premises applications and services. In fact, third-party vendors often develop applications to be used in conjunction with a popular SaaS application. In addition, companies often integrate their SaaS applications with other applications and platforms in their own data center and other cloud platforms. As businesses add their own business processes and third-party applications, they will become locked in to that platform.

As companies become experienced with SaaS, they'll see a pattern of characteristics that are common among the more successful SaaS solutions:

» SaaS applications are generalized to incorporate common services so that the applications meet the needs of different companies across multiple industries.

» *Multi-tenancy* means that a SaaS application serves many users with the same infrastructure while securely storing their data separately. (The next section dives deeper into the benefits of multi-tenant solutions.) However, in some situations, a business may insist on a single-tenant version of a SaaS application. In this situation, the vendor will isolate that business's version of the SaaS application at an additional cost.

» Highly elastic SaaS applications can easily scale up or down to support changing needs of a business. For example, if a company increases the quantity of documents being managed by an order of magnitude, the application will scale up new storage and the ability to search and manage it immediately.

» In many cases, SaaS vendors support a self-service option that allows users to provision resources and manage an application's deployment directly. Customers can go to the SaaS portal to add more licenses, renew their contract, or reduce their number of licenses in a matter of minutes. You no longer need to contact vendors and then wait for them to make the changes. Self-service includes built-in billing, monitoring, and usage information that gives customers a unified view of what they're paying for and receiving. However, when customers are using SaaS where there needs to be complex business process customization, there will need to be a direct relationship with the vendor or a third-party consulting firm. If you're implementing a corporate-wide license arrangement with a SaaS vendor, you'll likely work through the company's sales team.

>> Flexible SaaS applications are built to be modular and offer service-oriented interfaces, allowing complementary applications to be integrated into the SaaS application's ecosystem.

>> Some SaaS applications provide sophisticated business process configurators where each customer can change the process within the otherwise standardized SaaS application. For example, a company may add a process requiring a manager to approve the price being offered to a new customer. A built-in configuration tool enables this change to be done on an ad-hoc basis without programming.

>> SaaS applications need to constantly provide new features and new capabilities without interrupting the customer's ongoing work. SaaS vendors use a technique known as continuous development and deployment to accomplish this task. (See Chapter 11 for more details.)

A SaaS vendor must be able to ensure customers that their data and configurations are separate and secure from other customers' data and configurations. Imagine the possible consequences if your competitors use the same SaaS offering that you use, and they're able to access your customer lists or intellectual property. Vendors are aware of customer concerns and implement extensive security to prevent theft of customer data.

Multi-tenancy and its benefits

Multi-tenancy means that the SaaS application is serving many users with the same software instance at the same time. Multi-tenancy differs from a single-tenant solution where each user has their own exclusive use of one instance of the application running on a single machine.

So, how does multi-tenancy work? All users of the application use the same algorithms and programmed code, but each user's data is segregated from every other user's data. Further, the application is constructed with comprehensive security measures to ensure that each user's data is protected not only from hackers trying to gain access to the application, but also from other users who already have access to the SaaS application. In other words, SaaS processing is shared with all users, but their data is not shared.

Following are the advantages of a multi-tenancy SaaS over a third-party, hosted, single-tenancy application:

>> **Moving to the cloud saves on-premises capital expenditure costs.** With a single-tenancy, hosted solution, customers must build out their data center if new users are added, data needs grow, or other resources are required. In contrast, new users in a cloud environment get access to the same basic

SaaS software, so storage is likely to be the only resource that must be able to scale up per user — and those costs are relatively small and often bundled into the ongoing SaaS cost.

>> **Ongoing maintenance and updates are included.** End users don't need to pay separate maintenance fees to keep their software up to date. The costs of new features and updates are included with a SaaS subscription and are rolled out by the vendor on an ongoing basis.

>> **Configuration can occur while leaving the underlying code base unchanged.** In the on-premises context, applications and single-tenant-hosted solutions are often customized, but this costly endeavor sometimes requires changes to the application's code. Additionally, customizations can make upgrades time-consuming, because the new version of the application may not be compatible with your customization. In contrast, most multi-tenant SaaS solutions are designed to be configurable so that businesses can make the application perform the way they need without changing the underlying code or data structures. Because the code is unchanged, upgrades can be performed more easily. However, if the business customizes business processes, it will be more difficult to update code.

>> **Cloud vendors have a vested interest in making sure everything runs smoothly.** Multi-tenant SaaS providers have, in a sense, all their eggs in one basket. Although this approach may sound dangerous, it's a benefit to end users. In a single-tenant environment, a service disruption will affect only one customer, so the vendor may be slow to respond and fail to take the necessary steps to ensure the problem doesn't reoccur. In contrast, with a multi-tenant solution, a slight glitch can affect all customers of the SaaS application. Therefore, SaaS vendors invest significant amounts of money and effort into ensuring uptime, continuity, and performance.

THE STORY OF A SaaS PIONEER: SALESFORCE.COM

Although companies have offered software products as a service for many years, the current generation of highly sophisticated SaaS offerings can be traced back to Salesforce.com. The story of how this SaaS pioneer grew to become a market leader and a look at its current offerings provide insight into the market.

Marc Benioff, the founder of Salesforce.com, had been a marketing executive for Oracle for many years. After leaving and going off on his own, he started Salesforce.com. Being a marketing executive, Marc had a bold marketing moniker for his fledgling company: "No software." The plan was quite simple: Create a way to allow customers to use a popular application — customer relationship management (CRM) — over the Internet. Customers could purchase a seat and use the application over the web. The customer never had to update the software, didn't have to store data on a server, and never had to worry about maintenance fees. If that customer was traveling to a remote location, they could access sales leads from any PC. There were no capital expenses, with the exception of a PC or some endpoint, such as a tablet.

Initial Salesforce.com customers were small businesses that were willing to take a risk in exchange for not having to buy hardware or hire staff. Also, because there was only a one-month commitment, they knew they could simply take their customer data and go home if it didn't work out for them. Salesforce.com had a more difficult time separating large companies from their data-center focus. Sales and marketing departments at large enterprises began to implement Salesforce.com by placing the fees to run Salesforce.com on their expense reports. Slowly but surely, Salesforce.com made inroads into large companies that appreciated the ability to avoid buying equipment.

Salesforce.com opened its platform so that independent software vendors (ISVs) could build software that sits on top of the CRM application. Essentially, Salesforce.com built a Platform as a Service offering, which it named Customer 360 Platform. ISVs could create SaaS applications on the platform, and Salesforce.com was able to offer additional functionality, such as billing and monitoring, to its customers.

System integrators found that customers who were using Salesforce.com were not satisfied with Salesforce being a stand-alone application; customers needed to integrate Salesforce with the rest of their greater IT landscape. Companies needed to connect Salesforce.com to other, complementary systems, create workflow processes among independent applications, link to commerce networks, and so on. System integrators turned Salesforce.com into a hybrid environment that now interacts with data centers behind customers' firewalls, public clouds, and third-party applications built on its Platform as a Service offering.

The key to integrating all these components together is the service orientation of the underlying platform, accessible via a comprehensive set of standardized APIs. When integrators or other software vendors partner with a company like Salesforce.com, they create a dependency on the Salesforce.com development and deployment model. This dependency allows them to develop more quickly and efficiently, but it also locks them into a single platform.

The need for cloud native SaaS

The term *cloud-native* refers to the characteristics of a SaaS application where the application is based on a modular architecture where microservices are managed in containers. This approach results in better scalability and elasticity. With SaaS applications serving very large numbers of users at the same time, one might expect that SaaS applications must therefore be stingy with computing resources. Quite the opposite: Users can typically treat SaaS applications as though they have unlimited resources; users just do their work, and the application responds with whatever resources are needed. Compare this approach to applications in an on-premises data center where a sizable increase in demand can strain the resources of the data center. Users would then have to explicitly request additional resources from the IT organization, which could take days or weeks while approvals are secured, hardware is purchased, and systems are provisioned and deployed.

SaaS applications can meet increasing demands by using scalable resources that the cloud provides or designs into the application. What doesn't work for a SaaS application vendor is to simply move a legacy application to the cloud without building in the ability to scale. Although simply deploying a traditional application to the cloud has some benefits, the true advantage comes from re-architecting the application as a set of modular services.

The second major requirement for SaaS applications is to always be available. In on-premises data centers, applications can sometimes crash, be unavailable during maintenance windows, or be unavailable while an application is updated to a new version. None of those situations are acceptable in the cloud. SaaS applications are always in use, and new features must simply appear in SaaS applications without requiring downtime to be installed.

Keeping a SaaS application running all the time, even when new features are being deployed, requires a different approach to application reliability and a design that makes it easy to make updates on the fly. It also requires a development and deployment model known as DevOps. (See Chapter 11 for more details.) Containers and microservices are the modern tools that can help make SaaS applications be always available.

WARNING

The same characteristics that make SaaS applications so appealing also can cause problems. If the SaaS vendor has a technical issue when updating an application or infrastructure, there could be a service outage. This can lead to a crisis when users become dependent on the cloud-based application.

The Cloud Native Computing Foundation, an organization that drives adoption of the cloud-native programming paradigm, focuses on container and microservice technologies. It states that cloud-native applications and services should use an open-source software stack to meet the following architectural goals:

>> Each software component making up an application is packaged in its own container, which facilitates reproducibility, transparency, and resource isolation.

>> Containers are dynamically deployed and orchestrated — actively scheduled and managed to optimize resource utilization.

>> Applications are segmented into microservices, which significantly increases the overall agility and maintainability of applications.

For more information on containers and microservices, see Chapter 6.

Understanding SaaS Economics

Cloud SaaS applications have changed the way companies pay for and use software. The following are some of the most important things to think about when you consider budgeting for SaaS:

>> **Entry costs are lower with SaaS.** When implementing a SaaS application, customers are often able to get a free trial period to assess the software. Additionally, companies can slowly ramp up the number of *seats* (users) who have access to the application. With traditional on-premises implementations, a company must make a large capital expenditure upfront to acquire the application. It then must install the software and possibly purchase additional hardware to support the implementation.

>> **Maintenance and support are included in SaaS fees.** With on-premises applications, there's a perpetual license software model. With on-premises software, companies need to enter into a contract with a software vendor or services provider to keep software up to date and free from glitches and security vulnerabilities. With SaaS contracts, the costs associated with maintenance are not separated out from the monthly fees.

>> **Upgrades are no longer costly, prolonged procedures with SaaS.** Upgrading a traditional, on-premises application often requires months of testing, allocation of large budgets, and teams of consultants to ensure that the implementation runs smoothly. Companies often skip upgrades in order to reduce the headaches involved. In a SaaS model, the SaaS vendor performs upgrades behind the scenes by. All SaaS customers receive the new, updated software at the same time without having to manage a frustrating upgrade process. This ensures that SaaS users are always running the most up-to-date version of the software. However, a SaaS vendor could change an interface or software service that the customer doesn't like. That customer typically has no option to use the outdated interface or service.

Occasionally, SaaS updates cause problems. For example, if you're running a third-party application that gathers data from the SaaS, the application may fail because the SaaS has changed its data structure. However, these problems are typically kept to a minimum because SaaS vendors have to architect their solutions to support a wide variety of partners and their platforms.

Figuring Out How SaaS Fits into the Multicloud World

SaaS applications rarely operate completely independently. Companies often have an IT landscape that looks something like this: SaaS for CRM, a second SaaS for human resources, in-house analytics hardware behind a firewall, and AI for testing. Much of this information is fed into their enterprise resource planning (ERP) system that may be housed in their data center. Providing processes that allow information to securely flow among these systems is critical. Figure 9-1 illustrates this hybrid SaaS environment.

The environment described here truly is a hybrid cloud, and it is probably a multicloud as well. It's a hybrid cloud because the SaaS applications are in a public cloud while the analytics are on-premises. It may also be a multicloud because the SaaS applications may be in different public clouds. These applications ultimately need to work together to provide full business value. Of course, a hybrid or multicloud environment can be simpler or more complex than the one illustrated in Figure 9-1.

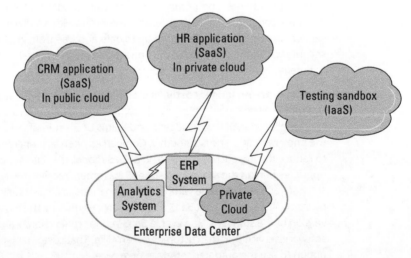

FIGURE 9-1:
A hybrid SaaS environment.

Where do SaaS applications run? A SaaS vendor might run its software in the physical data centers it operates. Salesforce.com did this originally out of necessity because it was an early innovator without other options. Other vendors — for example, SugarCRM — run their SaaS offerings in public clouds, such as Amazon AWS or Google Cloud Platform. A SaaS running in a vendor's data center isn't necessarily more stable, but great software on an unreliable third-party platform is useless. So, it's important to understand service level agreements (SLAs).

The ability of a SaaS application to run in different environments is important for many reasons, just as it is for almost any other application. Consider these examples:

>> **Physical location may make a difference.** Some SaaS applications need to be close to their users. For example, a high-speed video streaming server will provide a better user experience if the data does not have to travel long distances. In addition, some businesses have governance rules that require that their data be located in the country where the company is based.

>> **Software location may make a difference.** When SaaS applications interact with other applications, performance will benefit if they're both in the same cloud. This may not be necessary for simple interactions, but as data quantity and communication rates increase, it becomes more important. This is one of the reasons you may find the same SaaS application in different public clouds.

>> **Flexibility may make a difference.** Not all clouds are equal, and all clouds are constantly making changes to their offerings and prices. SaaS vendors should stay aware of each cloud environment and be ready to move their applications to the cloud (or clouds) that provide the best platform for their applications.

SaaS applications live in diverse environments, integrated with many services and other applications. Although this setup increases complexity, it also provides new opportunities.

TIP

So, when a division of your company wants access to all of an application's data so that it can run analytics, it is no longer reasonable to say, "Sorry, that's in the SaaS application." Instead, you can now replicate the data onto your private cloud where the analytics team can make a copy of the *golden master* (a single version of the truth for the data — the reference model) to run its sophisticated number crunching, and other groups, such as development, can make a copy of the data and use it for testing in a public cloud.

Using SaaS as a Platform

In order to create a more feature-rich application, some SaaS vendors have turned their application into a platform upon which partners and Independent Software Vendors (ISVs) can build applications that extend the SaaS platform. This model represents an ecosystem that extends the functionality and value of the SaaS application. Typically, these ecosystems are domain-specific, for example, addressing healthcare, CRM, or other business focuses.

This is how it works: A SaaS vendor with thousands of paying customers opens its APIs to ISVs. These ISVs can then build applications on top of the SaaS vendor's infrastructure. Therefore, they don't need to write and deploy an entire application, but can focus on their specific extension of the SaaS platform. By building general domain functionality into the platform, the SaaS vendor attracts other vendors within that domain. Further, the SaaS vendor that created the platform typically takes care of messaging middleware, business process services, and other complex programming.

Note: A SaaS platform is fundamentally a PaaS provider to the partners and ISVs who build applications in the SaaS ecosystem. (See the next chapter for discussion of PaaS.) When an application is built on the PaaS platform, there is no need to specify an operating system as would be required if the platform offered an IaaS service. By offering only the services that are consistent with the domain addressed by the SaaS. The SaaS vendor exercises control over the applications built on the platform, ensuring that they address the SaaS's domain.

Perhaps the most significant advantage to working in the ecosystem is that the SaaS vendor already has thousands of happy and paying customers. After a partner creates an application, it can market its software through the SaaS vendor's portal in addition to using its own traditional sales force. This has become a standard model used by SaaS vendors to build their brand and power in the market.

Discovering who builds applications on SaaS platforms

In this section, we take a closer look at the types of application developers that are suited to building their domain-specific applications on a SaaS platform. Partners and ISVs can be broken into two general categories: smaller startups and larger, established companies. It might be clear why a small company with limited resources might be motivated to build on top of, for example, the Salesforce.com platform, but if you're a large player with your own customer base, why would you be part of another company's ecosystem?

Established companies may want to join another company's online ecosystem for many reasons. Software vendors with successful on-premises applications are receiving pressure to offer a cloud version of their software. One challenge that these larger ISVs face is that in order to have a successful, enterprise-class application, they must create and establish their cloud presence. Joining an existing ecosystem that has already established their business and attracted customers shortcuts the path to customer awareness.

Both large and small companies benefit by using the PaaS environment of the SaaS platform, which can dramatically decrease the amount of software that must be created to form a mature application, thereby increasing time-to-market.

Consider Veeva Systems, a software vendor that has developed a cloud-based CRM solution for the pharmaceutical, animal health, and biotechnology industries. Veeva built its software in the Salesforce.com ecosystem. Without Salesforce.com, Veeva would have had to create a completely new platform from scratch — a monumental and expensive endeavor for a small company. Salesforce.com can't meet the unique needs of every industry, so where Salesforce.com falls short, partners like Veeva step in.

For example, pharmaceutical companies must comply with specific regulations. Veeva has built-in functionality to track and report the required information. Because Veeva controls software and process updates, when reporting requirements change, it updates the application so that all its users have access to the most up-to-date offering and are in compliance with government regulations and industry practices.

One might think that building a SaaS application in another business's ecosystem would devalue the application. However, the opposite is often more likely. You have no doubt noticed how food vendors at a mall are all located in the same area. Sometimes called the *food court model,* related businesses can do very well when colocated, not least because the customers attracted to the ecosystem are all highly qualified to do business with the vendors there.

Developing on a SaaS vendor's platform

Clearly, there are great benefits for ISVs that build applications in an established ecosystem, but these independent development companies may be at the mercy of the SaaS vendor. The SaaS vendor develops and maintains the platform, and the ISVs who have built applications on the platform are then dependent on it operating predictably. If the SaaS vendor does an update, the platform may possibly change its behavior in a way that destabilizes the ISVs' applications.

Of course, stability and consistency over time are important for any platform, from cloud infrastructures to operating systems. But SaaS platforms are relatively new, and SaaS businesses may not have as much experience in maintaining them. To protect themselves, independent vendors should have the opportunity to thoroughly test their application on a newly modified platform before upgrades are released to end users. ISVs should research a SaaS vendor before developing on its platform to verify it provides the stability required to safeguard applications.

However, in practice, the relationship between SaaS platform vendors and their ISV partners is symbiotic — each needs the other for success and growth. A SaaS platform should document its APIs and state how long they will be supported. The success of applications on a SaaS platform will benefit the SaaS vendor, just as failures will be attributed to the platform. Applications built on the SaaS platform will be branded with the creating company's name, and they will, therefore, also be credited with the application's success or criticized for failure.

Looking at examples of SaaS platforms

Like so many things cloud, SaaS applications have reached a certain degree of maturity — marked by users taking new SaaS applications for granted rather than marveling over every new SaaS application. In the following sections, we explore a selection of the major types of SaaS applications.

SaaS business applications

From accounting software to customer relationship management, supply chain management, financial management, and human resources, there are SaaS applications for all the standard business practices. Not long ago, many of these functions were custom-created and run in on-premises data centers. Now, they're in the cloud and generalized to make them suitable for the vast majority of businesses.

These products tend to have several characteristics in common: They're designed with business processes built in that customers can modify; they have published APIs so that third-party vendors and businesses can add functionality. These applications have moved in great numbers to the cloud because customers found the on-premises systems too hard to manage, and users need access to the application while on the go.

SaaS collaborative applications

SaaS is very popular for collaborative applications. This area is dominated by software that focuses on bringing people together — and most people are already in the cloud — to work together on shared activities. For example, web conferencing, document collaboration, project planning, instant messaging, and email and all collaborative applications. In a sense, it was inevitable that these platforms would move to the cloud. These tasks exist throughout the organization and need to be easily accessed from many locations.

SaaS development services

With more and more companies building software for the cloud, it's not surprising that many companies are building services that make it easier to build applications. *Services* means online software that is intended to be a part of an application, not an application itself.

Examples of development services include

>> **Monitoring as a service:** SaaS applications usually work well, but even the best can run into problems. Issues can come from bugs in the SaaS, reactions to unanticipated situations, or problems outside the SaaS. In each of these cases, the SaaS vendor needs to quickly understand what is going on and remedy it. They'll be lucky if they can fix the problem before customers start calling the support line. And if customers do call the support line, support personnel need to understand what the problem is so that they can help the customer work around the problem. Monitoring software examines many sources of information about the SaaS application and its operational context and delivers it to support, development, and other business units.

>> **Compliance as a service:** Compliance responsibilities are time-consuming and complicated tasks that large companies must perform. Because compliance is a well-defined activity, yet very involved with many special cases, many companies have implemented compliance solutions as a service so the SaaS company doesn't have to.

>> **Security as a service:** Almost without exception, vendors providing antivirus software are offering their products as a service. However, security extends much further than looking for viruses in communications. Increasingly, security is an activity that is part and parcel of software development and must be designed into software as it is being designed and built.

>> **Database (and other components) as a service:** Every application works with data and needs to store it, and databases (in this context, DBaaS, or Database as a Service) are the standard tool for storage and management of data. Every cloud environment offers many types and vendors of databases. Typically, it takes only a short time, perhaps minutes, to provision and launch a database and start using it. Other components used to build SaaS applications are also available for use in the cloud, including identity management, credit card processing, analytics, big data storage and analysis, and so on.

Chapter **10**

Standing on Platform as a Service

t makes sense that IaaS was the first offering for hosting applications in the cloud as it was a direct replacement for the hardware servers that had been hosting applications. The evolution from IaaS to Platform as a Service (PaaS) was a step that developers recognized quickly. After all, developers had been responsible for adapting their applications to different operating systems from time immemorial, and the ability to deploy applications without worrying about the differences between operating systems was an enormous breakthrough. By hiding the underlying operating system in a PaaS virtual machine and providing general services to replace operating system services, developers could focus on the business logic of their applications.

In this chapter, we discuss the value of the Platform as a Service model and its ability to make software development easier in a cloud environment.

Discovering the Business Value of PaaS

The efficiency of building software in a Platform as a Service (PaaS) environment (rather than an IaaS environment) allows developers to spend their time creating software rather than managing infrastructure. Rather than needing to create a

DevOps platform to give developers the tools they desire, PaaS environments provide the services that developers require. One of the primary benefits of the abstraction of the PaaS model is that it allows businesses to rapidly transform their software to meet new customer requirements.

While saving development time is an excellent tactical value, the bigger value is the opportunity to transform a business with forward-looking and efficient methodologies and practices. The role PaaS plays in this transformation is that it favors the use of container technology for packaging and deploying software, which in turn favors use of cloud capabilities to provide reach and scale, which in turn favors scalable and integrated business processes to manage it all. We touch on each of these symbiotic areas in this chapter.

Identifying the Characteristics of Platform as a Service

PaaS is a cloud-based computing environment where applications can be developed, run, and managed, but in contrast to IaaS, the compute environment includes an operating system. The services typically provided by an operating system, such as networking, file-systems, and I/O, are instead provided as abstracted services from the PaaS infrastructure. The PaaS model, in fact, sits on top of the IaaS services.

TECHNICAL STUFF

Other than using abstracted services instead of operating system services, applications running in a PaaS environment have essentially the same services and capabilities as applications running in an IaaS environment. Applications can communicate between IaaS and PaaS environments as easily as with another application within the same environment, with no application being aware of what type of cloud environment is associated with another application.

Using abstracted services instead of operating system services removes the need for expertise in each of those operating systems. Not having to worry any more about moving applications between environments with different operating systems simplifies software design and implementation, thereby reducing costs and time-to-market.

PaaS vendors create a managed environment that brings together a combination of systems and components that typically provide a complete ecosystem for application development, deployment, and operation. So, in addition to providing a computing environment for applications and services, PaaS often also provides tools that support the development effort and agile development methodology. In Chapter 11, we discuss the software development and operations platform that benefits from PaaS.

PaaS enables an organization to do the following:

>> Leverage important middleware services without having to deal with the complexities of managing different hardware platforms and operating systems.

>> Use a complete stack of development and deployment tools via the web. Many of these tools are in wide use and provide APIs for flexibility and standard use in different environments. Developers can often also access these tools and environments via legacy desktop applications.

>> Overcome the challenges of managing many individual development and deployment tools by providing a suite of integrated and standardized tools that meet company requirements.

PaaS can be viewed as having two fundamental parts: the platform and the management of the platform. In this chapter, we focus primarily on the platform itself — the actual software that's delivered to your organization.

The management, however, is a critical function that greatly increases the value of PaaS environments. The PaaS vendor doesn't just deliver the software making up the platform; it also continuously monitors the operation of the software to ensure that the platform performs as expected. Further, as new software updates and configurations become available, the PaaS vendor can immediately push them to its customers. Because of the abstractions of PaaS services, new software versions seamlessly provide their new features without requiring attention by the application owners.

One of the decisions you need to make before using PaaS is whether your business will manage its own PaaS environment, or you'll use a PaaS vendor's PaaS environment. If you choose to manage the PaaS environment yourself, you'll have to acquire, set up, configure, manage, and administer the PaaS (either in a public or private cloud). Of course, using a PaaS vendor who has constructed the PaaS environment and manages it is much more convenient. The downside of using a PaaS vendor is that it is probably a more generic solution; your organization may require different tools, more control over complicated systems, or support for different development methodologies. In those situations, your organization may find it necessary to build and control the complex PaaS environment itself.

Managing the Software Development and Deployment Life Cycle

PaaS computing environments are a technique for managing the cloud-based software development and deployment life cycle. With the movement toward adopting containers, a version of PaaS is particularly suitable for software that is deployed in containers. Indeed, container technology has been rising in popularity, and that growth intersects with the rise of PaaS technology — not only for deploying applications, but for development of applications as well. (For more details on containers, check out Chapter 6.)

Before the rise of cloud computing, the environment where software was developed was very different than the environment where that software was used. Now, in the cloud, software is developed in the same, or equivalent, environment(s) as where it is used, and that environment is almost always within a cloud. This change has had a profound impact on software development processes and methodologies as well as the operational processes for deployment of software to users.

The combined evolution of software development, use of the cloud, and the accelerated pace of deployment by operations staff is resulting in all those activities coming together into a single, more effective practice known as *DevOps*. Rather than software development and operations staff working independently with their own priorities as was normal not so long ago, now software development is merging with operations to form a single, integrated practice. Instead of development creating new features within new software releases and handing it over to an operations team for deployment to customers, DevOps focuses on developing the highest priority features needed by customers and immediately updating the cloud applications so that customers see the features they need right away.

In this new approach, software isn't deployed with release numbers on a 6- or 12-month schedule, but applications are updated with new features as soon as they're ready, sometimes multiple times a day. Of course, new software still has to be tested before it's released, but testing happens earlier and more often, so even though it's released more quickly, it's usually equally (if not more) robust and bug-free.

Success with this approach also requires more attention to the usability of the software so that new features don't require training and detailed explanation. All in all, implementing this new model for developing and deploying software requires a business to restructure its organization and change roles (for example, integrating development and operations), change processes (for example, feature prioritization, live software updates), and probably change relationships with their customers (for example, moving from a release schedule to delivering customer-prioritized features).

Managing an Agile Development Environment

To focus on customer needs and prioritize development activities to deliver features more quickly, companies are moving to an agile development and deployment process. In the traditional development and deployment model, features are developed over a fairly long period of time and eventually delivered to customers as a *release*, typically with a version number. Customers then usually examine the release, perhaps test it to make sure it still meets business needs and processes, and plan its installation, training, and introduction to users. From development to actual use would take at least months, and a year or more at the longest. With the high velocity of business and competition, that long lead time increases risks that needs will have changed in the interim or that a competing product reaches the market with needed features faster.

Agile development instead prioritizes swift development and deployment of new customer features, avoiding named releases (just update the SaaS application in place), and integrating development and deployment activities within a single team. Agile teams are typically composed of software developers, a product manager, sometimes an operations manager, a scrum master, user experience designers, and other specialists who may be brought in for special development tasks. An agile team works in *sprints* of typically two to four weeks in length, within which they produce a new, "shippable" product with new features.

NOT ALL PaaS ENVIRONMENTS
ARE THE SAME

Vendors provide various types of PaaS environments. A vendor may offer a PaaS environment within a SaaS application that allows other vendors to extend the SaaS application, just as Salesforce.com has done with Force.com. Public cloud vendors who provide IaaS services may augment these capabilities with PaaS services. Other vendors provide a dedicated PaaS environment that can operate across a multicloud environment. In addition to these vendor-supported public PaaS offerings, enterprises may decide to use the PaaS model when providing services to their internal users. Companies that follow this approach typically manage very large distributed data centers, and IT may take on the role of the service provider.

If you're using a public cloud-based PaaS, the vendor is responsible for managing the software services in the PaaS environment, as well as the overall development and deployment environment. If you decide to create your own PaaS environment, then, of course, the service management responsibilities will be yours.

A public PaaS platform is very different than a traditional development and deployment platform. These are some key differences between PaaS and an on-premises data center environments:

- In a PaaS environment, computing software resources aren't installed and managed by the business. Instead, the PaaS environment natively incorporates computing resources, and the PaaS vendor is responsible for platform management, performance, and software updates.

- When an application is built in a traditional on-premises environment, it must be packaged before it can be delivered to the customer's environment. An application built in a PaaS environment is already in the cloud and can be made available simply by publishing its location to customers (and perhaps opening up network access). On the other hand, a private cloud may be designed to support a PaaS environment and will have the same characteristics as PaaS on a public cloud.

- PaaS environments emphasize standardized computing services to replace operating system services, providing better portability between PaaS platforms for SaaS applications. PaaS environments may also offer development and deployment tools that are better integrated with the PaaS platforms, streamlining development activities. Some SaaS platforms provide their own proprietary PaaS environment to support their users.

In fact, the trend is to not only integrate teams, but to seek team members who combine related skills. In particular, *full-stack* developers are the ideal technical members of agile development teams because they can work on everything from the lowest-level server code to user interfaces, and all middleware services, such as databases, networking, security, and so on.

Agile teams who are operating efficiently can take a customer need for a new feature, turn it into a design, prioritize it for development, perform the development, test it, and deploy it to users via a SaaS application in as little as two or three days, and less time for simple things. (For more details on software development and deployment, see Chapter 11.)

Defining the Next Generation of Middleware in the Cloud

In the era of highly distributed cloud computing, middleware services are more important than ever. Middleware is the basic plumbing for all types of software environments in order to integrate services and data. All these middleware services are complicated. For these services to be useful, they require abstraction layers and APIs so that they can be plugged into a development effort to reduce the complexity.

These services sit on top of the operating system and provide critical services, such as:

>> Communications that facilitate interactions with other applications

>> Management of data, such as connectors to data sources, data transformation tools, and even databases

>> Correlation with business rules engines and security tools

Exploring Types of PaaS Platforms

All PaaS platforms provide a cloud computing environment without an operating system, but do include computing services that support building software using a complete set of services. However, PaaS platforms can be focused on specific computing contexts or markets, and that introduces interesting variants on the core

PaaS concept. This section discusses the most prominent PaaS contexts and explains why their focus is important to their consumers.

The specific PaaS contexts we explore in detail are

>> **Public PaaS:** A pure PaaS environment that is available as a public cloud

>> **Private PaaS:** A pure PaaS environment that is available as a private cloud within a business' data center

>> **Open PaaS:** Open-source software that enables building a PaaS where applications run in an open-source environment

REMEMBER

Each of these contexts supports building and running PaaS applications. Indeed, it's often possible to move an application from one PaaS to another PaaS without modification, a concept called *portability*.

Public PaaS

Public PaaS clouds provide the shortest path to development and deployment of a SaaS application. Granted, all PaaS platforms offer accelerated speed in developing applications, but public clouds have some advantages. For one thing, they're already operating and being managed by PaaS vendors — two advantages that will speed your development activities. The biggest PaaS clouds are, almost by definition, public clouds, with AWS's Elastic Beanstalk, Microsoft's Azure App Service, Red Hat OpenShift, and Google's App Engine as the most visible.

As public clouds, particularly those from larger vendors, these PaaS environments allow convenient access to deployed SaaS applications from around the world and provide the ability for applications to scale to sizes unsurpassed by private PaaS environments. This is to be expected, as public IaaS clouds offer the same reach and scale. For companies whose applications have mass market ambitions, public clouds should be the first considered, for either IaaS or PaaS-based applications. And if a company is already using a public cloud but just getting started with PaaS, using the PaaS platform offered by an IaaS platform vendor may have advantages. For example, an existing IaaS relationship will be easier to extend to their PaaS offering, and there may be more consistency of APIs and capabilities between the two platforms, simplifying training and application portability.

Startups and other companies have learned that they can run their entire businesses in the public cloud. Without having to invest in a physical data center of their own, they can perform all their IT and other activities using public cloud applications. If they're software companies, the public cloud will be the best place to perform their development activities. Companies that are located in different physical locations can collaborate effectively using the public cloud — as open-source companies, with their widely distributed contributors, have long known.

Having said that, sometimes companies have reasons, such as regulations, where parts or all of their business may not use the public cloud. For them, private PaaS clouds, which we discuss next, will be more appropriate.

Private PaaS

As with IaaS clouds, a PaaS cloud can be installed in your company's physical data center. Originally, responsibility for constructing and managing an IaaS private cloud fell to the business itself. It was a task that was overly complicated, because the private cloud was often as much a research project as a product in evolution. Nowadays, cloud installations have been streamlined and third parties are available to perform cloud deployments and sometimes management as well. The term *virtual private cloud* (VPC) describes a private cloud based on a third-party cloud provider's infrastructure, with a private cloud implemented over it.

PaaS platforms are generally much less complicated than IaaS platforms in their configuration and management, tasks which are often handled by the IT, development, or operations teams. It makes sense that those organizations would be responsible for management of private PaaS clouds, as they're the primary consumers of PaaS services and best understand what is needed. IT will use the PaaS cloud to develop, maintain, and support internal applications. Development will use the PaaS cloud to support agile development cycles and deployment of applications. Operations will manage the technical infrastructure, deployment of applications to the public cloud or directly to customers. For companies who use DevOps (combining development and operations responsibilities), the PaaS cloud must model the company's business processes for development and deployment of applications. It is, therefore, essential that these technical organizations be responsible for private PaaS cloud management.

Note: The infrastructure described in the previous paragraph is almost certainly a hybrid cloud, as the private PaaS is used as a path for deploying applications to the public cloud.

Although many public clouds have compelling PaaS cloud resources, some companies have good reasons not to use any public PaaS cloud. For example, companies in regulated industries may be required to have their computing resources audited in person by regulators. Public cloud vendors generally can't state exactly which of their many servers and disk arrays are used by the regulated company. Even if they could, they very rarely allow outsiders to enter the data center, let alone probe active cloud hardware. The rise of data sovereignty regulations can force companies to store their data in physical data centers in specific countries. And some companies still do not trust the public cloud to protect their data adequately.

Open PaaS

An open PaaS cloud is a bit different than the cloud platforms discussed in the preceding sections. Public, private, and enterprise PaaS clouds tend to be general platforms that allow a variety of proprietary and open-source services, resources, and underlying infrastructure. In contrast, an open PaaS is intended to promote open-source solutions and environment that isn't tied to a single cloud implementation — in other words, it fosters multicloud strategies.

Open-source software, and Linux in particular, is fundamental to most cloud environments. But where some proprietary cloud platforms bias their offerings to proprietary software, open PaaS favors open-source software. This provides a number of benefits, low cost being a primary value. But open-source is an engine of innovative value, and companies that take advantage of open-source solutions can stay at the crest of new products and methodologies, while spending much less on software costs. Granted, open-source use and development is practiced in a different culture than proprietary software development, but most businesses today see the need to be aware of open-source developments, and partake of open-source solutions to stay with, or ahead, of their competition.

Reaping the Business Benefits of PaaS

The potential cost savings of IaaS are clear: You pay for only the compute resources you actually use. PaaS has the same pay-as-you-go model, but that's just the beginning of cost and business advantages for PaaS.

Because PaaS removes a software dependency on operating systems and focuses on business logic, not only is software development simpler, but PaaS applications are easier to port to different PaaS platforms. Simplicity and ease of porting directly reduce costs that equivalent IaaS applications would require. Ease of porting also allows business to respond more quickly to lower cost (or higher performance) platforms.

Public PaaS shifts responsibility, and costs, of managing a PaaS platform to public PaaS vendors. With no hardware to procure and manage, no long-term software licenses to pay, and no ongoing platform management to handle, costs are cut to the minimum, and development and operations can focus on business issues instead of infrastructure costs.

By adopting a standardized platform across an organization, hardware and software conflicts are greatly reduced, resulting in simplified service and support. This level of standardization and automation allows organizations to reduce or refocus its teams on tasks that move customer relationships ahead rather than just keeping the infrastructure working properly.

A STARTUP FINDS SUCCESS WITH PaaS

Imagine a small services company preparing to roll out a mobile application for airline tracking. To create the application, the development team must bring together large amounts of data from a variety of sources, including airlines, weather forecast modeling, the Federal Aviation Authority (FAA), and local airport alerts. Being part of an emerging company, the team doesn't have an abundance of capital to spend on infrastructure, yet they must dealing with a massive amount of data. They choose to leverage cloud-based services.

The team is very technical, so they decide to use an IaaS platform and work with the tools they're already familiar with. Using an IaaS platform, they have to bring their own operating system, development tools, and middleware. They quickly found that the process was taking too long and was too cumbersome.

To speed applications delivery, avoid infrastructure coding, and save money by not hiring a system administrator, the company decides to use a PaaS platform. To save even more money, the company decides to use a PaaS platform that can be used both internally and as a public cloud service. Now, armed with an abstracted and well-integrated environment, the team finds that the focus on business logic (instead of infrastructure) keeps all the developers focused and working together.

The company is able to hit the market more quickly with the solution that customers are looking for. The management team quickly finds that it has to support a variety of different platforms and partners' ecosystems. The standardization and flexibility of the PaaS environment enables a relatively small development team to meet the demand from partners and customers. The company is on its way to what looks like a bright future!

4

Managing in a Multicloud World

IN THIS PART . . .

Develop and manage cloud applications.

Manage workloads across cloud services.

Understand cloud data storage.

Chapter **11**

Planning for DevOps in the Cloud

We're entering a new era where how applications are built and managed is changing thanks to the adoption of the cloud. To accomplish this transition is requiring that monolithic applications be turned into modular services. To be competitive, business leaders understand that the ability to change applications services quickly is crucial to create new business innovation. The cloud is a driving force to make this transition possible combined with a unified approach to software development, deployment, and delivery.

This modern approach to application development demands changes to culture, process, and technology. Many organizations that are forward-looking are focused on a cloud-first strategy for applications development and deployment, including a focus on continuous integration and delivery of software. In this chapter, we explain the changing landscape of applications development and deployment that is emerging based on cloud computing and the impact on organizations.

Entering a New Era of DevOps

The transition from traditional applications development and deployment is based on a change in culture within the business. This cultural change requires that developers and operations management collaborate to create seamlessness between development and deployment — not an easy task. Traditionally, separate teams have to work together. This new era relies on a combination of tools and best practices to accelerate the pace of application creation and enhancement.

The DevOps culture provides organizations a variety of benefits that make it a good match for today's IT environments. The most obvious is greater quality, resulting from the use of Continuous Integration/Continuous Development (CI/CD) concepts that find and correct defects early. *Continuous integration* focuses on constantly integrating and validating changes to software code and underlying services to ensure errors are identified and fixed as soon as they are introduced. *Continuous delivery* automates the software delivery process (nonfunctional testing, functional testing, security, deployment, and so on), ensuring that with each change, the application is release ready. Later in this chapter, we get into the details of the importance of CI/CD in the DevOps process.

The use of automation as a mechanism for operating and managing infrastructure and development processes makes managing at scale more effective. Finally, applications can be developed, changed, and delivered much faster, enabling a faster response to competitive conditions and potentially lowering costs.

The importance of agile development

DevOps is one more recent manifestation of an approach to software development known as agile, the principles of which are related to a number of software development frameworks (examples include Scrum and Kanban). The foundation of DevOps from an agile perspective is that it supports seamless collaboration across a variety of functional teams. These teams have to include not only developers, but also operations professions, security leaders, and end users.

When agile principles are adopted, individual stakeholders and their interactions through collaboration are more important than adhering to strict methodologies and highly structured tools. The emphasis on speed and agility as a means to respond to rapid change brings the resulting software to the forefront, even if rigorously documenting every process step has to be put on the back burner.

Transforming security

Despite the continued adoption of DevOps processes, security is still often handled traditionally. In contrast to the philosophy of a DevOps approach, security is implemented sometime within, or even at the end, of a DevOps process as opposed to being embedded in the development process at the beginning. A solution to this issue is a discipline known as *DevSecOps.* In brief, DevSecOps is the process of integrating security into the software development process.

DevSecOps begins with a change in culture founded in ongoing learning (to raise security awareness with developers who may already be entrenched in DevOps processes), the identification of security-savvy people within the organization who can champion the change in the security approach, and the empowerment of those working on security to determine how best to embed robust security into the clouds they support. Tools can then be used to automate security testing, detect vulnerabilities early, and raise security as a gate to blocking forward progress, and even the deployment of a release, if problems are found.

Examining Changes for DevOps in the Cloud

While many existing applications can serve your business needs quite well, other applications need to be modernized and modularized in order to meet new business requirements. While some applications can't be modernized, other applications can be transformed through modern APIs and modularization of existing code into services.

The cloud environment also makes it possible to begin creating new cloud native applications that are designed for the unique characteristics of the highly distributed world of the cloud. This new generation of DevOps addresses the need to have application services that are designed specifically for a hybrid and cloud native environment. Modern cloud native application development addresses the issue of flexibility so that businesses can add new services and change applications to keep up with changing customer demands. Firstly, modern application development decentralizes many tasks in the development and deployment chain. Software services can be developed across the globe and may involve multiple teams each working on a portion of an application. Secondly, there is a need to break down silos across departments within the business. While this decentralized model may seem to be contradictory, the software development revolution taking place today provides developers with the freedom and agility to innovate with a focus on business goals, rather than organizational or functional silos even though teams may be geographically dispersed.

Over the past decade, organizations have moved to a cloud-based IT infrastructure to reduce cost, lower administration overhead, and gain flexibility. The early transition to the cloud was mostly focused on costs, however. Today, companies now look to the cloud for a strategic advantage. The cloud gives teams rapid access to a scalable infrastructure that can support a new model of development. The economic benefits of the cloud in the forms of lower costs, reduced capital investment, and greater flexibility are undeniable. Yet the growing adoption of the cloud among organizations also changes both the development and deployment landscapes. For example, when hybrid clouds and/or multiple public clouds are involved or a single monolithic architecture is decomposed into cloud-based microservices, creating and managing applications and data can turn into very complicated tasks.

Developers and IT managers will need new tools and capabilities to effectively navigate this terrain. They'll need to review and analyze their current data center applications and policies, the relationship among IT, business units, and executive management, and how these factors affect IT decisions. And, more importantly, IT leaders need to reevaluate their current development and deployment practices. They must assess how all the business and IT stakeholders work together and the processes, tools, and technology that can help modernize their business.

Forward-looking IT leaders ask questions about how they can create agile and advanced approaches to customer engagement to implement new innovative strategies. They look at new development approaches, and new deployment and delivery models, from cross-functional agile teams using cloud-based tools to highly decomposed and distributed applications. In short, insightful developers are moving away from developing monolithic code and applications to creating standards-based business services incorporating agile code and a microservices-based architecture. These services can be linked together to create business value.

An agile microservices based approach to DevOps is becoming the new normal. This transition won't happen overnight. Some organizations will be able to move quickly, while others, because of technical and organizational constraints, may require more time.

Discovering the Value of Demand-Driven Applications

As more and more customers rely on next generation mobile and web applications to execute and manage transactions (purchases, correspondences, shopping, and so on), businesses need to make the customer experience as efficient and satisfying as possible. Customer-facing systems must be easy to use and provide access to all functions and capabilities relevant at any point in time. They must be transparent and integrate with other core services, such as billing, sales, and so on. All of the services, no matter where they physically reside, need to work together seamlessly. However, there must be a high degree of flexibility so necessary changes can be executed quickly as customer expectations change.

The new generation of agile application development and deployment means software services can be developed and deployed virtually anywhere. Microservices enable applications to be developed as services linked together through lightweight interfaces. Therefore, small independent teams can develop and deploy each service. This flexibility provides greater benefits in terms of performance, cost, and scalability. Being able to build modular services, packaging them together, and managing them consistently and predictably, demands a new approach to software development and deployment.

Examining the Role of CI/CD in Agile Development

When we discuss the concept of agile development and deployment in the cloud, it is critical to put this process in perspective with CI/CD.

While continuous integration and continuous deployment (CI/CD) are linked together as though they are a single practice, it is important to understand both of these processes separately. The following sections explain the two processes, how they relate to each other, and their value in dynamic application development, delivery, and deployment.

Continuous integration

Continuous integration is a software development practice in which developers frequently commit source code changes to a central repository, and the changes are continuously built and validated. This practice differs from the traditional development process where changes to the code may not be integrated until right before a planned release or at the end of the development cycle.

Continuous integration saves time and increases quality because errors are immediately uncovered, closer to the point they were introduced, allowing them to be corrected earlier and more easily.

Continuous testing

To meet the goal of continuous everything, a new approach to testing is needed. Testing should no longer be thought of as a stop along the delivery pipeline. Instead, testing must be an automated part of the continuous delivery pipeline. By continually testing, you can spot and remedy potential problems at the earliest possible point.

Continuous delivery

Continuous delivery extends continuous integration principles and practices further downstream in the software delivery process. With each change, continuously testing and deploying code ensures that software is in a release-ready state.

Continuous delivery enables changes to be moved into preproduction or production environments, and eventually into the hands of users, in a rapid, repeatable, and reliable way.

Continuous deployment

Continuous deployment is a process where software code changes are automatically deployed into preproduction or production staging. Continuous deployment requires that there is automation along each step of the delivery pipeline.

Exploring the Role of Opinionated Continuous Delivery

Starting from scratch with CI/CD is a difficult proposition. As the adoption of continuous delivery practices increases at a rapid pace, a growing demand for simple solutions allows developers and development teams to get started quickly. These fast, quick-start solutions provide an opinion on how continuous delivery should be achieved.

An opinionated solution serves as a starting point for teams, without the need for developers to get slowed down by complexity of process design and custom pipelines. An opinionated solution is also attractive to small teams and organizations with limited staff or expertise. These smaller, more lean teams need to focus on delivering value, not building and maintaining custom pipelines.

Continuous delivery is ideally built on a foundation of microservices, containers, container orchestration, and other elements that make it possible to modularize applications for flexible deployment across multiple environments, including the cloud. It's important to note that while cloud native applications are where the industry is going, existing assets (applications, tools, and systems) will continue to be part of the mix with which new applications must interact.

One of the most challenging tasks in implementing continuous delivery is determining the ideal workflow, including integrations, supply chain management strategy, environments, gates, and so on. This task requires a deep knowledge, multiple iterations, and manual scripting.

What if developers had a tool that could detect a project's type and then build a pipeline automatically? What if a developer did not have to directly interact with Kubernetes (see Chapter 6) to deploy an application to a particular environment, but rather have a tool automate that step for them? These are some examples of how the right Kubernetes platform can in effect make orchestration decisions for developers, freeing them to focus on creating business value through IT.

Understanding the Challenges to CI/CD Adoption

Despite the obvious advantages and benefits, some obstacles to adopting continuous delivery exist. Some of these obstacles involve human factors, while others are more technical and involve both the legacy of an organization's technology base and the tools they use to build and deploy applications.

Change always involves risk or at least a perception of risk. IT likely has processes and techniques in place to build applications, many of which, while manual, represent a known and comfortable approach. The benefits are obvious, but the path to adoption is not comfortable. This discomfort may also be reflected in a skills gap, and the time and effort involved in bridging that gap can often be seen as a distraction from what developers know are their deliverables. Additionally, those involved in the software development and delivery process, who are invested in manual steps and gates, often see risk in trusting these steps to automation. Even with the promise of modern approaches and practices, such as microservices and CD, the technology, tools, and more importantly, culture can stand in the way.

Continuous Delivery and the Importance of a DevOps Culture

While continuous integration, delivery, and deployment are recognized as required components of today's face-paced, highly competitive, software-driven market, they require organization-wide changes to how software development and delivery is approached. Organizations have discovered through trial and error that a DevOps culture does not just happen. The process of creating the level of teamwork and collaboration requires these teams spend the time to build a culture that breaks down technical and organizational silos. Successful organizations have discovered a set of best practices for DevOps, which includes a focus on outcome, the ability to continuously innovate, delivery value, and learning from customer input.

DevOps, which is a combination of the terms "development" and "operations," is an approach to software development and delivery that emphasizes a culture of collaboration to deliver software rapidly, reliably, and repeatedly. DevOps is an extension of the agile movement, and although it is focused on culture, a major component of DevOps is automation. Achieving the transformation to a DevOps culture requires collaboration and orchestration between all stakeholders, including development, deployment, operations, and business teams.

Security must be an integral part of the DevOps process. Therefore, it is not surprising to see the emergence of DevSecOps. This approach brings the IT security team into the DevOps process. Rather than having an application security team review an application after it has been developed, a DevSecOps methodology integrates the security into every step of the process.

The Challenge of CI/CD in the Cloud Era

The challenge of creating collaboration between application development and deployment has been an issue for decades, but the rapid growth of the cloud as a foundation for modern software development has upped the sense of urgency. Innovative IT leaders understand the only path to success is through the use of cloud native applications supported by containers and microservices. The mandate for cloud native applications, containers, and microservices can be successfully implemented only with CI/CD based on a DevOps culture.

CI/CD allows developers to quickly identify defects as they're introduced so they can be corrected as soon as possible. When application defects are identified close to when they are introduced, it is much faster and cheaper to correct versus having to go back and reexamine the entire application. CD is in effect an extension of CI that focuses on the process of delivering changes after they are "committed" as part of the CI process. In other words, software code that passes automated tests can be considered ready for production. Continuous delivery is often used interchangeably with continuous deployment, in which all changes are automatically released to production. For CI/CD to be effective requires that the two major steps in application development — development and deployment — cannot be separated as they were when employing traditional development models. This is the foundational concept behind the DevOps movement.

Clouds, Containers, and Microservices

The change in how the industry approaches software development can be attributed to the advent of cloud computing and the availability of features and capabilities offered by cloud providers and tool vendors. In many cases, developers create applications that functionally span an organization's data center, one or more public clouds, and a variety of platforms and deployment models. With the advent of containerization, for example, applications can be deployed virtually anywhere.

The cloud has therefore given rise to a variety of architectures and technologies developers need to use and tools that support their use. Microservices, as an example, can facilitate the development of large, complex applications by breaking them down into a set of loosely coupled services. Each service can be developed by a relatively small team of developers — or even a single developer — allowing for parallel development that can make the process more efficient and development time shorter in addition to simplifying testing. Microservices in a very real sense serves as an enabler of CI/CD.

The decentralized, modular architecture that characterizes many cloud-based implementations has also encouraged the adoption of containers. Containers provide a means of packaging applications such that they are abstracted from their run-time environments. Developers can now spend their energies on creating the application logic and dependencies. Operations can focus only on how and where the logic is deployed and how it is managed without worrying about version numbers and application-specific configuration issues. Containers build on the virtualization concept by virtualizing at the operating system level, allowing for one or many containers to run directly on top of the operating system kernel.

Modern application development requires new thinking, new platforms, and tools. Without a CI/CD approach supported by important standards such as Kubernetes, teams will be bogged down in complexity. Therefore, most organizations consider Kubernetes, a standard container orchestration platform, as a good way to meet these challenges. In simple terms, Kubernetes is an open-source container orchestration system for automation of the tasks.

Defining Cloud Native Applications

As the cloud matures and becomes more sophisticated, it, too, evolves to support the way cloud applications are defined. This brings us to the value of cloud native applications. In brief, *cloud native applications* are software offerings designed with microservices, containers, and dynamic orchestration as well as continuous delivery of software. Every part of the cloud native application is housed within its own container and dynamically orchestrated with other containers to optimize the way resources are utilized.

Taking a step back, the concept of cloud native changes the way we think about application creation and management. The Cloud Native Computing Foundation, an organization founded in 2015 under the auspices of the Linux Foundation, "builds sustainable ecosystems and fosters a community around a constellation of high-quality projects that orchestrate containers as part of a microservices architecture." The Cloud Native Computing Foundation defines cloud native as follows:

Application services are containerized so that resources can be managed in a more efficient manner.

Services are dynamically managed in a consistent and standardized way in order to be able to discover, deploy, and scale up and down containerized applications.

A microservices approach helps organizations decompose the application into modular, independent services that interact through well-defined service contracts.

Scalable cloud computing requires the infrastructure to be in place to support the needs of continuous integration and continuous delivery. To be successful, developers need some fundamental capabilities to achieve resilience by being able to discover reusable services.

Achieving Resilience

It's critical for cloud applications to adhere to a service level guarantee regardless of where their services run. Historically, cloud services relied on virtual machines tied to a specific server environment. But as more cloud services become customer facing, resiliency is imperative. However, with virtual machines (VMs) you cannot assume the VMs or the network services you deploy will be permanent. Too often these VMs will disappear because of a systems error or because an administrator deletes that VM. The consequences can be significant because without any warning, your applications may not gracefully shut down. While it may be possible to restart the VM, the problem may not be resolved. This means you have to architect for failure and assume that any services you interact with could disappear at any given time.

Discovering Reusable Services

Because cloud native applications are designed to take advantage of containers and microservices, it is imperative to be able to locate services that have been vetted so that they can be used in other applications. Therefore, any services your applications interact with need to be found, usually from a run-time registry.

Moving from VMs to Cloud Native

Cloud computing has evolved significantly over the past decade, making it easier for developers to quickly gain access to compute and storage capabilities and create a platform for applications creation and deployment. Traditionally, developers have relied on virtual machines as a technique to create cloud services. In essence, virtual machine software makes a single system act as though it were a discrete collection of independent services. However, virtual machines sit on a layer of software, including the operating system, middleware, and tools, which makes the VM more complex and slows down the process of continuous integration and rapid applications development.

The cloud native application fully exploits the benefits of cloud technology. It is important to recognize that a cloud native application is not defined by where it is running, but rather how it is built. Because a cloud native environment is based on containerization, it is not physically tied to a specific hardware or operating system. Therefore, cloud native applications are designed to work on a variety of cloud environments.

Open-Source Cloud Native Applications

If you're going to adapt an agile continuous integration and continuous delivery model for your cloud applications, you need to explore innovative tools and techniques that apply to the full life cycle of applications creation and deployment. Most of the most important innovations in native cloud tools are based on open-source technologies from a vibrant community of contributors. For example, the Cloud Native Computing Foundation focuses on projects designed to create and deploy cloud-native applications and services. The foundation's work has resulted in a number of projects (completed or underway), including Helm (for package management), Harbor (a registry), and, of course, Kubernetes (for container orchestration).

One only has to look at continually evolving companies, such as Facebook, Netflix, and Uber, to name a few, that must constantly change their platforms to adapt to changing user expectations. All these companies take advantage of continuous delivery, immutable containers, and microservices to help achieve the elastic scaling capabilities needed to cater for an unpredictable competitive landscape. The sense of urgency is palpable: Adapt quickly or die.

Indeed, Netflix's transition to cloud native when it spun off a part of its business from the physical DVD rentals to a profitable streaming service is a case in point. After the company suffered from a massive database corruption episode, the service was out of commission for three days. As a result, the company determined it needed a new architecture that could utilize the horizontal scaling capabilities of a public cloud and a microservices approach to software development.

Differentiating Cloud Native Applications

Traditionally, many organizations considered the cloud because of lower costs — a valid reason, but a limited one. Prior to being able to build cloud native applications, cost savings was often the main driver. Cloud native applications enable businesses to shift from focusing exclusively on cost savings to being able to quickly build applications that bring a competitive advantage. In a highly fluid business environment, this is critical for success.

Cloud native applications are built to run on hardware that is modular and automated, allowing them to become both resilient and predictable. Performance and scalability become important benefits, resulting from the ability to flexibly deploy workloads wherever they need to be. Traditional applications simply do not offer those benefits.

The technologies used to create and deploy cloud-enabled applications (covered in more detail in the next section of this chapter) provide an abstraction layer away from the underlying software and hardware infrastructures, including the operating system. Developers can focus exclusively on building their applications without the need to deal with dependencies of the underlying infrastructure. By creating applications that do not rely on the underlying infrastructure, development and deployment teams can deploy applications on the most pragmatic platform.

Well-designed cloud native applications automatically provision and configure tasks and can dynamically allocate resources based on application requirements. This automation is one way that scalability can be achieved and how applications can balance themselves to prevent failures.

While DevOps methodologies are not unique to cloud native application development, DevOps is a necessary component of cloud native applications. The collaboration associated with a DevOps approach involves the integration of processes, tools, and of course, developers. DevOps creates an environment in which software can be written, tested, and released quickly and as often as needed with minimum disruption. DevOps can be the enabler of an organization's CI/CD goals because the software modules created for a cloud native application can be released continuously and in an automated fashion.

The Foundation of Microservices

Creating true native cloud applications requires different thinking, collaboration, and manageability approaches. Cloud-enabled applications are designed to be modular, distributed, deployed, and managed in an automated way. These characteristics require technologies that go beyond what was typical for the development of traditional software.

The technologies start with an architectural style that incorporates the modularity concept. Cloud native applications are built as a collection of multiple, independent microservices. Each of these microservices is designed to support one discrete, bounded piece of application functionality. Although these microservices are independent, they can be linked together in a coordinated fashion to provide all the functionality the application is intended to deliver.

Microservices provide a number of significant benefits:

>> Application development is simplified because each microservice is built to serve a specific and limited purpose. Small development teams can focus on writing code for narrowly defined and more easily understood functions.

>> Code changes will be smaller and less complex than with a complex integrated application, making it easier and faster to make changes, whether to fix a problem or to upgrade a service with new requirements.

>> Scalability, both up and down, makes it simpler to deploy an additional instance of a service or change that service as needs evolve.

Microservices are fully tested and validated. When new applications leverage existing microservices, developers can assume the integrity of the new application without the need for continual testing.

The Imperative to Manage Microservices

It's easy to see how microservices can help organizations fully exploit the advantages of the cloud. Microservices are designed to be packaged within containers that are then managed through orchestration services. These orchestration services are needed to manage both process and logic as well as data services. In effect, it is a game of numbers – there are often many microservices, and many instances of microservices that are distributed over many systems. Keeping track and consistently documenting all of these microservices is a challenge.

The Value of the Container Model

Cloud-enabled software is generally built using containers, which are software elements packaged with everything needed to execute it: an application's code, the run-time environment, required system tools, and libraries and settings. Each container runs in a virtualized environment, but completely isolated from the underlying infrastructure.

A container's abstraction makes it possible to port the service to virtually any system. Containers can be spun up or down based on the user load present at any given time. Clearly, containers are a critical foundational element for building and running cloud-enabled applications.

The Role of APIs

Of course, in a highly distributed environment composed of microservices, the ability to communicate between services is critical if the benefits of the cloud are to be fully realized. Application programming interfaces (APIs) serve this purpose and have special applicability to the cloud. In fact, they are the mode of communication among microservices and containers using interprocess communication mechanisms.

APIs have been used extensively in the past for communicating with and connecting various IT assets. They are an important connectivity mechanism for the way services are combined to create an application. In addition, at the IaaS level, APIs are used to provide control and distribution mechanisms for resources such as provisioning, for example. At the application level, SaaS APIs furnish the ability to connect applications with the underlying infrastructure and, when applicable, cloud resources.

APIs become even more critical when one or more cloud providers are involved. In these multicloud cases, your API strategy needs to consider the APIs provided by the cloud providers themselves to allow connectivity and communication with their clouds. Many cloud providers are offering more generic (HTTP) integration capabilities to make it easy for their customers to integrate and access resources.

With microservices typically deployed in the form of containers, the interprocess communication mechanisms used with microservices are different from traditional applications. Because the microservices are more granular, so, too, are the APIs. This means client data requests may span a number of microservices, requiring the request to follow a one-to-many form of interaction.

A number of API platforms, including API management platforms, are available today that address a variety of needs in the cloud. Choosing the right API platform involves a careful assessment of the application environment.

This new generation of applications require a more agile approach to development and deployment. Why is change necessary? Cloud computing requires the infrastructure to be in place to support the needs of continuous integration and continuous delivery. To be successful, developers need some fundamental capabilities, including achieving resilience, being able to discover reusable services, and providing the organization with the ability to scale on demand.

The typical enterprise utilizes many applications. Some of these may be large, monolithic legacy applications that are built in-house and customized. There may be smaller homegrown applications as well. You may also use SaaS applications purchased from a service provider. There's also a good chance that, if you've embraced the cloud as an organization, you'll make the decision to actually build some new applications that will run in it.

There are numerous scenarios in which you might want to write an application for the hybrid cloud. Here are a few:

>> You want to write an application for the cloud that will work with the customized applications you already have in place.

>> You want to write applications that can work both on-premises and in the public cloud.

>> You may want to write applications for the cloud that can be leveraged across multiple clouds.

If you look at any one enterprise, there's a good chance you'll find a mix of development environments and processes. Development may be done in silos for siloed applications. Developers may be restricted by the lack of resources. Perhaps the tools they're using were developed to handle the most complex problems. As companies transition to developing in the cloud, it's important for them to begin understanding how to abstract away some of the complexity. Of course, doing so will take time.

Big benefits of developing and deploying applications to the cloud are its elasticity and scalability. The infrastructure you need for development and deployment can be automatically scaled up or down, based on the requirements of the application. This field is evolving, however, and it pays to do the math. Many vendors will charge based on the utilization of underlying resources, which might include usage per hour, processing, bandwidth, and storage.

We've been talking about developers in both medium- and large-sized corporations that are building applications to run complex businesses. There's a whole different class of developers — the Internet-scale developer — who may be interested in different sets of problems than enterprise developers. These Internet developers address problems that, from the get-go, are ready for scale and building for performance and failures of the Internet. One example of an Internet-scale developer is a social media analytics services company that develops analytics that cull through massive amounts of social media data.

Chapter **12**

Managing Multicloud Workloads

Managing the deployment and operation of applications and other workloads is critical for meeting customer expectations for availability and performance of the software tools they depend on every day. Managing applications and storage is hard enough in this relatively small context, but the challenge of predictably managing workloads becomes even more challenging in a distributed cloud environment — you must consider new challenges and new technologies. Furthermore, in addition to the public, private cloud, and hybrid cloud (a combination of the public and private cloud), the new computing horizon is multicloud where you can deploy and operate workloads in all cloud contexts.

In cloud computing environments, you can to deploy workloads across many global regions, using many different cloud providers. As you can imagine, keeping track of all those workload deployments, monitoring and managing workload health, and staying aware of whether cloud providers are meeting your SLAs and cost targets is a difficult task. Moreover, companies want to use the cloud's flexibility and ease of use for running applications and not be burdened with managing the details. Thankfully, cloud management solutions can handle the low-level platform details, allowing companies to focus on their strategic needs.

In this chapter, we discuss the nature of cloud applications and workloads, and the challenges and approaches for managing workloads in multicloud environments.

What Is a Workload?

Workloads are software programs that run on-premises, in a private cloud, on a mainframe, or in a public cloud. Workloads can be applications that people use directly, services used by applications to solve particular needs (such as handling credit card payments), or even operating systems or middleware — the software tools that provide platforms for all the other workloads.

As workloads comprise the full set of software used by people or other software, it's no surprise that matching workloads to computing resources can be a very complicated task. Moreover, workloads change over their lifetimes by adding features, serving increasing numbers of users, and interacting with other workloads. At the same time, computing resources are evolving as well, offering new capabilities in new contexts at different price levels.

All workloads aren't the same

There is a huge variety of workloads. For example, you may want to move your inventory database to the cloud, use the cloud for machine learning applications, or deploy a customer-facing mobile application in the cloud. As you can imagine, these different workloads each have their own considerations. For example, a data science workload that relies heavily on machine learning may perform best in an environment that has access to Graphic Processing Units (GPUs). In addition, you may even want a cloud that offers specific proprietary data science tools. Likewise, for transactional workloads, your priority may be speed, and you'll want an environment that offers the lowest latency. On the other hand, for some projects your focus may be on reducing costs, and in those instances, you may just want the cheapest option, even if that means it could take several days to access data.

Here are some of the types of workloads that are being moved to a multicloud environment:

>> **SaaS workloads:** Software as a Service (SaaS) workloads are the applications that run on the cloud. Some of the most widely used SaaS applications include Workday, Slack, Google's G-suite, and Office 365. These SaaS applications are able to handle many simultaneous users with a multitenant architecture. (See Chapter 9 for more details on SaaS and multi-tenancy.) Typically, SaaS applications rely on back-end server services to satisfy user requests. For example, when a user enters a Google search, it is Google's back end that searches millions of web pages to return the pages the user was looking for. Because users expect quick responses, SaaS applications must be optimized to perform user tasks and repaint the screen to show results quickly. With many users, popular SaaS applications depend on the elastic capabilities provided by the cloud environment to scale up and out as needed to meet high demand.

» **Batch workloads:** These workloads are designed to operate without human interaction and typically without a user interface. Typical batch workloads perform repetitive tasks such as backups and process large volumes of data. As these tasks run asynchronously, they may not be time-sensitive. However, there are many exceptions. For example, backups must run every day and must complete before the next backup starts. Otherwise, the regular daily schedule will be thrown off. Automating batch workloads is relatively easy. Batch workloads are usually run on a regular schedule and can take advantage of the economies of scale of public cloud services. Again, as in any cloud environment, the decision of where and when to execute batch workloads is determined by business rules, governance, and security regulations.

» **Transactional workloads:** Transactional workloads are business processes such as billing and order processing. With the increasing use of electronic commerce that reaches across partners and suppliers, transactional workloads must be managed across various partners' computing environments. These workloads are both compute- and storage-intensive. Traditionally, transactional workloads were deployed on-premises where the computing and storage was secure. In the new world of the cloud, these workloads may now be placed into private clouds to gain scalability. Also, public cloud security has become as trustworthy as on-premises security, so cost-benefit analysis may recommend that complex transactional workloads are deployed to a public cloud.

» **Analytic and big data workloads:** Organizations use big data analytic services in a cloud environment to make sense of the vast amounts of data across complex multicloud environments. This requirement isn't simply a technical one; in the world of big data, one can find business insights by holistically analyzing data embedded in many data sources across public websites, private clouds, corporate data warehouses, and so on. For example, organizations examine their own businesses operational data, and that of their partners, to benchmark the success of their partnerships and to make adjustments to increase success. These types of analytic workloads tend to require much more real-time computing capability and lots of storage.

» **High performance workloads:** These workloads have specialized processes with scientific or technical requirements, are complex, and typically require significant compute capabilities. Thus, they're well suited for specialized public clouds optimized for performance.

» **Back-end workloads:** Applications have back-ends that perform the heavy data analysis, business transactions, and other processing that users have requested via the application's front end. Back-end workloads employ architectures and services appropriate to the application's functionality, and these can be very diverse. Back ends can be as simple as a single workload that drives storage and recovery of data, or as complicated as many workloads that cooperate to provide complex solutions.

>> **Database workloads:** These workloads are the most common type, as every application needs to store and retrieve data. A database workload must be tuned and managed to support the service that's using that data. Database workloads tend to use a lot of I/O (Input/Output) to get data into or out of the database. In some situations, data workloads are small and self-contained; however, in other situations, the data workloads are huge, and their operation requires a sophisticated approach. For example, high-performance database workloads may be implemented across many scaled-out database nodes.

Table 12-1 provides a summary of the different types of workloads and why you might consider using those workloads in the cloud.

TABLE 12-1   ## Workloads in the Cloud

Workload Type	Focus	Why Cloud?
SaaS workload	Manage user interactions, communicate with back-end services	Easy access for customers to start using and to scale up
Batch workload	Repetitive processing of large volumes of data in the background	Access to large amount of storage and automation tools
Transactional workload	Focuses on large volume of current transactions	Access to scalable storage and leverage cloud analytics tools
Analytic workload	Affects large amounts of data for decision making	Access to specialized hardware like GPUs, and scalable compute and storage
High-performance workload	Has scientific or technical focus	Can quickly build large computing environments without building on-premises
Back-end workloads	Serve needs of the SaaS front end	Compute intensive workloads that can use less expensive resources at lower demand times
Database workload	Is highly tuned to application needs	Easy access to a variety of database types to support a variety of data, including structured and unstructured data

Workloads not suited for the cloud

REMEMBER

Just as some workloads are appropriate to run the cloud, some are not. Although in general these workloads might be poorly suited for the cloud, it is important to keep in mind that cloud vendors are offering more and more specialized cloud environments to meet the requirements of different types of workloads. A few examples of workloads that you don't want to move to the cloud include

>> **Applications that have not been architected for the cloud:** Older, often large and monolithic applications that were designed for physical servers will not be able to take advantage of cloud capabilities, such as scaling out to provide better performance. These applications should be rearchitected to take advantage of cloud innovations before being moved to the cloud.

>> **Workloads that need very high-performance storage:** Because data needs to be accessed very quickly, these workloads may not be suited for the cloud, where you're dependent on the Internet for network speed.

>> **Application workloads that require very low latency:** Often, legacy workloads weren't architected to run in a distributed computing environment. They may have stringent performance requirements, and it may not make sense to move them to the cloud.

>> **Applications in regulated domains where storage must be secure and auditable:** Because public cloud storage is almost always stored in data centers that do not allow visitors, auditable data must be stored in an on-premises or third-party data center so that auditors can visit the storage to verify that security measures are in place.

Resource abstraction and workloads

Private and public clouds offer a virtual computing environment for running workloads. Although the cloud is internally composed of physical computers and networks, what is exposed to consumers of cloud resources are abstracted resources that represent the physical resources. For example, the cloud places a workload on an abstracted server called a virtual machine (VM). Behind the scenes, the workload is actually placed onto a physical server, but the cloud selects which physical server is used (based on the VM type selected by the consumer) and provides the user with a means to connect to their server. This notion of abstraction is critical for providing workloads with the resources they need to run in the cloud. The only way to create a distributed computing environment consisting of multiple services in multiple locations is to use well-architected, abstracted resources.

Note that some clouds provide bare metal servers as well as virtual machines. This allows workloads to be placed on traditional physical servers by management and deployment frameworks using the same tools, application programming interfaces (APIs), and procedures as used for virtual machines.

Workload Management

TIP

Workloads need to be managed throughout their life cycles. Management starts as applications and services are designed and built, continues as they are deployed to a physical data center or cloud, and includes monitoring and controlling workloads when they run.

Here are a few things to consider as you think about managing workloads in a physical or cloud context:

» Understand your workloads' needs. If your application is home-grown, talk with the architect of the application. Manageability of a workload must be designed into the software, and verified to be effective while the workload is developed. Application test suites should be able to provide performance and resource usage information. You need to pay attention to all of the resources your workload will require: CPU, storage, network, and so on. If you purchased the application from a third party, it should be able to provide the information you need.

» Understand the configuration of your workloads. Most applications are composed on multiple, cooperating workloads. These sets of workloads must be deployed together. There may be manifest or other configuration files or settings you need to provide so the application's family of workloads will be able to find each other and work properly.

» Determine the capacity you need in your cloud computing environment. When selecting resources for your application's workloads, remember that the environment will have to handle not just normal usage, but also peaks during high usage times. Either verify that the cloud will automatically scale when more resources are needed, or, if not, overprovision the resources so they are always ready for usage peaks.

» Define how workloads will be deployed. Before cloud technology was prevalent, software was usually released on CD or other media, and each release was designated with a release number. Often, updating software would be a laborious and expensive processes. Increasingly in the cloud, software is continually updated. Applications might be updated several times a week in response to user feedback, security issues, or other issues. These changes in how software is released are often due to software development methodologies like DevOps (a merging of development and operations; see Chapter 11). Regardless of the development and deployment path that software takes, it is the result of careful decisions and business processes.

THE LOAD BALANCER

In distributed computing environments, such as the cloud, a load balancer is often deployed to help ensure that no single machine is overwhelmed. Load balancing is the process where IP traffic is distributed across multiple servers. The figure illustrates a simple example of load balancing. Here, the load balancer sits in front of three servers and distributes the load across them. All three servers utilize the same database. The load balancer helps to optimize resource allocation across the servers.

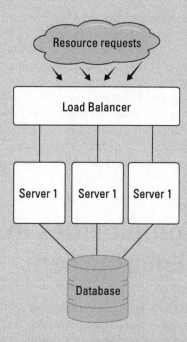

How does the load balancer do this? First, it needs to know where the data is coming from. Second, it needs to know which servers it's supposed to distribute the load across. Then it uses an algorithm to determine which machine to give the load to. For example, a popular algorithm is the round-robin algorithm, where the first database request goes to the first server, the second request goes to the second server, and so on. After serving the third server, the cycle starts over again with the first server. Of course, there are algorithms that can be used to balance workloads across servers. A good alternative is for the load balancer to monitor the work queue of each server and direct new requests to the server with the least backlog of requests to service.

» Use automation whenever possible. In the cloud, everything is scaled beyond what it was in an on-premises data center. There are more workloads, more places the workloads can be deployed, quicker pace for deployments, and so on. Cloud management is simplified by providing automated processing of all these issues. Workloads can be automatically ushered through development, and deployment processes and selection of where to deploy a workload can be automated by letting the workload define its computing needs. Only by automating your standard processes will you be able to stay ahead of the demands of running many workloads in the cloud.

» Ensure your workloads can be monitored. Once your applications and services have been deployed and are in use by your customers, you need to ensure that those workloads are working properly. Workloads can have all kinds of failures including performance problems, incorrect results, data loss, or outright failure to run. Organizations who run software need to monitor the health of their applications and services, so they can, ideally, fix problems before customers encounter them. However, if customers encounter problems, you can be sure that they will contact the support organization. Support should constantly be watching the state of deployed software so they can help customers when they run into problems.

Workload Complexities in the Multicloud Environment

The world is a lot more complicated with multicloud environments than it was with a single on-premises computing environment. With the advent of the multicloud world, many more applications and services will be deployed across geographies. Some workloads are permanent and need to run constantly, such as an online commerce site or a control system that manages a critical environmental process. Other workloads come and go as needs require. Business services and various application models are added into the mix as well.

REMEMBER

In a multicloud environment, your workloads may be running on different clouds, running different kinds of infrastructures using different operating systems. You're bringing together workloads from different environments that, generally, should behave as though they're a unified system.

Operationalized workloads

How important is workload management in the cloud? It's critical to ensure that you have a well performing cloud environment. This is true whether you are a service provider offering a public or private cloud to customers, or if you're managing a hybrid cloud to benefit internal customers and external customers and partners.

It is easy to underestimate the challenges of managing a multicloud environment that performs at a sufficient level of quality while meeting security and governance requirements. These are not static requirements; from an operational perspective, organizations need to be able to dynamically change workload management policies based on changing business requirements.

Suppose that a workload is being used within a geography that has data sovereignty rules for where data must be stored and, sometimes, processed. If the data has to be stored within the country where the data is used, that workload has to be managed differently than the same workload running in a country without this type of governance requirement. With fewer restrictions, IT operations are free to move workloads to any locations that have the bandwidth or capacity to meet the quality of service required by the business. In fact, the ability to change and move workloads based on business requirements is at the heart of operational issues in the cloud.

APIs: Keys to cloud resources

Application programming interfaces (APIs) enable a software product or service to work with another product or service. More specifically, an API is a formal entry point into an application or service that can be used by another application or service to get some work done. For example, if you're a software developer who has created a SaaS application that sells pictures, you can use a credit card processing service to handle customer payments by calling its API. The credit card processing service will document how you can use its API, probably by specifying the credit card information, the amount of the payment, and the account that should receive the payment. The developer doesn't need to know how the service does its work, just the information the service needs to be able to complete the payment.

There are two dominant forms of APIs:

>> **Programmatic APIs** are typically used between applications and software services that are run together in the same server. They are written in the programming language used by the application and service and are analogous to function calls within a program.

>> **RESTful APIs** are used when applications and the services they use are running on different servers. RESTful APIs are written in XML and use the web HTTP protocol for communicating, which allows services to be accessed in any context that supports web communications.

TECHNICAL STUFF

RESTful APIs are particularly important because of their ability to be used in many contexts that programmatic APIs cannot work (such as between servers), and because they use a "stateless" protocol that encourages simple and consistent programming patterns. *Stateless* means that each API call is independent of every other call. A service is not required to remember previous API calls and can treat each API call as a single request which can be processed and then "forgotten." Stateless operation simplifies processing and eliminates problems that can arise when multiple calls would otherwise be needed to process one operation (transaction).

REMEMBER

An API defines a standard interface that workloads use to document the services they provide to other workloads. The interface typically only specifies what work must be done, so the API effectively hides how the work is done. For example, callers of a service shouldn't know the details of how the service implements internal security (if they did, the service might be less secure).

All cloud providers offer APIs for their customers to use in IaaS and PaaS environments. Everything is great as long as you manage your workload within the environment where you created it or where you will deploy it. However, many organizations are beginning to find that APIs are not always consistent across different computing environments. For example, the API for using storage resources in one cloud environment may be different than the storage resources API in a different cloud environment. Applications can handle this situation by including software that can communicate with both APIs, but the application will have to be aware of which cloud environment it is running in so it uses the right API. This inconsistency of APIs limits the ability to move workloads between different cloud environments.

To better understand the complexities of the problem, consider what happens when you create workloads in the Amazon Web Services (AWS) IaaS platform. Here are three common scenarios you might encounter:

>> **AWS lets you create a set of connections to the network as a security group by assigning a permanent IP address.** If you try to connect this public service with a private cloud service, you'll find incompatibilities at the networking level.

>> **You create a workload for storage on AWS and a second workload for storage in another public cloud for redundancy.** You have a third storage workload running in the private cloud. When changes to your application occur, you don't have a standard way to manage these three different storage services. This situation increases the chance that errors are introduced to your application on one or more of the cloud platforms.

THE NEED FOR STANDARDIZED ACCESS TO APIs

As you see from the previous discussion, no single standard API exists that can be used to support access to services offered by different cloud providers. What is needed is a standard access layer that creates compatibility among cloud workloads. For example, in service oriented architectures, a standard XML model allows for interoperability among business services. There's no equivalent model for multicloud environments.

Of course, you can always find ways to work around complicated problems. For example, in the cellphone market, vendors end up implementing both the U.S. and the European wireless connectivity standard into each phone set. Likewise, in multicloud workload management, companies offer capabilities to create customizable templates that allow developers to make allowances for the differences in APIs and thus are able to deploy and migrate workloads.

>> **Cloud APIs are all different.** Although AWS APIs have become a de facto standard, many more APIs have emerged in the market. For example, there is the Open Cloud initiative, the Open Cloud Stack, the IBM Smart Cloud, and the Microsoft Windows Azure market. None of these cloud APIs are compatible with each other.

The question remains, how can you handle these incompatible APIs in your management tools?

Workload Portability

Discussing APIs and standards is essential because of their impact on workload management. One of the goals of multicloud computing is *workload portability*, to be able to move workloads between cloud environments at any time, for whatever reasons a business may have. Examples of why a business might want to move their applications to other clouds include

>> **Avoiding vendor lock-in:** If you rely on a single vendor, you run the risk of being stuck with higher fees if the vendor raises prices or changes its licensing agreements, or lagging your competitors if the vendor fails to innovate as quickly as competitors.

>> **Taking advantage of best of breed technology:** Your development teams want to use the best technology for the task at hand. Additionally there are financial constraints, and in many instances, you want to find inexpensive options that still meet the requirements for a specific workload.

>> **Increasing productivity by giving teams the tools they want:** Teams can use the platforms and tools that they are familiar with. You want them focused on creativity and productivity, not needing to learn new tools.

>> **Creating an ecosystem that meets compliance and governance regulations:** To comply with various industry, governmental, and international regulations, you may need to have certain types of data and workloads in different locations. For example, some data might need to reside in a particular country or behind your firewall.

>> **Creating a flexible environment to support changing business dynamics:** Businesses constantly change, and you need to plan for change by having flexibility. For example, you may be using a cloud provider that begins to reposition its company to compete against you. You'll want to have the freedom to move your workloads to a different cloud provider that is not also your competition.

In today's multicloud world, a lot of manual intervention is needed to achieve workload portability. However, we anticipate future standards and well-defined approaches that will make multicloud workload portability and management a reality. Until the vision of universal workload portability is realized, we recommend building your own portability layer to hide the differences between cloud APIs from your workloads. When APIs are eventually standardized, you'll be able to replace your portability layer with the new standard without having to make changes to your applications or services.

Note that container technology is making it easier to create portable workloads. See Chapter 10 for details.

Chapter **13**

Managing Data Storage in the Cloud

D ata storage is a prime concern for businesses and can be complex and expensive. There are many considerations when it comes to data storage. A small sampling of the typical storage questions includes

» How often will the data be accessed?

» When should the data be deleted?

» Where geographically should the data be stored?

» What is the data backup plan?

These concerns don't go away within a cloud environment. In fact, in many ways the movement to the cloud can complicate data storage because there are many more choices in the cloud, the scale of data may be much greater, and managing data across on premises and private, public, and hybrid clouds can be much more challenging.

While many businesses are investigating a multicloud approach to data storage, many questions need to be answered. When should you keep data in your private cloud or data center? When is it appropriate to store data in a public cloud environment? How are the storage options going to impact important issues such as latency, availability, security, and governance?

In this chapter, we explore the evolution of storage requirements leading to the hybrid cloud strategy approach. In addition, we consider how companies can streamline their organizations' IT capabilities by leveraging both public and private cloud storage options.

Understanding Cloud Storage Fundamentals

The design of cloud storage is very similar to other cloud services in terms of self-service, elasticity, and scalability. Cloud storage is based on abstracting physical storage with a well-defined interface so it can be managed in a self-service manner. In addition, cloud storage needs to use an architecture that protects each consumer's cloud data from other consumers.

Of course, one of the most important characteristics of cloud storage is how it integrates with IaaS, PaaS, and SaaS clouds. Today, hard disks are connected to physical servers using a SATA interface, which is rapidly replacing older IDE and SCSI protocols. However, in the cloud, scalable storage services are typically not connected directly to physical servers, but use interfaces that transfer data over Ethernet or other communication technologies. We explore how storage connects with virtual machines in the cloud in the upcoming "Elements of storage" sidebar.

The following sections address four key fundamentals of cloud storage: access protocols, usage scenarios, functions, and benefits.

Cloud storage access protocols

TECHNICAL STUFF

One important issue in cloud storage is the speed and ease of accessing data when it's needed. In order for cloud storage to be a viable alternative to on-premises data storage, you need to be able to access your data at a competitive cost and at a speed that is appropriate for the situation. Today, there are four types of cloud storage access methods:

>> **Web services application programming interfaces (APIs):** These use RESTful APIs (following the principles of Representational State Transfer) to integrate with applications.

>> **File-based protocols:** These protocols are used to transfer files and provide integration independent of the application being connected. They also generally provide faster service than web service APIs. Different types are

- Network File System (NFS)

- Common Internet File System (CIFS)

- File Transfer Protocol (FTP)

» **Block-based APIs:** These use iSCSI (Internet SCSI) to connect an application to storage middleware that support services such as storage for databases, data replication, and data reduction.

» **Web-based Distribution Authoring and Versioning (WebDAV):** This is based on Hypertext Transfer Protocol (HTTP).

THE ELEMENTS OF STORAGE

New mobile and digital technologies are among the many market factors that are responsible for an exponential rate of increase in the quantity and type of data that companies need to store. Some data needs to be readily available, and some needs to be stored for five to seven years or longer for compliance purposes. In addition, new technologies like virtualization have helped companies to become more efficient and save money but have also created new and costly storage challenges. For example, some companies found that the savings they expected from consolidating and increasing the utilization of their servers was eaten up by increased spending on storage for a rapidly growing number of virtual machine images. Companies want to find new cost-effective and flexible storage solutions to help meet their evolving storage requirements. So while we expect new methods and innovation in the approach to storage, the following summarizes how large-scale storage is typically managed:

- **Direct attached storage (DAS):** In this model, storage is generally connected to a server's local bus. In other words, your storage may be a hard drive that's internal to your machine or an external drive like a USB storage device. DAS is not directly accessible to other servers.

- **Storage area network (SAN):** This is a high-speed network of interconnected storage devices that provides block storage to its users. These storage devices might be read/write disks, optical disk drives, or other storage media. There can be a large number of them, depending on your company's requirements. Databases are one of the primary users of SAN block storage, and they impose their data structures on the storage (for example, not a file system). SAN communication protocols do not use TCP/IP (typically used to connect servers to a LAN), but require servers to connect to SAN networks using HBAs (Host Bus Adapters). SANs can require significant configuration and support to install.

(continued)

(continued)

- **Network addressable storage (NAS):** NAS is often implemented as a specialized kind of computer that provides file-based storage to other computers over a LAN. It's generally easier to install and not as highspeed as a SAN. The difference between a NAS and a SAN is that a NAS provides storage for files, whereas a SAN provides block storage.

There are different types of data storage and they tend to fall into different tiers of performance. The fastest storage tends to be able to store less information (and costs relatively more), while storage that holds lots of data tends to be slower to access (and costs relatively less). Storage that is used as a cache in a server (to be able to quickly serve recently used data) must be faster than the storage of all the data. Otherwise, there would be no need for the cache. For example, although rarely used nowadays, tape storage was very slow compared to disks, but stored lots of data and was much less expensive.

Understanding the tiers of storage performance is critical when designing and software applications and services. Application data that must be used very quickly (such as, when placing a stock purchase at a specific price in a volatile market) must use very quick storage and processing. On the other hand, archiving data for long-term storage does not require quick access time, and the lower cost is well-suited to storage of lots of old data for long periods of time.

Here are the three tiers of data storage:

- **Tier 1:** Refers to data that has been recently accessed or is mission-critical. In other words, you want to have it readily on hand. It's generally stored on high-quality media. Think of your bank account data. It's likely that you want to view the last several months of this data.

- **Tier 2:** Refers to data that's rarely accessed. This might be backed up on a periodic basis in a corporate environment. Data stored in databases, for example, is often mirrored (copied) by another sever. In a corporate environment, data might be stored this way for three to six months.

- **Tier 3:** Data that's almost never accessed. This data may need to be stored for a long period of time for compliance reasons. In the brokerage industry, for example, the Securities and Exchange Commission (SEC) requires that all transactions and emails are stored for up to seven years. The amount of tier 3 data can be huge for a large company.

The most common method for accessing cloud storage is by using web service APIs such as REST (Representational State Transfer). Cloud storage vendors implement this technology because it's dynamic and simple to use in the cloud. In addition, because of the use of virtualization in cloud environments, there's a requirement for a more stateless (no set location for any code) access protocol. Web service APIs support this requirement for statelessness. This access method is used by Amazon Simple Storage Service (Amazon S3), Windows Azure (Microsoft's Cloud Platform), and others. However, Web service APIs need to be integrated with a specific application when used for cloud storage, which can create some challenges. If you want to avoid the need to integrate with an application, file-based protocols and block-based APIs can be used as alternative access methods. Another connection protocol is WebDAV, a specification designed to create an efficient cloud storage interface.

Delivery options for cloud storage

How will your cloud provider deliver your storage capability? You can use an appliance within your data center, or connect to a public or remote storage service.

Although latency is a major issue for primary (tier 1) cloud storage, particularly for data used frequently, vendors are currently offering a different class of products called hybrid cloud storage solutions that may ultimately address primary storage. (Because we talk about hybrid clouds in general throughout this book, some of the terminology may be confusing, but bear with us.) The idea is to use local and cloud-based resources to address performance issues associated with storage in the cloud. Generally, these offerings consist of two things:

>> An appliance that is a physical or virtual server where the hardware and software are preconfigured so the user doesn't have to understand the details

>> A connection to a remote storage service

The appliance intelligently handles the movement between the local storage and the cloud; to the end user, all the data seems to be in one place.

A cache is a block of memory for temporary storage on the appliance that provides a high-speed buffer between your client and the cloud service. The cache uses a host of algorithms to keep the most frequently used data on the local, expensive hardware. For read requests, attributes such as the age of the data, time since last accessed, time since last updated, and so on are used. For write requests, the appliance may write the data locally on the machine and then burst it out to the cloud storage provider.

The data is generally encrypted when it's transported. When you request data from the provider, the data is first deduplicated to make it faster to retrieve.

Functions of cloud storage

The type of information you need to store and how quickly you need to access data both have an impact on the type of storage you will use. You can use policy-based replication to enable more granular control over how and where data is stored.

Cloud storage can serve multiple purposes:

>> General-purpose storage for day-to-day or periodic use

>> Data protection and continuity, which can include data replication and backup and restore functionality

>> Archive and records management, meaning recoverable long-term data retention to support compliance and regulatory requirements

Benefits of cloud storage

Some of the benefits of cloud storage include

>> **Agility:** The elastic nature of the cloud enables you to gain potentially unlimited storage in an on-demand model.

>> **Fewer physical devices to purchase and maintain:** When you're storing data in a data center, you have to plan for the servers that will be part of this storage solution. This means you need to plan for purchasing the machines and maintain them during their life cycle. Additionally, you must make sure that you have enough space and can meet power requirements. In the cloud, you don't have to purchase physical devices or deal with environmental issues. The cloud provider should do this for you (but it pays to do your homework on the services that your provider offers).

>> **Disaster recovery:** The cloud can serve as a good replacement for tape or other backups and can minimize concerns about your own data center capacity to support your backups. Instead of continuing to expand your on-premises storage, your information can be backed up to the cloud. If your systems go down, you can retrieve your data from the cloud.

>> **Cost:** Although DAS is relatively inexpensive, NAS and SAN devices require significant capital expenditures. The cloud storage model is based on usage, so you only pay for what you use. This is similar to how you use your telephone — generally speaking, you pay for what you use.

Deploying Hybrid Cloud Storage

You might consider various scenarios for a storage architecture when you deploy a cloud. Remember that in a hybrid and multicloud model, some of your resources and assets might be on-premises while other will live in one or more clouds. Here are some possible scenarios:

>> Your applications and data are on-premises, and your tier 2 and 3 data is stored in a public cloud.

>> Some of your applications are in a public cloud, your data is on-premises, and your storage is in a public cloud.

>> You have a private cloud within your enterprise, and you're managing a private cloud that's hosted elsewhere.

>> Some of your applications are in a public cloud along with your data. Some of your applications and data are on-premises. Your storage is both in the cloud and on-premises.

You get the idea. In a hybrid world, there can be multiple permutations in terms of how you architect your applications, data, and storage. So, here's what you need to be thinking about in terms of storage as you deploy a hybrid cloud.

Interfaces

To store and retrieve data, your applications need an API that connects your local system to the cloud-based storage system. Users should be able to send data to the cloud storage device and access data from it. You need to ensure that the APIs the cloud provider uses are interoperable with your own, because there are few standards for cloud storage. (See Chapter 5 for more on standards.) In other words, vendors like to use their own APIs.

According to experts, what users want is a standard like the ubiquitous TCP/IP for the network used across all storage interfaces. However, this may be difficult because each vendor may define its own APIs based on SOAP and REST. So, for the near term, there may be similarities, but vendors won't be completely interoperable.

Security

Security is always a concern. Make sure security measures are in place when data is transferred between storage and on-premises locations, as well as access-control measures once the data is stored. Files need to be secure while in storage, too.

Reliability

Data integrity is also a piece of the hybrid cloud environment. You need to make sure that your data gets from point A to point B and that it maintains its integrity. Your cloud provider might index your data. Its integrity also needs to remain intact when it's in storage. For example, if indexes are corrupted, you can lose your data. We talk about the why and how of security in Chapter 15.

Business continuity

Planned and even unplanned downtime can cause problems for your business. Your storage provider needs to include snapshots, mirroring, and backups, as well as rapid recovery so that if the provider's system goes down, you're covered. You also need to make sure that the right service level agreements are in place (see Chapter 19).

Reporting and chargeback

Because cloud storage is a pay-as-you-go model, you need to know what your bill will be at the end of the billing cycle. This will include any transactional charges the provider might charge you as well as storage costs.

Management

In a hybrid cloud environment, if you choose to store some of your data on-premises and some in the cloud, you'll need to be able to manage the environments together. How will service levels be monitored and managed across these environments? How will you know if there's a problem with your storage provider? It would be nice to be able to manage all of this together, in one spot, in one single "pane of glass." However, the industry is not there yet, because it's continuing to evolve its offerings in this space. See Chapter 12 for more on managing a hybrid and multicloud environment.

Performance/latency

Once you put your data in the cloud, you are subject to *latency* (delays that occur when processing data) issues. The questions to ask here are these (which we explore more deeply in the next section):

>> How quickly will your applications need data?

>> What are the risks if data isn't available in a reasonable time frame?

>> Will your applications experience time-out and thus problems?

>> Does the cloud storage provider match or exceed your network speeds?

>> Are there any bottlenecks?

Data and network speed

Once you start moving your data into the cloud, you may need to address latency concerns, depending on the amount of data you're storing there and how often you need to access it. In a hybrid model, you're not just utilizing your LAN or WAN for data access, you're now going across the Internet to access it. So, you really need to think about the kind of data you're willing to store in the cloud based on how often you need to get to it and the network speed that you're dealing with. Although storage may be unlimited (for a price) in the cloud, the network is not. Two issues you need to consider are amount of data and network speed.

Amount of data

Say that you want to store a large amount of tier 3 data in a storage cloud provider. It may not make sense to actually try to transport the data over the Internet. Remember, *the bandwidth of a truck is greater than any existing network.* It might make sense to provide the data to the vendor in another way. Calculate transfer rates based on the amount of data you have and then decide which leads to the next point regarding network speed.

Network speeds

Bandwidth is just one element that contributes to network speed. Latency is another one. Latency refers to a delay in processing data as it moves from one part of a network to another. For example, when a singer's mouth moves on a video but the words don't seem to match, that's because of latency. Low latency is when there's a short delay; high latency is when there's a longer delay. So, although the speed of your network should be fixed according to the bandwidth of the network connection, it doesn't always work that way because of latencies. A number of factors contribute to network latency, including data collisions, contention for bandwidth, encryption, as well as routers and computer hardware delays, to name a few.

A good corporate LAN/WAN is a gigabit network, which means that your internal network might be faster than the Internet. So, after your information gets to the Internet, you may experience a bottleneck as the information moves to your provider. This bottleneck will affect how quickly you can get your data off your premises and, more importantly, back to your premises. If you have a petabyte of data in a provider's cloud and want to analyze it on-premises, be aware that it's going to take a while to get the data back. You need to consider this issue when planning your hybrid deployment. For instance, you may decide not to store tier 1 data in the cloud because network speeds may not match your requirements for use.

Planning for Cloud Growth and Change

Planning for cloud growth and change involves understanding your data, devising a strategy to deal with the growth, and choosing a provider. We discuss each step in this section.

Understanding your data

In a cloud environment, as with any environment, you need to understand your rate of data generation. Of course data is being generated at faster and faster rates with the advent of newer technologies like the Internet of Things (IoT) and social data as well as the technical ability to store all of this data.

In a multicloud world, this data is being generated in multiple cloud environments and on-premises.

Devising a growth strategy

The second step is to devise a strategy to determine how you're going to deal with the growth of data and the move to the cloud. As part of this strategy, you need to understand how much storage growth you want to support internally and how much you can support outside your corporate walls. You need to do an analysis that compares your investment in corporate infrastructure to a potential cloud strategy. This analysis includes the following:

- » **What kind of applications and data you're willing to store in the cloud versus what you want to keep on-premises:** This includes data issues associated with regulatory compliance and other risk factors. Although you may be thinking only about archive and backup applications, experts advise considering other applications that may not be mission-critical. However, make sure that your provider can adhere to any regulatory or compliance issues your company has in place. You also need to make sure they are willing to change if something changes in your industry.

- » **A risk assessment:** Every company has its own tolerance level when it comes to risk. Aside from technology risks, you may also want to consider how your processes might change in the cloud. For example, you need to determine whether there are any people, processes, or cultural issues to consider.

» **On-site data storage costs:** Include all costs associated with on-site data storage: hardware, software, maintenance, environmental costs (such as electricity), and so on.

» **Cloud storage costs:** Include all costs associated with cloud storage, including data migration costs and storage costs associated with these applications and data.

Choosing a provider

When you've decided that you want some of your applications and data in the cloud, you need to pick your provider with due diligence. Read the fine print in terms of costs associated with the storage and what contract termination looks like. You also want to make sure that the provider puts recovery-time objectives in place, in case there's a problem with its service. Also, make sure the vendor you select is viable. For example, what happens to your storage if your service provider goes out of business? Will you be able to recover your assets?

Experts also advise to ensure that an escape clause is in your contract, in case your provider doesn't perform as advertised.

WARNING

These concerns boil down to trust and doing your homework. Do you trust your vendor and have you put the right contracts in place to protect yourself? Have you done your homework? If you haven't, you need to.

The hybrid cloud storage model offers many advantages to organizations that want to maintain the security of storing their highly confidential data within a private cloud and then selectively store data with fewer confidentiality requirements in the public cloud. Ultimately, the right mix between public and private environments is one that maximizes cost savings while maintaining security and geographic storage requirements.

5

Developing Your Cloud Strategy

Chapter **14**

Managing and Integrating Data in the Cloud

S uccessfully managing data in a hybrid environment is critical to your business and the satisfaction of your customers. One of the complexities of data management is the variety and diversity of data within your business. There is highly structured transactional and customer data. There is a huge amount of unstructured data that exists in documents and images. The ability to manage and integrate data sources across on-premises data centers and hybrid clouds is at the core of any data strategy.

In this chapter, we discuss the need to deal with the massive amount of information that defines your business.

Ensuring Trustworthy Data

Increasingly, businesses are grappling with the problem of leveraging the flexibility and economics of the cloud while protecting their data. The movement to the cloud is causing companies of all sizes and in all industries to think about how to keep business data that was previously secured inside a firewall safe and compliant. Although cloud providers must have the proper controls in place to ensure the security and privacy of your data, you are ultimately responsible for your company's data. This means that industry and government regulations created to protect personal and business information still apply even if the data is managed or stored by an outside vendor. For example, the European Union (EU) has implemented a complex set of data protection laws for companies that process, store, or otherwise use EU citizen data. In addition, industry regulations must be followed whether or not your data is in the cloud. For example, the Health Insurance Portability and Accountability Act (HIPAA) was created to secure the privacy of individual healthcare information. Healthcare organizations must require their subcontractors to comply with HIPAA privacy considerations and use reasonable security measures.

Controlling customer data privacy

Many businesses are rushing to acquire more and more data in an effort to create better analytics models. It is increasingly easy for businesses to enrich customer and prospect data with various third-party data sources. For example, there are technology vendors that will help companies match customer information with customers' social media postings. The business can also shop for data from specialized data brokers who possess data on individuals who are not customers. It has been a common practice in marketing to acquire email lists or to access consumer data on social media sites such as Google, Facebook, or LinkedIn. However, as you begin to amass more data, you must think about how you can ensure that customer privacy is maintained.

Businesses now must be aware of enhanced regulatory controls on data privacy when reaching out to consumers via acquired data. In most cases, permission must be granted from the consumer to use the data via an opt-in process. But gaining such permission is difficult if there is no preexisting relationship between a business and the consumer.

Assessing cloud data risks

You should be concerned about a number of issues in hybrid and multicloud environments. Of course, the level of risk depends on the kind of data that you're trying to secure. Data can range in type from credit card transactions to product catalog information to internal social network site data. You need to understand the impact of not being able to access the data or having your data compromised; then you can decide where you'll store those different types of data. You may want to keep some data on-premises so that it can be physically audited, some might go to the public cloud to drive catalog sales, and some could be part of hybrid cloud configuration when your on-premises application's data must integrate with a SaaS application. Here are just a few data-related risks to think about:

>> **Data multi-tenancy:** As we mention in Chapter 15, in a public cloud, there's a good chance that your data will be stored on the same system as other companies' data. Typically, each tenant is well isolated.

>> **Data deletion:** If you end your contract with your service provider and ask it to delete your data, the deletion may not be thorough. The result may be that some of your data is still be on the provider's system.

>> **Data breaches:** You need to do your homework and determine how good the security environment of your cloud provider is. If the cloud and related elements such as the network aren't well secured, customer data can be stolen. Data protection laws that protect personal information can vary by country and state.

Securing data in the cloud

The three key areas of concern related to security and privacy of data are location, control, and secure transport of your data.

REMEMBER

Cloud providers must ensure the security and privacy of your data, but you are ultimately responsible for your company's data. Industry and government regulations created to protect personal and business information still apply even if the data is managed or stored by an outside vendor.

It's important to note that some experts believe that certain kinds of data are just too sensitive for the public/hybrid cloud. This might include highly regulated data, such as medical information. Others believe that if the right level of transparency and controls can be provided, consumers can be protected. In some circles, this is an ongoing debate. Clouds that host regulated data must meet compliance requirements such as Payment Card Industry Data Security Standard (PCI DSS), Sarbanes-Oxley, and HIPAA. We devote Chapter 15 to cloud security.

Location

After data goes into the cloud, you may not have control over where it's stored or how it's used unless you specifically contract with the cloud provider for a specific location for your data. Numerous issues are associated with this situation:

>> **Specific country laws:** Laws governing data can differ across geographies. Your own country's legal protections may not apply if your data is located outside it. A foreign government may be able to gain access to your data or keep you from having full control over your data when you need it.

>> **Transfer of data across country borders:** A global company with subsidiaries or partners (or clients) in other countries may be concerned about cross-border transfer of data because of local laws. Virtualization makes this an especially tough problem because the cloud provider might not know where the data is at any particular moment either.

>> **Optimized performance:** There are times when you want to have your data in close proximity to the user. Users have a variety of requirements, including the ability to quickly optimize application performance. In other situations users need to be able to avoid moving data for performance and security reasons.

>> **Secondary use of data:** In public cloud situations, your data or metadata may be vulnerable to alternative or secondary uses by the cloud service provider. Without proper controls or service level agreements in place, your data may be used for marketing purposes. It could be merged with data from other organizations for such alternative uses.

The control of data in the cloud

You may or may not have heard the term the *Confidentiality, Integrity, and Availability (CIA) Triad.* These three attributes have been around a long time in the world of auditing and management controls; they're critical for data in the cloud environment for the following reasons:

>> **Confidentiality:** Only authorized parties with the appropriate privileges can access certain data, so there's no theft of the data.

>> **Integrity:** Data is correct, and no malicious software (or person) has altered it; there is no tampering with the data.

>> **Availability:** Network resources are available to authorized users.

These three attributes are directly related to controlling data. Controls include the governance policies set in place to make sure that data can be trusted. The integrity, reliability, and confidentiality of your data must be beyond reproach. This holds for cloud providers, too.

REMEMBER

You must understand what level of controls will be maintained by your cloud provider and consider how these controls can be audited.

Here are some types of controls designed to ensure the confidentiality, integrity, and availability of your data:

>> **Input validation controls** to ensure that all data input to any system or application is complete, accurate, and reasonable.

- » **Output reconciliation controls** to ensure that data can be reconciled from input to output.

- » **Processing** controls to ensure that data is processed completely and accurately in an application.

- » **Access** controls to ensure that only those who are authorized to access the data can do so. Sensitive data must also be protected in storage and transfer. Encryption can help.

- » **Reidentification** (the process by which anonymized personal data is matched with its true owner) **controls** to ensure that codes are kept in a separate location to prevent unauthorized access to reidentification information.

- » **Change management controls** to ensure that data can't be changed without proper authorization.

- » **Data destruction controls** to ensure that when data is permanently deleted, it is deleted everywhere, including all backup and redundant storage sites.

TECHNICAL
STUFF

The concept of controls in the cloud is so important that the Cloud Security Alliance has put together a list controls called the Cloud Controls Matrix (CCM) to guide cloud vendors and assist potential cloud customers in assessing the overall risk of the provider. The matrix outlines the controls, architectural implications, and the kinds of cloud delivery models that the control pertains to.

TIP

Your company needs to develop and publish a consistent set of rules and policies regarding the creation, capture, management, transmission, access, storage, and deletion of confidential and business-critical data. Use techniques such as encryption and tokenization to reduce exposure to data theft and misuse. We recommend speaking to your cloud provider regarding what controls it provides for your data.

Secure transport

Suppose that you've decided to move some of your data to the cloud. Regarding data transport, ensure two things:

- » No one can intercept your data as it moves from point A to point B in the cloud.

- » No data leaks (malicious or otherwise) occur from any storage location in the cloud.

These concepts are not new. The goal of securely transporting data has been around as long as the Internet. The issues you face moving your data from one point to another are the same kinds of issues you might have faced moving your data from a data center in Pittsburgh to one in Miami.

In the multicloud world, the journey from point A to point B might occur any number of ways: within a cloud environment, over the public Internet between an enterprise and cloud provider, or even between clouds.

The security process may include segregating your data from other companies' data and then encrypting it by using an approved method. In addition, you may want to ensure the security of older data that remains with a cloud vendor after you no longer need it.

A virtual private network (VPN) is one way to manage the security of data during its transport in a cloud environment. A VPN essentially makes the public network your own private network instead of using a dedicated physical connection. A well-designed VPN needs to incorporate two things:

>> A firewall to act as a barrier between the public Internet and any private network

>> Encryption to protect your sensitive data from hackers; only the computer you send it to should have the key to decode the data

In addition to transport, in a multicloud world, there will be many touchpoints between your data and clouds. Therefore, it's important to deal with the storage and retrieval of this data. It's important to note, however, that a lot of research has been done over the past decades on storage and retrieval of sensitive information. Some of these techniques use a form of encryption to prevent information leakage. Researchers and experts in the field are now working on other techniques to deal with the challenge of the server performance degradation because of encryption. They're addressing issues related to data partitioning between your on-premises data and a service provider. They're investigating how to deal with distributed query processing over unencrypted and encrypted data.

Integrating Data across Environments

As soon as you start dealing with the cloud, you must establish a way to deal with the fact that you have data that potentially spans multiple environments. Of course, your data probably does span multiple environments today, but it's under your control. How do you integrate all this data? Most companies very quickly find that they must contend with many different integration scenarios.

Three integration scenarios

The three most common cloud integration scenarios are

» On-premises data center to cloud

» Connectivity between (or among) clouds

» Connectivity in clouds

We discuss each of these scenarios in this section.

On-premises data center to cloud

Connectivity from the data center to the cloud is one of the fundamental tools used to build cloud integrations. The typical IT organization manages its enterprise resource planning (ERP) system within its data center and uses a SaaS application to manage sales leads. Data from sales, order, invoice, and inventory data systems must be synchronized for the company to function properly. This can be a major cultural shift for an organization that's used to having full control over its line-of-business applications.

Users have little or no control over the architectural structure of the SaaS environment, so the IT organization needs to establish new processes to manage integration of a data center application and a cloud-based application. IT management needs to separate the data elements within the line-of-business applications from unnecessary dependencies. For example, there may be a business process that controls a specific circumstance that interferes with your ability to easily connect between data sources on the cloud.

In addition, specific issues related to using cloud computing environments affect the style of integration. For example, although your company gains huge value from using a SaaS-based customer relationship management (CRM) system, governance requirements may demand that customer data be stored behind your firewall. So, when a prospect becomes a customer, the company moves the data into the data center for additional security. This company now has a hybrid environment to manage. The company needs to automate data mobility across clouds in order to transfer and transform customer data to migrate between public and private clouds.

Connectivity among clouds

Companies may need to integrate a private cloud and multiple public clouds. One common example of this occurs when a business uses several public clouds across departments. In some cases, a variety of public clouds are used to manage data storage or to support advance analytics.

For instance, an entertainment organization is testing the introduction of a new game that supports on-demand group participation. The online gaming community has already shown a great deal of interest surrounding this new capability.

The entertainment company wants to test how its web application scales from 20,000 to 1 million concurrent users before going live. They know they need more cycles and more power than they have available on-premises, so they expand their environment by leveraging public cloud resources. After the testing was completed, the company signed an agreement with a public cloud service in order to ensure that the application could scale as the game became more popular.

Connectivity in clouds

A third type of integration occurs when you need to create multidirectional integration with multiple SaaS applications in order to support a business process. In this case, the connectivity capability itself is in the cloud. For example, a services organization uses sales automation to keep track of its prospects and a different SaaS application to manage commission and salary payments. Many sales situations exist where a cross-brand sales team collaborates in closing a large sales opportunity.

As a result, the sales commission must be split among different sales people. The data in the CRM system needs to be consistent with the data in the payment application, or the people who closed the deal won't be paid accurately. Automating this process requires the synchronization of the data between the two SaaS applications.

Because both of these applications are in the cloud, the most efficient approach to synchronizing the data is to use a cloud-based integration capability. Public cloud offerings include connectivity in the cloud for this type of situation.

Choosing an integration method wisely

When considering a hybrid cloud, you need to understand that you will lose control over how many things are done. Use an integration method to monitor these connections and make sure standards are met. For example, the SSL/TLS industry standard handshake will authenticate using X.509 certificates to ensure that users are legitimate. Part of this handshake process includes creating an encrypted tunnel, which protects against security threats such as eavesdropping and man-in-the-middle attacks. Secure communication protocols exist that should be followed when communicating with endpoint applications and databases.

Options for cloud data integration

Various options are available for cloud data integration. The option that you choose should be based on the business problems you're trying to solve and the kind of cloud deployment you're dealing with:

>> **Software solution:** In this approach, vendors can provide a preconfigured integration pattern or template that jump-starts the effort of integration between applications. One of the benefits of working with a standardized template is that the same template can be reused for other integration projects. The template is typically designed to cover about 60 percent of the requirements for a particular integration. The packages usually also provide a way to visually map the data between source and target systems.

For example, in your on-premises ERP system, your customer ID might be called ID, and in your cloud application, it's called CUST ID. The visual mapping interface makes this easy to specify that the two fields refer to the same entity. You just draw a line between the two to specify that they're the same. Some packages also allow you to work with more complex mappings as well as provide a way to set up rules for data integration.

>> **Cloud-based tool:** This option is similar in many ways to traditional tools, such as connectors, that can be used to connect specific applications. In this case, end users can buy different components from a provider based on what they need to do. For example, you could buy a component for database connectivity or to transform data going into a database.

>> **Cloud-based solutions:** In this case, data integration is offered as a service or set of services. For example, a vendor might offer a data replication service to copy data from one source to another and then automatically update it. Or it might offer data quality and assessment services, or services to load data from various format types (such as flat files or databases) into target applications. Or it might offer a packaged web application server and database.

>> **Data virtualization solutions:** Recently, vendors have begun offering the option of leaving data in its original location and moving the algorithm to the data. This approach means that data does not have to be moved, which can avoid potential security risks.

You can find a number of vendors offering solutions in this space. Some offer packaged solutions, some offer cloud solutions, and some offer both. The solution you choose will depend on the problem you're trying to solve.

No matter what approach you use, an overriding issue is going to be to make sure that your data maintains its integrity by being complete, accurate, and up to date. You will still have to make sure that you have a master version of your data in place that serves as what is often called a single version of the truth — an agreed-upon golden master.

Managing Big Data in the Cloud

When we use the term *big data*, we are referring to the massive amount of data that is available in many forms and complexity. The existence of big data is not new. Organizations have long had to content with large volumes and complexity of data. The difference with the advent of the commercialization of the cloud where the cost and efficiency of both compute and storage is a small fraction of the costs in the era of the traditional data center. In an earlier era, businesses were limited by how much data they could afford to storage and analyze. With those limits removed with the cloud, organizations can now afford to manage big data as never before. Big data technologies allow people to analyze and utilize this data in an effective way. The ability to store and analyze massive amounts of data is revolutionizing the way organizations can understand data that was once inaccessible. This has opened the door to the renaissance in advanced analytics, machine learning, and artificial intelligence.

Master data management

Master data management (MDM) is a technique that helps companies establish consistent and accurate definitions of data across their IT assets. It is about transcending data silos to reach a single version of the truth. For example, you might have multiple systems in your company, each containing customer information. But what is a customer? In the pharmaceutical industry, in one system, a customer might refer to a physician. In another system, it might be a group practice. In yet another system, it might be a hospital that buys drugs in bulk. So, if you're mapping this data together, you need to understand what you're calling a customer, or you'll end up with data that doesn't make any sense when you go to analyze it. That's what master data is all about.

Big data characteristics

Big data generally has three characteristics:

>> **Volume:** Big data is big in quantity, and although the word *big* is relative here, currently we're talking on the order of at least terabytes. Many big data implementations are looking to analyze petabytes of information.

>> **Variety:** Big data comes in different shapes and sizes. It includes these types of data:

- *Structured data* is the typical kind of data that analysts are used to dealing with. It includes revenue and number of sales — the type of data you think about including in a relational database. Structured data is also being produced in new ways in products such as sensors and RFID tags.

- *Semi-structured data* has some structure to it but not in the way you think about tables in a database. It includes EDI and JSON formats.

- *Unstructured data* includes texts, images, and audios, including any document, email message, tweet, or blog internal to a company or on the Internet. Unstructured data accounts for about 80 percent of all data. (Note that *unstructured* is a bit of a misnomer; it's not as consistently structured as data that fits conveniently into a relational database.)

» **Velocity:** This is the speed at which the data moves. Think about sensors capturing data every millisecond or data streams produced by medical equipment. Big data often comes at you in a live stream, so it has a real-time nature associated with it.

The cloud is an ideal place for big data because of its scalable storage, compute power, and elastic resources. The cloud model is large-scale; distributed computing and a number of frameworks and technologies have emerged to support this model, including

» **Apache Hadoop:** An open source distributed computing platform written in Java. It is a software library that enables distributed processing across clusters of computers. It's really a distributed file system. It creates a computer pool, each with a Hadoop file system. Hadoop was designed to deal with problems where there's a large amount of complex data. The data can be structured, unstructured, or semistructured. Hadoop can run across a lot of servers that don't share memory or disk. For more information, visit http://hadoop. apache.org.

» **Spark Core:** The Spark framework was designed to manage complex data at scale and support a variety of languages and Application Programming Interfaces (APIs). One of the benefits that distinguishes the Spark framework from other distributed models is the ability to use machine learning algorithms in an efficient and predictable way. The Spark Core is distributed in memory architecture that is significantly faster than disk based implementations. One of the foundational services that is built on top of the core is a machine learning library.

Supporting an Analytics Strategy

What good is lots of data if you can't do anything active with it? The lure of analytics in the cloud is cloud elasticity. Your data can be processed across clusters of computers. If you need more compute power, you can get it from the cloud.

Big data analytics

Here are some examples of where analytics get big and may require cloud resources:

>> **Financial services:** Imagine using advanced analytics technologies like predictive analytics to analyze millions of credit card transactions to determine whether which might be fraudulent. On the unstructured side, picture the text in insurance claims being analyzed to determine what might constitute fraud.

Take a worker's compensation claim submitted by a worker who may have been reprimanded several times by his boss. This data (or the claim), which came from unstructured sources, can be used with structured data to train an analytical system on what patterns might indicate fraud. As new claims come in, the system can automatically highlight the ones that may need to be investigated.

>> **Retail:** Just think about the recommendation engines from Amazon and eBay. They've become more sophisticated. Amazon uses advanced technologies that will look at what you're purchasing, and then, based on models it has of the numerous purchases of other people, make a recommendation.

Another example is the use of advanced analytics over massive amounts of data in real time at big-box stores. Using your loyalty card, based on what you're buying, what you have bought in the past, and what others with similar profiles like you have bought, the store will provide you with coupons for different products you might like.

>> **Social media analysis:** Imagine all the data being collected across the Internet. This includes blogs, tweets, and news feeds. Companies are mining this unstructured data to understand what is being said about them. A consumer packaged goods company might mine this data to determine what is being said about it and whether this sentiment is positive or negative. Numerous companies are providing this kind of service in the cloud.

Writing the code to process this data across clusters of machines requires highly trained developers and complex job coordination. With a technology like MapReduce, the same MapReduce job that was developed to run on a single node can distribute this analytic processing power to a group of 1,000 nodes. Say you need immediate analysis of sensor data or social media data that is streaming into your data center or your cloud provider. Parallel processing across multiple computing resources can help do this by spreading the analysis across the environment. It gets you to insight faster.

Other cloud analytics

The cloud can be useful in supporting an analytics strategy when your data isn't that big (by contrast with the previous examples of big data). Say you work at a company that wants to predict what action your customers will take. You want to use predictive analytics to do this, but you don't have the skills in-house. In this case, you can turn to analytics providers that offer SaaS-based services for help. You provide them your data, and they provide you with the analysis.

A number of cloud-based offerings on the market can either help you analyze your data or provide software in the cloud for you to do the analysis yourself. Maybe you're using a cloud-based CRM and ERP system, and you want to analyze the data that's being generated there. There's a cloud service for that.

REMEMBER

If you're thinking about using some of the data services in the cloud, before you sign the contract, remember that data (especially your company's data) is a precious asset, and you need to treat it as such. We recommend discussing certain topics with your potential vendor. We describe those issues in the next section.

Talking to Providers about Data Control

In addition to issues surrounding security and privacy of your data as covered earlier in this chapter, we recommend talking with your potential vendors about the following issues because when your data leaves your premises in a cloud model, you need to ensure that the proper controls are in place to protect it:

>> **Data integrity:** What controls does your provider have in place to ensure that the integrity of your data is maintained? Are there controls in place to make sure that all data input to any system or application is complete, accurate, and reasonable? What about processing controls to make sure that data processing is accurate? Also, output controls need to be in place. This dovetails into any compliance issues that your particular industry might have.

>> **Compliance:** You are probably aware of any compliance issues particular to your industry. You need to make sure that your provider can comply with these regulations.

>> **Loss of data:** Your data is a precious asset. Key to any decision to go with a cloud provider is to find out what provisions are in the contract if the provider does something to your data. If the contract says simply that your monthly fee is waived, you need to ask some more questions.

- » **Business continuity plans:** What happens if disaster strikes and your cloud vendor's data center goes down? What business continuity plans does your provider have in place, meaning how long is it going to take the provider to get your data back up and running? For example, a SaaS vendor might tell you that it backs up data every day, but it might take several days to get the backup onto systems in another facility. You need to determine whether this meets your business requirements.

- » **Uptime:** Your provider might tell you that you will be able to access your data 99.999 percent of the time; however, read the contract. Does this uptime include scheduled maintenance?

- » **Data storage costs:** *Pay-as-you-go* (you pay for what you use) and no capital purchase is appealing, but you need to read the fine print. For example, how much will it cost you to move your data into the cloud? What about other hidden integration costs? Then how much will it cost to store your data? You should do your own calculations so you're not caught off-guard. You need to find out how the provider is charging for data storage. Some providers offer a tiered pricing structure. Amazon, for example, charges you based on the average storage used throughout the month. This includes all object data and metadata stored in buckets that you created under your account.

- » **Termination of contract:** How will data be returned if the contract is terminated? If you're using a SaaS provider and it has created data for you, will any of that data be returned? You need to ask yourself if this is an issue for you. Some companies just want the data destroyed. So, you need to understand how your provider will destroy your data, in order to make sure it doesn't continue to float around in the cloud.

- » **Data ownership:** Who owns your data once it goes into the cloud? Some service providers may want to take your data, merge it with other data, and do some analysis.

- » **Data access:** What controls are in place to make sure that you and only you (or whoever has access rights) can access your data? In other words, what forms of secure access controls are in place? This includes identity management, where the primary goal is protecting personal identity information so access to computer resources, applications, data, and services is controlled properly.

- » **Threat management:** What software and procedures does your provider have in place to counter a variety of security threats that might affect your data? This includes intrusion protection.

MACHINE LEARNING IN THE CLOUD

While the cloud has been important in the big data revolution in general, it has a profound impact on the evolution of advanced analytics. The scalability of the cloud enables data professionals to gain insights and understanding of data at a deeper level than is possible with traditional data analysis tools.

Increasingly, organizations are investing in machine learning and artificial intelligence in order to leverage data to improve decision making. While organizations have consistently used advanced analytics tools to optimize decision making, the commercialization of the cloud has made the ability to use machine learning algorithms with massive amounts of data affordable. This has led to an explosion of emerging vendors as well as well established companies focused on providing cloud-based tools. While the area for machine learning and AI is still emerging, there is huge potential to help businesses leverage the cloud to gain true insights from data that is transformational.

Chapter **15**

Promoting Cloud Security and Governance

Security is one of the most important issues facing IT leaders when they begin their transition to the cloud. Whether you're looking at creating a private cloud, leveraging a public cloud, or implementing a hybrid environment, you must have a security strategy. Security is something you can never really relax about because the state of the art is constantly evolving. Hand-in-hand with this security strategy needs to be a governance strategy — a way to ensure accountability by all parties involved in your cloud deployment.

Managing security in the cloud needs to be viewed as a shared responsibility across the organization. You can implement all the latest technical security controls and still face security risks if your end users don't have a clear understanding of their role in keeping the cloud environment secure. Cloud services provide non-IT professionals with more control over their IT environment than ever before. As a result, the organization benefits from increased efficiency, flexibility, and productivity. However, there is also a much greater likelihood that end users can impact security if they don't understand the implications of their actions.

In this chapter, we examine the security risks and governance considerations for companies working in hybrid cloud environments. There is a lot to consider, and understanding security is a moving target. Ultimately, education is key to ensuring that everyone in the organization has an understanding of his or her roles and responsibilities with regard to security.

Exploring the Risks of Operating in the Cloud

According to the National Institute of Standards and Technology (NIST), a government standards body, computer systems are subject to many threats ranging from loss of data to loss of a whole computing facility because of fire or natural disaster. These losses can come from trusted employees or from hackers. Sensitive data can be accidently exposed through an innocent mistake or stolen by criminals. NIST divides these security risks into the following categories:

>> Errors and omissions, including data errors or programming errors

>> Fraud and theft

>> Employee sabotage

>> Loss of physical infrastructure support

>> Malicious hackers

>> Malicious code

>> Threats to individual personal privacy

Many of the same security risks that companies face when dealing with their own computer systems occur in the cloud, but there are some important twists. The Cloud Security Alliance, an organization dedicated to ensuring security best practices in the cloud, noted in its recent publication, "Security Guidance for Critical Areas of Focus in Cloud Computing," that significant areas of operational security risk in the cloud include the following:

>> **Traditional security:** A hybrid cloud environment changes traditional security because you're no longer totally in control. Some of the computing assets you're using aren't on your premises. Now, you must ensure that strong traditional security measures are being followed by your cloud provider. Traditional security includes

- Physical security covers security of IT equipment, network assets, and telecommunications infrastructure. CSA recommends both "active and passive" defenses for physical security (see the section, "Assess your cloud vendor," which also includes equipment protection and location).

- Human resource security deals with the people side of the equation — ensuring background checks, confidentiality, and segregation of duties (that is, those who develop applications don't operate them).

- Business continuity plans need to be part of any service level agreement to ensure that the provider meets its service level agreement for continuous operation with you.

- Disaster recovery plans must ensure that your assets (for example, data and applications) are protected.

>> **Incident handling:** A hybrid cloud environment changes incident handling in at least two ways. First, whereas you may have control over your own data center, if an incident occurs, you'll need to work with your service provider, because the service provider controls at least part of the infrastructure. Second, the multi-tenant nature of the cloud often makes investigating an incident more complicated. For example, because information may be commingled, log analysis may be difficult, since your service provider is trying to maintain privacy. You need to find out how your service provider defines an incident and make sure you can negotiate how you'll work with the provider to ensure that everyone is satisfied.

>> **Application security:** When an application is in the cloud, it's exposed to every sort of security threat. The CSA divides application security into different areas, including securing the software development life cycle in the cloud; authentication, authorization, and compliance; identity management, application authorization management (for updating application and the like), application monitoring, application penetration testing, and risk management.

>> **Encryption and key management:** Data encryption refers to a set of algorithms that can transform text into a form called cyphertext, which is an encrypted form of plain text that unauthorized parties can't read. The recipient of an encrypted message uses a key that triggers the algorithm to decrypt the data and provide it in its original state to the authorized user. Therefore, you can encrypt data and ensure that only the intended recipient can decrypt it.

In the public cloud, some organizations may be tempted to encrypt all their information because they're concerned about its movement to the cloud and how safe it is once it's in the cloud. Recently, experts in the field have begun to consider other security measures besides encryption that can be used in the cloud. (We tackle a few of those security measures in the later section that deals with encryption options.)

>> **Identity and access management:** Identity and access management (AIM) is a broad topic that applies to many areas of technology. The goal of AIM systems is to manage identity information so that access to computer resources, SaaS and on-premises applications, data, and other IT services is controlled properly. Identity management changes significantly in the cloud. In a traditional data center, you might use a directory service for authentication. The cloud often requires multiple forms of identity to ensure that access to resources is secure. (We also cover this topic in a bit more detail in the identity management section, later in this chapter.)

With the increasing use of cloud computing, and mobile devices, you no longer have well-defined boundaries regarding what is internal and what is external to your systems. On an ongoing basis, you must assess whether holes or vulnerabilities exist across servers, network, infrastructure components, and endpoints, and then continuously monitor them. In other words, you need to be able to trust your own infrastructure as well as a cloud provider's.

Cloud provider risks

A company planning to secure its IT environment generally focuses on a broad range of vulnerabilities in order to safeguard sensitive corporate, customer, and partner information, whether it is located in a public or private cloud or the data center. Regardless of where your workloads are running, it's your company's responsibility to protect and secure your applications and information. There are a number of challenges that arise when you're working with an external provider. Here are a few of those challenges:

>> **Multi-tenancy:** In a multi-tenant architecture, a software application partitions its data and configuration so that each customer has a customized virtual application instance. However, your applications and data exist on the same servers as other companies using the same service provider, and these users are accessing their resources simultaneously. You may not know the names of the other companies that are sharing these servers. So if one company's data or application is breached or fails for any number of reasons, your application may be affected.

>> **Attacks that affect you, even though you aren't the target:** If your company makes use of a public cloud, you may be the collateral damage in an attack, even if it wasn't meant for you. Consider a virus attack, for example. Because you're sharing an environment with others, even though you may not be a target, your resources may be affected, resulting in a service interruption or worse.

>> **Incident response:** In a cloud environment, you may not have control over how quickly incidents are handled. For example, some cloud providers may not tell you about a security incident until they've confirmed that an actual incident occurred. As a result, you won't know something has happened until it affects your business. Additionally, if you become aware of an incident, you may not have access to servers to perform an analysis of what went wrong.

>> **Visibility:** In many cloud environments, you may not be able to see what your provider is doing. In other words, you may not have control over your visibility into your resources that are running in the cloud. This situation is especially troublesome if you need to ensure that your provider is following compliance regulations or laws.

>> **Non-vetted employees:** Although your company may go through an extensive background check on all of your employees, you're now trusting that no malicious insiders work at your cloud provider. This concern is real because close to 50 percent of security breaches are caused by insiders (or by people getting help from insiders). If your company is going to use a cloud service, you need to have a plan to deal with inside as well as outside threats.

>> **Data issues:** If you're putting your data in the cloud, you need to be concerned about a number of issues including the following:

- Making sure no unauthorized person can access this data

- Understanding how this data will be segregated from other companies' data in a multi-tenant environment

- Understanding how your data will be destroyed if you terminate your contract

- Understanding where your data will be physically located

- Understanding how your data is treated as it moves from your location to your provider's servers.

Data issues are so important in a hybrid cloud environment that we devote Chapter 14 to them.

>> **Multiple cloud vendors:** Some cloud providers may be storing your data on a different cloud provider's platform. For example, cloud provider A may need extra capacity and move your account to a separate cloud environment supported by cloud provider B. It is therefore important to understand where your data in the cloud is actually located. Once you gain this information, you must make sure all the parties are complying with your security requirements. You need to make sure that providers A and B are both doing a thorough job of vetting employees.

Different applications and resources might demand different levels of security. If you're not providing time-sensitive data to the cloud, for example, you may not be as concerned about incident response time as someone who does. The point is this: You need to ask yourself how much you have invested in what you're putting into your cloud environment. If you're very concerned about what happens if there's a service interruption or what happens to your resources, you need to practice due diligence. What happens in the cloud can affect your cloud resources as well as those on your business's premises. It's best to be prepared.

Even when cloud operators have good security at the physical, network, operating system, and application levels, your company is responsible for protecting and securing its applications and information.

End-user risks

The cloud has helped to bring IT into the hands of the non-IT professional. It is easy, fast, and cheap for a business user to contract with any number of cloud services. And with the increase in the use of mobile devices, business users can easily access and share company data wherever they are located. The IT team no longer holds all the control. This democratization of IT brings with it the problem that non-IT professionals are just not aware of the risks that cloud computing can have. This is not their fault; they've never had to think about IT security in the past. Some of the reasons why include

>> For the most part, their interactions with cloud computing are through various SaaS programs ranging from enterprise-level applications like Workday and Salesforce.com to consumer applications like Facebook, Yelp, LinkedIn, and many others. Users of these SaaS offerings typically take for granted the complex security that is built into each level of the application.

>> Employees are used to acquiring compute resources from the IT team. The IT team is of course well aware of security risks and follows best practices for things like systems configuration, software maintenance, and access control.

>> Compute power that teams were traditionally acquiring from IT were from an internal data center that has strong security measures in place.

The reality is that non-IT teams typically don't know why the data center is secure, nor have they ever cared; all they need to know is that it "works." They don't realize that most of the technologies involved in making the data center secure are not built into basic public cloud virtual machines. In fact, some cloud vendors make it very clear in their service level agreements that users are completely responsible for securing their cloud environment — not something somebody pulling out their corporate card to spin up a virtual machine is likely to appreciate.

Security measures taken by the IT department can be easily undermined by well-meaning business users who do not have an understanding of best practices for maintaining security in cloud environments. For example, sharing of passcodes for a SaaS application is a common practice in some companies and can lead to secure information ending up in the wrong hands.

Developing a Secure Hybrid Environment

A thoughtful approach to security can succeed in mitigating against many security risks. Here are some pointers about how to develop a secure hybrid environment.

Assessing your current state

In a hybrid environment, security starts with assessing your current state. We recommend that you begin by answering a set of questions that can help you form your approach to your security strategy. Here are a few important questions to consider:

>> Have you evaluated your own traditional security infrastructure recently?

>> How do you control access rights to applications and networks — both those within your company and those outside your firewall? Who has the right to access IT resources? How do you ensure that only the right identities gain access to your applications and information?

>> Can you identify web application vulnerabilities and risks and then correct any weaknesses?

>> Do you have a way of tracking your security risk over time so you can easily share updated information with those who need it?

>> Are your server environments protected at all times from external security threats?

>> Do you maintain your own keys, if you are using encryption, or do you get them from a trusted, reliable provider? Do you use standard algorithms? Does your cloud vendor have access?

>> Are you able to monitor and quantify security risks in real time?

>> Can you implement security policies consistently across all types of on-premises and cloud architectures?

>> How do you protect all your data no matter where it's stored?

>> Can you satisfy auditing and reporting requirements for data in the cloud?

>> Can you meet the compliance requirements of your industry?

>> What is your application security program?

>> What are your disaster and recovery plans? How do you ensure service continuity?

Assessing your cloud vendor

A hybrid cloud environment poses a special set of challenges when it comes to security and governance. Hybrid clouds utilize your own infrastructure plus that of your service provider. For example, data may be stored on your premises but processed in the cloud. This means that your own on-premises infrastructure may be connected to a more public cloud, which is going to affect the kinds of security controls you need to have in place.

Controls must be in place for perimeter security, access, data integrity, malware, and the like — not only at your location, but also with your cloud provider. Cloud service providers each have their own way of managing security. They may or may not be compatible with the compliance and overall security plan of your organization. It's absolutely critical that your company not bury its head in the sand by assuming that the cloud provider has security covered.

You need to verify that your cloud provider ensures the same level of security that you demand internally (or a superior level, if you're looking to improve your overall security strategy). You must ask a lot of hard questions to guarantee that your company's security and governance strategy can be integrated with your provider's.

Here are some tips that can get you started and that may also be useful in assessing your security strategy:

>> Ask your cloud provider what kind of companies they service. Also ask questions about system architecture in order to understand more about how multi-tenancy is handled.

>> Visit the facility unannounced in order to understand what physical security measures are in place. According to the CSA, this means walking through all areas, from the reception area to the generator room and even inspecting the fuel tanks. You also need to check for perimeter security (for example, check how people access the building) and whether the operator is prepared for a crisis (for example, fire extinguishers, alarms, and the like).

>> Check where the cloud provider is located. For example, is it in a high crime area or an area prone to natural disasters such as earthquakes or flooding?

>> What sort of up-to-date documentation does the cloud provider have in place? Does it have incident response plans? Emergency response plans? Backup plans? Restoration plans? Background checks of security personnel and other staff members?

>> What sort of certifications does the provider have in place? Do cloud security personnel have certifications such as CISSP, CISA, and ITIL?

>> What companies have provided your third parties with certifications? Are those certification companies reliable?

>> Find out where your data will be stored. If your company has compliance regulations it must meet about data residing in foreign countries, this is important to know. Refer to Chapter 14 for more about data management issues.

- Find out who will have access to your data. Also check to see how data will be protected.

- Find out more about the provider's data backup and retention plans. You will want to know if your data is commingled with other data. If you want your data back when you terminate your contract, these issues may be important.

- How will your provider prevent denial-of-service (DoS) attacks?

- What sort of maintenance contracts does your provider have in place for its equipment?

- Does your cloud provider utilize continuous monitoring of its operations? Can you have visibility into this monitoring capability?

- How are incidents detected? How is information logged?

- How are incidents handled? What is the definition of an incident? Who is your point of contact at your service provider? What are the roles and responsibilities of team members?

- How does your provider handle application security and data security?

- What metrics does your cloud provider monitor to ensure that applications remain secure?

This list proposes a lot of questions, and we don't expect you to be able to answer them in a few seconds. We present them because the information you'll gather should be the foundation for assessing your current security environment.

Given the importance of security in the cloud environment, you might assume that a major cloud service provider will have a set of comprehensive service level agreements for its customers. In fact, many of the standard agreements are intended to protect the service provider — not the customer. So, your company really must understand the contract as well as the infrastructure, processes, and certifications your cloud provider holds.

You must clearly articulate your cloud security requirements and governance strategy and determine accountability. If your cloud provider doesn't want to talk about these items, you should probably consider a new cloud provider. On the other hand, your cloud provider may actually have some tricks up its sleeve that can improve your own security! In fact, it probably does.

Completing this assessment will give you a lot to think about. At that point, you'll have an idea about the strengths and weaknesses in your own security environment, as well as any issues you need to discuss with your cloud provider. You'll have a better idea of the tools and techniques you may have to put in place, both on your own premises as well as in the cloud. And, your provider may surprise you.

STRATEGIES FOR A SECURE ENVIRONMENT

TIP

Here are some additional pointers:

- If your company is large and you are implementing a complex cloud environment, it makes sense to have security people on staff who can help you do your assessments and assess security products.

- In most circumstances, approach cloud security from a risk-management perspective. If your organization has risk-management specialists, involve them in cloud security planning.

- Try to create general awareness of security risks by educating and warning staff members about specific dangers. It is easy to become complacent; however, threats come from within and from outside the organization.

- Regularly have external IT security consultants check your company's IT security policy and IT network and the policies and practices of all your cloud service providers.

- Stay abreast of news about IT security breaches in other companies and the causes of those breaches.

- Continue to review backup and disaster-recovery systems in light of your security strategy. Apart from anything else, security breaches can require complete application recovery.

- Review your governance strategies on an ongoing basis to make sure that your cloud security strategy is enforced. We discuss governance in section "Creating a Cloud Governance Strategy," later in this chapter.

Cloud providers are now making it their business to understand the ins and outs of security. This means that you should not be surprised if they have a much better handle on security than you do!

Digging deeper into identity management

Identity management helps prevent security breaches and plays a significant role in helping a company meet IT security compliance regulations. In a cloud environment, where you don't own the infrastructure and may not control the applications, you may need to think about identity management in a slightly different way. For example, you need to think of identity as more than just an individual user's identity. Identities also exist for devices, code, and other resources that exist off premises. A username and password simply aren't enough. Perimeter security with a firewall isn't enough. For example, many financial services companies are using advanced security techniques for access and identity. If you've ever signed onto your bank or credit card's account page on a new computer or from a new geographic location, you've probably been presented with challenge questions. In addition, these AIM systems can detect other characteristics about the device you are using. If somebody tries to log into a bank account from a phone that has been turned off for six months, the system may infer that this login attempt is fraudulent and could completely block access.

In the cloud, identity and attributes (that is, facets of identity that link to the identity) can come from many systems. These facets may feed into an entitlement layer that contains the rules for authorization and access to the different layers at a provider's site. These layers include the network layer, the system layer, the application layer, the data layer, and the process layer.

Think about the cloud. Machines can be decommissioned quickly and then brought up online again. New machines can be provisioned on the fly. Data can be moved to different machines when the need arises. Your company may want to communicate with different partners and cloud providers. All of this can affect security and identity management practices.

Understanding data protection options

Some experts believe that different kinds of data require different forms of protection and that, in some cases in a cloud environment, data encryption might, in fact, be overkill. You could encrypt everything. You could encrypt data, for example, when you write it to your own disk, when you send it to a cloud provider, and when you store it in a cloud provider's database. You could encrypt at every layer.

Encrypting everything in a comprehensive way reduces your exposure; however, encryption poses a performance penalty. For example, many experts advise managing your own keys rather than letting a cloud provider do so, and that can become complicated. Keeping track of too many keys can be a nightmare. Additionally, encrypting everything can create other issues. For example, if you're trying to encrypt data in a database, you will have to examine data as it's moving (point-to-point encryption) and also while it's being stored in the database. This procedure can be costly and complicated. Also, even when you think you've encrypted everything and you're safe, that may not be the case.

One of the long-standing weaknesses with encryption strategies is that your data is at risk before and after it's encrypted. For example, in a major data breach at Hannaford Supermarkets in 2008, the hackers hid in the network for months and were able to steal payment data when customers used their credit card at the point-of-sale. This breach took place before the data was encrypted.

Maintaining a large number of keys can be impractical, and managing the storing, archiving, and accessing of the keys is difficult. In order to alleviate this problem, generate and compute encryption keys as needed to reduce complexity and improve security.

Here are some other available data safeguarding techniques:

>> **Anonymizing the data:** When data is anonymized, all the data that describes the data (called metadata) is removed. This might include someone's name or Social Security number or address. Although this technique can protect some personal identification, hence privacy, you need to be really careful about the amount of information you strip out. If it's not enough, hackers can still figure out who the data pertains to.

>> **Tokenization:** This technique protects sensitive data by replacing it with random tokens or alias values that mean nothing to someone who gains unauthorized access to this data. This technique decreases the chance that thieves could do anything with the data. Tokenization can protect credit card information, passwords, personal information, and the like. Some experts argue that it's more secure than encryption.

>> **Cloud database controls:** In this technique, access controls are built into the database in order to protect the whole database so that each piece of data doesn't need to be encrypted.

Sharing security responsibility with your cloud provider

If you are using the public cloud, your company is sharing common infrastructure with other companies. This concept of sharing is at the heart of the cloud model; you get access to advanced virtual server environments at a lower cost because you share this infrastructure with others. But in addition to these benefits, you are also sharing security risks. Your cloud provider has the responsibility of securing the physical and logical aspects of the infrastructure and operation system in the cloud environment. You can minimize some of your security risks by choosing the right cloud provider. However, in some cloud environments, you need to share security responsibilities with your cloud provider. For example, if you are using IaaS, you are responsible for the security of your virtual resources once they have been provisioned.

The cloud provides your business users a greater level of control over their IT environment. IT users also have much greater control over provisioning IT assets.

Without understanding the risk involved, users have the potential to easily provision images without providing the right level of attention to security. You need to manage resources provisioned in the cloud with the same attention to security as used in your internal data center. All users of cloud virtual machines need to understand that all provisioned instances must adhere to your company security standards.

After you have provisioned an image, you need to take responsibility for the patch management of that instance as well as additional images you create from that instance. For example, you need to keep up-to-date with vendor bulletins and apply required security updates, fixes, and patches to your software.

Having an inadequate identity management process opens up vulnerabilities that can impact the security of your environment. You can also put other customers of your cloud provider at risk if you have a weak identity management process and create vulnerabilities and open points of entry for hackers. You will need to have a process for

» User ID request process

» User ID approval process

» User ID revalidation process

» User ID revocation process

» Password management guidelines

» Password strength guidelines

If you fail to maintain the right level of security, your cloud provider may decide you are a poor risk and can refuse to provide you with services.

Creating a Cloud Governance Strategy

An effective cloud security strategy requires enforcement and accountability. This is where governance comes in. Basically, governance is about applying policies — the organizing principles and rules that determine how an organization should behave — relating to using services. In the cloud world, governance helps to define how multiple organizations behave, because multiple parties across different companies will be part of the governance plan.

IT governance is really a combination of policy, process, and controls. The role of IT governance is to implement, maintain, and continuously improve these controls. IT governance does the following:

>> Ensures that IT assets (systems, processes, and so on) are implemented and used according to agreed-upon policies and procedures

>> Ensures that these assets are properly controlled and maintained

>> Ensures that these assets are providing value to the organization

IT governance, therefore, has to include the techniques and policies that measure and control how systems are managed. However, IT doesn't stand alone in the governance process. In order for governance to be effective, it must be holistic. It's as much about organizational issues and how people work together to achieve business goals as it is about technology. A critical part of governance is establishing organizational relationships between business and IT, as well as defining how people will work together across organizational boundaries. So, the best kind of governance occurs when IT and the business are working together.

Understanding governance risks

Each industry has a set of governance principles based on its regulatory and competitive environment and its view of risk. There are different levels of risk. For example, in certain companies, information cannot be shared across international boundaries. In financial services, certain data practices need to be followed. In software development, there are risks associated with getting the product on the market on time. In the healthcare industry, there are patient privacy concerns.

Although a business's CIO may work with the business to put together a certain set of rules to manage risks, everyone in the business must understand the risks. To make our point, suppose you have a corporate policy stating that no data from a credit card system can be used by the company's marketing analysis systems. Now, suppose that the CIO discovers that the marketing analysis system used this information. In this case, the business is put at risk, and IT governance fails. Clearly, not only the CIO needed to know the rules set in place to manage risks.

Here is a list of risks to consider as you move into a hybrid model:

>> **Audit and compliance:** Include issues around data jurisdiction, data access control, and maintaining an audit trail.

>> **Security:** Include data integrity and data confidentiality and privacy.

>> **Performance and availability:** Include the level of availability and performance your business requires to successfully operate — for example, alerts, notifications, and provider business continuity plans. In addition, does the provider have forensic information, in case something does go wrong?

>> **Interoperability:** Associated with developing a service that might be composed of multiple services. Are you assured that the infrastructure will continue to support your service? What if one of the services you're using changes? What policies are in place to ensure that you will be notified of a change?

>> **Contract:** Associated with not reading between the lines of your contract. For example, who owns your data in the cloud? If the service goes down, how will you be compensated? What happens if the provider goes out of business?

>> **Billing:** Associated with ensuring that you're billed correctly and only for the resources you consume.

>> **Other:** Include protection of intellectual property.

Implementing a governance strategy

How does governance typically work? IT governance usually involves establishing a board made up of business and IT representatives. The board creates rules and processes that the organization must follow to ensure that policies are being met. These rules and processes might include the following:

>> Understanding business issues such as regulatory requirements or funding

>> Establishing best practices and monitoring these processes

>> Assigning responsibility for things such as programming standards, proper design, review, certifications, and monitoring applications

When you move into a hybrid cloud environment, you want your governance board to deal with issues related to how your computer resources are handled on your premises, as well as deal with your cloud provider. Cloud governance is a shared responsibility between the user of cloud services and the cloud provider. Understanding the boundaries of responsibility and defining an appropriate governance strategy within your organization require careful balance.

A successful governance strategy in a hybrid environment requires a negotiated agreement between you and your cloud provider(s). Generally, several goals are involved in cloud governance, including risk and monitoring performance.

Your governance strategy needs to be supported in two ways:

>> **Understanding the compliance and risk measures the business must follow:** What does your business require to meet IT, corporate, industry, and government requirements? For example, can your business share data across international borders? These requirements must be supported through technical controls, automation, and strict governance of processes, data, and workflows.

>> **Understanding the performance goals of the business:** Perhaps you measure your business performance in terms of sales revenue, profitability, stock price, quality of product or service provided, and timely delivery. Your cloud provider needs to be able to support these goals and help you optimize your business performance.

Making governance work

We believe that effective management of the cloud will be part people and processes and part technology. It's really a three-part solution:

>> Your organization needs to set up a governance body to deal with cloud issues and to put processes in place to work with the business around enforcement (this body can be your existing governance board, if you like). This board will have oversight responsibilities and will collaborate with the business (it should include business members). It can also develop best practices.

>> Your organization needs to have governance bodies in the cloud that deal with standardization of services and other shared infrastructure issues. You need some sort of interface to this group. Your level of involvement depends on your level of involvement in the cloud.

>> Your organization also needs to have technology in the mix that helps your organization automatically monitor what happens in the cloud.

Measuring and monitoring governance performance

You can measure business performance by comparing production, sales, revenue, stock price, and customer satisfaction with your goals. Likewise you can measure IT performance by comparing server, application, and network uptime; service resolution time; budgets; and project completion dates with your goals. However, measuring the success of a governance program is much more difficult. At the end of the day, the rules that you put in place should help provide guardrails so that teams do not get in trouble, while also giving teams the flexibility to innovate.

Of course, your own internal governance committee needs to answer the following types of questions to get started:

>> How can a governance strategy help to support the business? Can you create a policy that keeps your organization safe while also giving teams flexibility?

>> What should management measure and monitor to ensure successful IT governance?

>> Are internal and external users of IT resources getting their questions resolved quickly?

>> Is customer data safe from unauthorized access? What persons within your organization can view customer data? Can employees do their jobs effectively while also seeing less specific customer data?

>> Can you demonstrate to business management that your organization can recover from anticipated outages without damaging customer loyalty? What will happen in a worst-case scenario if your business or a partner's systems are breached? Do you have a rapid response plan to handle security incidents?

>> Are you able to monitor systems proactively so that you can make repairs before faulty services affect rules and regulations?

>> Can you justify your IT investments to business management? As your investments in governance, privacy, and security increase, do you need to think about new ways to justify the costs?

These questions need to be answered whether or not you're using a cloud.

Chapter **16**

Breaking Down Cloud Economics

One of the most confusing issues that a business faces when moving to cloud services is understanding and planning for the costs and the economic impact on the business. It is not surprising.

First, costs can change dramatically when a business begins to use a cloud service for a limited set of functions, such as testing, creating an application, or storing data in a cloud service. These initial costs can be quite reasonable and often dramatically less expensive than using data center services. However, management is often taken by surprise when the use of cloud services expands dramatically. There may be a logical reason for the costs of the cloud services.

Balancing Costs with Requirements

It is imperative that you be able to understand the costs and benefits of leveraging different models of computing. When you begin your thought process around the economic impact of the cloud, you realize that there are no simple answers. You have to consider a variety of issues that impacts your decision-making process. The costs of running an application, such as ERP, is more complicated to calculate than looking at just how much you pay for the software and the expense of employing the required staff to run the application. You must also consider issues such as cooling, floor space, and capital expenses versus operating expenses — the list goes on. The reality is that organizations — from small and mid-size to the largest global enterprises — are moving toward cloud environments to increase flexibility and cost efficiencies. Correctly balancing the use of different public and private cloud services is critical to creating long-term longevity to support your business goals. The hybrid cloud allows an organization to leverage a variety of computing models based on current and future needs of the business in order to support changing customer requirements.

Striking the Right Balance of Environments for a Hybrid Cloud

Operational performance, security, economics, and flexibility all have a great impact on an organization's cloud strategy. Striking the right balance among public cloud services, private cloud, and the data center requires a pragmatic planning process. Planning must take into account the needs of a variety of business units as well as an understanding of the future business strategy. Finding the right combination of environments is critical for your organization to achieve the best value when creating a hybrid cloud strategy. Consider the following:

>> Public clouds offer amazing capabilities for scalability and a variety of third-party tools and applications. However, just because you are using a third-party service does not mean that you are off the hook for security, governance and compliance. Therefore, you want to make sure that you have the right services to protect your assets and ensure that you are placing data in the appropriate location.

>> You can't leave the selection of your cloud services to chance or whim. Rather you need to establish a set of guidelines that applies to central IT as well as business units. For example, what is your policy on the type of data that you can store on a variety of public clouds? Which data needs to be behind your firewall? Which data needs to remain in the country of origin? Are there data sources that you need to have near immediate access for analytics? Don't assume that everyone will agree with your plan without a well executed communications plan.

>> You have strategic line of business applications that run in your data center and you have a mandate to move to the cloud. This can offer you potential

cost savings and agility. However, you need to do your homework. For example, it is far more expensive to move an aging monolithic application to the public cloud. So, before you start a migration, do your homework so that you understand your own applications that are critical to the day-to-day operations of your business. Have a well thought out plan.

>> Your organization may become too reliant on a single vendor. While this may give you clout and economies of scale, it may also leave you at risk. Sudden pricing increases may impact your budget. Also, if that vendor has a sudden outage, you have no recourse. Many organization are selecting several public clouds in order to reduce financial as well as technical risks.

THE ECONOMICS OF THE ONLINE GAMING MARKET

Consider an example of one of the players in the exploding market for online games. Our hypothetical vendor hit the market with the right online games that suddenly took the market by storm. The company had to move fast in order to meet the heavy demand for its compute resources if it hoped to maintain its market lead. The tipping point came when the company's newest online game went from zero users to 10 million in six weeks and then to 25 million in five months. It was abundantly clear that the company's on-premises infrastructure could not hope to keep up with demand for compute, storage, and networking bandwidth.

Judging by the experience of some of its weaker competitors, management understood that it had to move fast. Therefore, the company selected a popular public cloud service that would automatically scale during peak usage hours. After the first year of successfully using the public cloud, the company began to recognize that costs would rise at unacceptable rates. It decided not to abandon the public cloud but to create its own private cloud to manage data and to handle compute intensive requirements. This hybrid environment helped the company balance the need for instant scaling from its public cloud provider combined with private cloud that was efficient in managing unique mobile social gaming workloads.

At the same time, as the company became powerful, it was able to create an ecosystem of independent software vendors that created new games and support services based on its gaming platform. This brought additional revenue and customer growth. Over time, the company has added new internal capabilities as well as using a variety of public cloud services that ensure consistent and predictable growth.

>> As your business strategy evolves, you may decide to become a service provider to your own customers. In this case, you need to review the costs of exclusively using a single public cloud to deliver services to customers. What are you able to charge your customers for your services? Do you have a robust internal IT organization that can transform itself into a commercially viable service provider? What are the risks of either using a public cloud provider or creating your own internal cloud? There isn't one right answer. You need to weigh all the factors and come to a well considered decision.

Computing is not a simple environment. It is dynamic and rapidly changing as new technologies become available and as standards emerge that transform how vendors offer their services. Costs can change in the blink of an eye. A new service emerges that will cause you to rethink your execution plan. Therefore, it isn't enough to simply set a strategy and plan in motion and execute blindly. You need to be ready to reevaluate your plan often as the market for cloud computing market matures.

Reaping the Economic Benefit of the Cloud

An organization typically has many different types of workloads to manage in its data center, and some of these workloads will be a better fit than others for a cloud environment. Therefore, to optimize your economic benefit from the cloud, you must first have a good understanding of your workload requirements.

Commodity workloads, such as everyday email, collaboration, and messaging applications, are straightforward and well-defined business processes executed over and over again. The economic benefit for workloads with these characteristics comes from leveraging cloud capabilities such as standardization, optimization, and scalability. A commodity workload such as email, analytics, and cloud native applications are a good fit for the cloud.

A customer-facing financial application in the heavily regulated financial industry may be better suited for a private cloud environment. While there may be a well designed SaaS application that can handle the task quite well, there may be cultural and governance reasons that a business will chose a private cloud. Therefore, any potential economic benefit from the public cloud is outweighed by security and compliance issues. An organization may have specialized workloads that are used occasionally by a select group of users. These specialized workloads may have run effectively for many years in the internal data center, so there may be no economic benefit in moving them to the cloud.

After you evaluate your mix of workloads, however, you will find many situations where the standardization, flexibility, and scalability of the cloud can deliver outstanding economic benefit.

A move to the cloud is likely to deliver an economic benefit if you need

» **Increased capacity:** Your organization is ramping up for a new but short-term initiative, and you temporarily need some extra CPU capacity and extra storage.

» **A Software as a Service (SaaS) solution:** As your company has grown and diversified, everyone on your distributed sales force seems to be running a different version of your internal sales automation tool. You have recently lost out on some big deals based on discrepancies in customer and prospect data across different sales teams. You decide that implementing a SaaS solution to run your sales automation will ensure that all members of the sales team have consistent and accurate information when they need it. (See Chapter 9 for more on SaaS.)

» **Scaled application service:** Running your email system requires more and more servers and lots of system administration time spent on maintenance and upgrades. You decide that a massively scaled application service in the cloud will deliver the performance you require and allow you to move the skilled administration team to focus on other projects.

The next few sections look these scenarios from an economic perspective.

Filling the need for capacity

Some pragmatic workloads fit perfectly into the Infrastructure as a Service (IaaS) model. These include basic computing services to support unexpected workloads or test and development requirements.

Considering IaaS for workloads that are outside the normal day-to-day operations makes sense for these reasons:

» Building out a full infrastructure for these unpredictable requirements isn't economical. An organization would have to purchase much more capacity than is otherwise required. Given that these resources would be dramatically underutilized, this approach doesn't make fiscal sense.

» Being able to procure a resource when it's needed streamlines planning and allows for much faster go-to market models. The IT staff can be more conservative in projecting requirements knowing that if needs expand, it will be able to respond to those changing needs in real time.

So an IaaS model is an economic choice because organizations can access what they need right away, without having to buy new hardware or go through the long process of manual provisioning. In practical terms, this means you must consider the following:

>> **Software:** Building new software is both a cumbersome and a long-lived process. Typically, developers need to acquire servers and specialized development software. Although this is a necessary process, it doesn't add to the bottom line of revenue. It can be time-consuming and expensive to evaluate new software. If that software is available as a service, an organization is more likely to try innovative software because it can quickly evaluate it. In addition, new approaches to continuous integration and continuous deployment (IC/CD) models (see Chapter 11) require the flexibility and economic model of the cloud.

>> **Cloud-native application services:** Increasingly, developers are using next generation DevOps tools within a PaaS environment to create cloud native applications. These are highly modular and containerized services with well defined APIs. This means that the services can be moved across different public and private clouds based on circumstances. With this architecture, a business can operate certain workloads in the public cloud and others in the private cloud or data center.

>> **Expanding need for storage:** As organizations expand the amount of data they need to store and manage, it's logical to use inexpensive cloud storage services. Considering the scalability of cloud storage services, it makes sense businesses often save considerable costs. However, in some situations, a business's storage needs are so expansive that an internal cloud storage environment may be more economical.

>> **System testing:** Similar to software evaluation, resources are required for a relatively short time when testing a system. Despite this, testers typically want to own their own resources, which isn't cost-effective because they will sit idle most of the time. In addition, if someone is testing a fast-growing workload, he has to spend much more money to achieve the same thing than he could via a service for a fraction of the cost. Testing as a service also means that the IT organization can test for situations that cannot be easily replicated within the data center.

>> **Seasonal or peak loading:** Some companies are already using IaaS for cloud-bursting when there are unexpected or planned high-load periods. The flexibility of using IaaS means that the company doesn't have to overinvest in hardware. These companies must be able to adapt to higher loads to protect themselves.

Selecting a SaaS for common applications

Not all SaaS applications are the same in terms of costs to the organization. If the application is fairly independent of the overall applications and information environment of the company, SaaS is an economical way to quickly implement core services. Also, because many SaaS vendors make their application programming interfaces (APIs) available to other vendors and customers, they are able to work in conjunction with third-party SaaS offerings or on-premises offerings. Moreover, SaaS has enormous benefits for organizations that don't want to support their own hardware and support environment. However, depending on the number of users using the SaaS application, costs may skyrocket. Therefore, it is important to analyze the costs of the SaaS application before signing an agreement.

WARNING

Make sure that you understanding the pricing model of the SaaS vendor. Is it charging for each user per month? Does it offer volume discounts? Does the vendor have a free version of the product so you can test whether the SaaS application will be useful before buying? There will be vendors that create pricing models that are not obvious at the outset. You need to do your homework to make sure you can anticipate future costs.

Reducing your hardware requirements may seem like an obvious benefit, but you may not have considered the additional economic benefit that accrues based on reductions in support and maintenance after you cut back on infrastructure. For example, when you implement a SaaS application, you shift the responsibility of managing new versions and updates to the SaaS provider. You can realize many economic benefits as a result of this shift:

>> You can cut back on IT staff or reposition members of the team to other projects.

>> End-user productivity improves with a SaaS model that is consistent with more frequent application and seamless upgrades.

>> Improved data accuracy is based on the consistency and improved automation and availability of the SaaS solution.

However, one of the economic implications of SaaS is that they can create even more silos of applications and data in the IT organization. It is, therefore, important to evaluate the SaaS approach and choices based on how well Software as a Service needs to be integrated with other applications — both in the cloud and in the data center. A SaaS application can easily lead to even more costs if the IT organization has to go back and rearchitect the integration between various on-premises and cloud applications.

OpEx VERSUS CapEx

When the value of cloud solutions are discussed, the conversation often revolves around these ideas of CapEx versus OpEx:

- **Capital expenditures (CapEX):** These are investments made by a company to acquire or significantly upgrade assets. These assets could be vehicles, real estate, equipment, software licenses, networking equipment, or servers. Companies either lay out the money up front or pay over time (a capital lease) for the ability to out-right own the resource. The company can then depreciate the value of the asset over time.

- **Operating expenses (OpEx):** These are funds that must be paid for the ongoing operation of a business. Examples include wages, repairs, utilities, and supplies, as well as cloud services like Infrastructure as a Service, Platform as a Service, and Software as a Service.

OpEx versus CapEx is important because companies are limited in the amount of capital expenses they can make. Organizations often try to avoid sinking capital into resources that do not produce income. This is the reason why many companies choose to lease rather than purchase office space and why many utility companies elect to lease their trucks and other vehicles. They do so primarily for two reasons. First, a company can redirect CapEx to other projects that might be more lucrative; second, companies gain greater agility — a company can easily cut its losses if a project is not successful or can quickly ramp up if it gains traction.

The CapEx versus OpEx discussion often leads to the CapEx person arguing that over a period of three years (the time to depreciate servers) a server costs less than a cloud virtual machine (VM). Of course, you must take into account the fact that you might not be running your VM 24 hours a day, 365 days a year; the physical server has associated costs for maintenance, administrators, power, and so on. The cloud VM has additional costs like storage and bandwidth. However, even if there is a premium for the cloud VM, utilizing cloud services likely still makes business sense because that choice frees up capital for other projects like research and development or marketing and the increase in flexibility and agility.

Selecting a massively scaled application

Some of the earliest cloud adopters are large companies that wanted to take a massively scaled application (such as email) and put it into a cloud. Companies are finding that approach to be a more cost-effective approach. In essence, this is the type of cloud application where the economics can't be matched by the data center. When applications support this type of massively scaled infrastructure, the cloud will often win out. Because massively scaled applications such as email and social media are relatively simple, a vendor can easily standardize and optimize a platform, making it cost-effective to support vast numbers of users at a low cost. By taking advantage of the economies of scale in cloud environments, a massively scaled application is a win-win in the cloud.

When it's not black and white

Not all situations are clear-cut. Accurately forecasting the economics of the cloud can be complicated. The problem for many organizations is that they don't have an accurate picture of data center costs that allows them to consider cloud propositions on an apples-to-apples basis. For example, because companies pay per user per month for a typical SaaS application, the costs over time may appear to be greater than the costs of owning an application outright. The same argument could be made about IaaS services where the customer pays for a unit of work by volume or time. However, it's important to consider the flexibility and agility of the organization to change based on the needs of customers and partners. Some companies are willing to increase their operating costs in exchange for reducing their capital expenses because it gives them long-term flexibility.

THE EMERGENCE OF ON-PREMISES PUBLIC CLOUDS

A new model of computing is taking shape. This model offers customers the same infrastructure and capabilities of the public cloud but located within a data center.

AWS Outpost is an early example of this emerging model. With Outpost, you lease a rack of servers from Amazon that include the same hardware and software technology as the AWS public cloud but lives within your data center. All services are controlled and managed by Amazon. You don't purchase the hardware or software. The Outpost service connects directly to the AWS public cloud.

This becomes yet another economic model that customers that want hybrid computing will consider. It is early in the development of this model so you'll have to spend time gaining an understanding of the short- and long-term costs of this model.

There are other situations where an application designed for an earlier era is not well suited for the cloud. These applications often have dependencies to other applications in the data center. The applications are not optimized since they were built in an era where code had to be designed for a specific hardware and networking environment. If that application is simply moved to the cloud it will require an enormous amount of compute, storage, and networking resources just to operate. Only when the application is modernized does it make sense to move it to the cloud.

Understanding the Economics of the Data Center

It's hard for most organizations to accurately predict the actual costs of running any given application in the data center. A particular server may be used to support several different applications. For example, how do you accurately judge how many personnel resources are dedicated to a single application? Although there may be a particular month when your staff is updating one application, those same staff members may be troubleshooting a different application in another month. In some organizations, there may have been attempts to tie computing costs to specific departments, but if so, the model is likely to have been very rough.

Consider, as a simple example, the use of email. Some departments are very heavy users, whereas others barely touch it at all. Pockets within a single department may be heavy users. Although technically you can monitor individual use, doing so would require more overhead than it's worth. In addition, overhead costs associated with supporting customers when they forget their password or accidently delete an important message can surpass expectations and add to the overall costs of running an application such as email.

Latency is a key consideration when considering the cost and benefit of computing services. There may be some surprising instances where using a cloud service might cause problems. Take the example of a business that requires its employees to take qualifying exams every month. The online service is well designed and able to execute on the testing. However, there are often peak periods when too many people in too many companies are all doing the testing at the same time. The vendor may not have architected its cloud service to handle the load. This could result in slow performance or outages. Not all cloud vendors have a well designed architecture that can handle the requirements of its customers. The bottom line is that you need to evaluate your vendors based on your own needs today and in the future.

To prepare for your evaluation of on-premises data center costs, you need to look at the costs that are directly and indirectly related to the application or type of workload you want to move to the cloud (public or private). Some of these indirect costs are hard to evaluate, making it difficult to accurately predict the actual costs of running any given application in your company. Here is a fairly comprehensive list of the possible costs, with notes:

» **Server costs:** With this and all other hardware components, you're specifically interested in the total annual cost of ownership, which normally consists of the cost of hardware support plus some amortization cost for the purchase of the hardware. Additionally, a particular server may be used to support several different workloads.

» **Storage costs:** What are the management and support costs for the storage hardware required for the data associated with this application? Storage costs may be very high for certain types of applications, such as email.

» **Network costs:** When a web application you host internally, such as email or collaboration, is moved to the cloud, the strain on your network may be reduced. However, keep in mind that ensuring that users in your company have on-demand access from anywhere to cloud services requires substantial bandwidth. Consider how the cloud vendor will charge for use of networking services. When you move data or workloads in and out of the cloud how does the vendor charge for that service?

» **Backup and archive costs:** The actual savings on backup costs depend on what the backup strategy will be when the workload moves into the cloud. The same is true of archiving. Say that you're thinking of moving some workloads to the public cloud. Will all backup be done in that cloud? Will your organization still be required to back up a percentage of critical data? There are many different options for storing data in the cloud. (For more on cloud storage, you should flip to Chapter 13.)

» **Business continuity and disaster recovery costs:** In theory, the cloud service will have its own disaster recovery capabilities, so there may be a consequential savings on disaster recovery. However, you need to clearly understand what your cloud provider's disaster recovery capability is. Not all cloud providers have the same definition of disaster recovery. IT management must determine the level of support the cloud provider will offer. This can be an added cost from the provider, or you might seek out a secondary vendor to handle disaster recovery and procedures. Many organizations have redundancy and diversity built into their cloud strategies to mitigate business continuity concerns.

>> **Data center infrastructure costs:** A whole series of costs — including electricity, floor space, cooling, building maintenance, and so on — go into the data center. Because of the large investment in data centers, moving workloads to a public cloud may not be financially viable if you're only utilizing 40 percent of the data center's compute power. (Of course, you can deploy a private cloud to take advantage of the underutilized space and the advantages of the cloud.)

However, if your data center is 80 percent full and has been expanding at 10 percent a year, you'll soon need a new data center. At that point, you may have to build a costly data center. The cloud will be a much more economical choice in order to divert workloads away from the data center.

>> **Software maintenance costs:** What's the annual maintenance cost for the software you may move to a cloud-based service? Although the answer to this question may seem simple, things can easily get complicated if a specific software license is part of a bundled deal or if an application is integrated with other applications in your environment.

>> **Operational support personnel costs:** A whole set of day-to-day operational costs is associated with running any application. Some costs are general ones that apply to every application, including staff support for everything from storage and archiving, to patch management and networks, to troubleshooting and security. Some support tasks, however, may be particular to a given application, such as database tuning and performance management. Costs may be offset by emerging cloud management and automation tools.

>> **Infrastructure software costs:** A whole set of infrastructure management software is in use in any installation, and it has an associated cost. For example, management software is typically used for many different applications and can't easily be divided across specific applications.

Evaluating Costs in the Hybrid Environment

In order to make a smart economic choice about running workloads in your internal data center versus implementing a public or private cloud, you need to understand some of the subtleties of the cost factors. You also need to consider potential hidden costs associated with the cloud and, in particular, a hybrid cloud. There's always a cost to change, including the following:

>> **Management:** Management of a hybrid environment brings additional challenges. You no longer need to simply manage the data center, or even

one cloud, but instead multiple environments — on-premises, in your private cloud, and on one, if not multiple, public clouds. People, processes, and software can help with management, but they each have their own costs involved. See Chapter 4 for more details on multicloud management.

» **Data transfer:** When you transfer data, say from your premises to an application in a public cloud, costs are involved. This includes the fee to initially move your data to the cloud. These costs can quickly mount if you have large amounts of data requiring lots of bandwidth. Furthermore, depending on your cloud vendor, you can incur networking fees when moving data between different VMs within the same cloud (for instance, during backup or replication).

» **Customization:** If you're migrating an application to the public cloud that was on-premises, there may be costs associated with customizing the application so that it can now work in the hybrid environment. Most likely, some configuration work and testing will be done first. In addition, that application may not be well designed for the highly distributed nature of the cloud environment in its current form, and it may need to be rewritten.

» **Integration:** In a hybrid model, you will probably want to integrate various applications. For example, your off-premises CRM application might integrate with your on-premises business intelligence application. Sure, you might have to integrate them if they were both on-premises, but it will probably take you more time to figure it out in a hybrid model.

» **Storage:** As you move data and workloads to a hybrid cloud, you will really have to balance and think about your long-term storage costs.

» **Compliance:** Compliance (external or internal) can be an increased cost when using the cloud. It may be necessary to have the cloud service audited to see that it meets the appropriate requirements, which may relate to IT security or recovery procedures or any other such IT activity that must obey compliance standards. This is in addition to your existing on-premises audits. Compliance requirements might come from several sources:

- Vendors and partners: An example would be credit card companies requiring companies who accept credit cards to comply with the Payment Card Industry Data Security Standard (PCI DSS).

- Customers: Customers may require that you produce an SSAE 16 or similar report to evidence various compliance requirements.

- Governmental bodies: Your organization may need to comply with local, national, or international compliance standards. These include Health Insurance Portability and Accountability Act (HIPAA), and Sarbanes–Oxley (SOX), along with dozens of others.

- Internal compliance: You may have compliance requirements that your organization has established. These may be even more specific than externally required compliance.

- Server: If an application is relatively small, running in a virtual server, or perhaps only running occasionally, it's unlikely that moving it to the public cloud will result in any server hardware savings.

>> **Storage:** Similarly, if very little storage is consumed by the application, there may be no reduction in SAN costs.

>> **Data center infrastructure:** The floor space in the data center will not be reduced by the removal of a few servers, and it may make little difference to cooling costs. The change usually needs to be significant in order to bring down these costs.

>> **Operational support personnel:** Savings occur here only if there's a possibility of saving the cost of a staff person or delaying the recruitment of another person.

>> **Infrastructure software:** Infrastructure management software costs may not come down with the movement of a few workloads into the cloud.

CALCULATING COSTS: CLOUD BROKERING

Cloud pricing changes constantly which makes it difficult for a business to be able to do the type of financial planning that management requires.

- **Estimating charges:** Some vendors provide monthly calculators for their web services. For example, a calculator might ask you a series of questions about the number of compute instances, storage needs, data transfer, load balancing, and IPs needed, and then provide you with a monthly estimate. Of course, your monthly usage and, therefore, the charges, may vary from the estimates that the calculator provides.

- **Calculating total cost of ownership (TCO):** Other vendors offer TCO calculators. These calculators might ask you a series of questions about the type of deployment, the number of servers, storage requirements, and load volatility (for example, the kind of demand you have). Then the calculators will estimate how much you might be able to save versus a data center deployment over five years. These calculators look at such factors as server utilization; facility, power, and hardware costs; the cost of downtime, reduction in deployment, and provisioning time; and cloud administrative costs.

Warning: Of course, you should not base your decision to move to the cloud simply on these calculators. Some of these calculators are marketing tools, at best. However, they can help you wrap your head around some of the costs associated with the factors inherent in the move to the cloud.

From a policy perspective, companies shouldn't simply take an action because it seems cheaper. You need to have a policy on what must stay in the traditional data center or in a private cloud and why (for example, privacy and complexity and singularity of the workload). You should have a policy that states that automation and self-provisioning will support the business and enable it to react quickly to opportunities. There also needs to be a policy that specifies when a workload can safely be moved to a public cloud — and whether the data is safe enough in the private cloud. All these questions are part of the larger economic decision-making process.

Chapter **17**

Planning Your Cloud Strategy

Planning your hybrid strategy is a journey, not a simple set of steps. The right planning strategy is imperative to getting your plan to be operational. So, you need to look at the technical components, the business strategy, and the organizational plan. You have to focus on bringing all constituents to have a common understanding of how the cloud provides an opportunity for success. Remember that cloud computing can offer a dramatic change in the pace and style of computing as well as business strategy. Therefore, although costs will, of course, be imperative, you also need to think about the benefits that may help transform the customer experience. Your overall strategy will include a hybrid of different types and models of computing, so planning will be integral to your path forward.

In this chapter, we give you an idea about what to expect as you begin your journey, along with the important issues you need to consider.

At the Beginning: The Move to the Cloud

In the initial decade of cloud computing, very few businesses had a strategy. Primarily, departmental developers tired of having to wait for IT to provide them with the resources they needed to get the job done turned to public cloud services. These capabilities were inexpensive, elastic, and based on a self-service model. This approach to computing caught on across organizations across the globe. While this ad hoc approach to using the public cloud was pragmatic, it began to cause problems.

Because no planning occurred, financial managers began to see the cost of computing skyrocket. While an individual developer wasn't paying much to build an application in the cloud, when all those bills were aggregated together, the costs began to spiral out of control. In addition, there was little control over security and governance. Business units began to use SaaS applications at an ever increasing pace.

IT initially ignored the cloud and assumed that its use would not last. Managers viewed the use of this third-party service as a threat to the role of IT in the business. In addition, many business leaders were concerned that security in the public cloud was flawed and would put the business at risk. Some managers tried to sabotage the acceptability of cloud services. This approach was typical of any new technology that threatened to change the status quo.

What changed? In simple terms, the pace of business. Well established businesses began to notice the emergence of a new generation of companies that relied on the cloud and would therefore create new business models without having to requiring the lead time to create a new physical infrastructure. In many competitive markets, there was only one option: Move to the cloud.

Starting the Plan

Many companies have either begun their move to the cloud or in the planning stages. It can be overwhelming to come up with a strategy that enables the organization to select the right services, the clouds that are best suited for the workloads, and create an environment where change is the norm.

WARNING

It is not easy to determine what to do first. Do you pick a single product and select a cloud platform? Do you get rid of your data center and move all of your existing services to a public or private cloud? Do you select a single public cloud vendor to support all of your workloads? Do you hire a staff of experienced IT professionals to build a private cloud, or do you hire a consulting firm to make all the decisions for you?

REMEMBER

There isn't simply one option that will handle all of your business situations and all of your workloads. Therefore, there best approach is to come up with a staged plan that will help you achieve your business and technical objectives.

An overall cloud computing strategy is like any other business strategy; it must be planned within the context of your business goals and objectives. So, before you begin your journey to the cloud, we suggest that you take the five steps, outlined as stages, described in the following sections.

Stage 1: Assess your current IT strategy

Your first step is to assess the current state of your IT strategy and how well it serves the business. IT organizations have typically grown in a relatively unplanned fashion. Although they likely began as well-orchestrated sets of hardware and software, over time they have grown into a collection of various computing silos.

You might think of them as being like a typical two-car garage. In the beginning, the garage held two cars and a few necessities such as yard tools. Over the years, the homeowner began to store lots of different paraphernalia in the garage, ranging from unused pots and pans to an array of old furniture. Suddenly, that well-planned, purpose-built space became crammed with so much stuff that it's hard to use the garage for its initial intent — storing cars!

Today, is your IT infrastructure like that garage, or is it a well-planned and well-orchestrated environment? Does it provide the type of flexibility and manageability that supports new initiatives and business change? Or is it an assortment of different servers, different software products, and a variety of disconnected tools? Do you have many different departments that are taking advantage of a variety of public cloud services from different vendors? Do you already use third-party cloud services for specialized needs? Most likely your business has a combination of all of these environments.

Your first step is taking an honest assessment of where you are today. What is working well and what is holding you back? You can't undertake this process in isolation; you need to create a task force that brings together business and IT leaders along with those who will develop and deploy services across the business.

You should look at what systems are critical to the operations of the business and which applications no longer support changing business needs. You need to consider the flexibility of your existing infrastructure. What happens when the business requires a change in processes? How does the IT organization support partnership initiatives? Take a look at the cloud services including SaaS applications as well as cloud applications built in different divisions. In addition, you need to assess the data that is critical to managing your business. Where does the data reside? Is it tied to a specific application? Do you store your data across various parts of the environment? Does some of your data reside in public or private clouds? You need to understand your data and the process that you use today to control that data.

Stage 2: Imagine the future

Once you understand what you have today and how effective your IT environment is in executing your strategy, it is time to look into the future. What will your business look like in six months and in three years? Who were your competitors two years ago and who are your competitors now? Do you anticipate that your industry is changing dramatically that will impact your ability to compete and collaborate? Are there technological approaches that your emerging competitors are starting to implement that you will have to embrace? Are there opportunities to offer new business strategies that are driven by emerging technologies? It may be that your industry is changing, and without new technology approaches you will not be able to sustain a competitive advantage.

This process, which is imperative to planning for a hybrid and multicloud strategy. You will most likely have workloads that live in your data center or in the private cloud. You will need to prepare for your hybrid cloud strategy so that you are ready for the unanticipated changes in your business. Through the planning process, both the business and IT organization will have a deeper understanding of both the changes to the business and the technologies that will help manage that change in a predictable manner. This process of imaging the future and tying that future to innovative technologies isn't a one-time effort. Rather you should assume that you will continue to update your plan as new competitors enter your market and as new innovative technologies emerge.

Stage 3: Explore what's out there

Armed with the knowledge of the current state of your business and the supporting IT infrastructure and where it is headed, now is the time to learn and experiment with cloud computing options. Although plenty of organizations will be happy to do all the work for you, it's important that you spend the time understanding the landscape of best practices, as well as different cloud computing options that can help the business.

Spend time with your peers and see what type of cloud strategy they have adopted and the type of dividends it's paying. What are the best practices that have worked well for companies in your industry or of your size? What are the new innovations coming to market from young companies? How can you offer a new approach to business that will allow you to effectively compete with much larger companies in your market?

TIP

The wonderful thing about cloud computing capabilities and offerings is that you are free to experiment. Almost every company in the cloud market offers free trials of its technology. There are many open-source offerings as well that will give you the opportunity to test out whether different options will serve your business now or in the long run. This education process is critical so that you know what questions to ask. Even if and when you turn to a service provider for help, you will be able to make better decisions about how you approach your cloud strategy.

Stage 4: Create a hybrid cloud strategy plan

At this stage, you're ready to start creating the actual plan. Again, this should be based on a joint effort between the business and IT. If your company has done planning for a different way to think about your technology services.

REMEMBER

You won't be building monolithic applications. Rather, you will be building microservices that will be building blocks to create new creative services that will keep you ahead of the competition.

While you are spending your time rethinking your business and imaging the future, don't lose sight of what you actually know about your industry and business. Take advantage of the strategic planning you have already done.

TIP

Always leverage the knowledge and expertise inside your company as a starting point. It's also a good idea to get your most strategic partners involved in the process. Your best partners, suppliers, and customers will help you better understand how they want to collaborate with you in the future. Use all this as the foundation for your hybrid cloud strategy. We use the term hybrid because more than likely you will not leverage a single deployment model for your workloads. You will have some public clouds, some private clouds, and a data center. Your strategy needs to take into account where you want to run your workloads.

Where you deploy your workloads will depend on issues related to latency, costs, and reliability. At the same time, you need to take into account your security, privacy, and governance policies that your company needs to adhere to. These issues need to become part of how you approach cloud computing in your company. For example, different industries have different regulations that you will have to conform to. Some countries have laws that restrict where and how customer information can be managed and stored. This must be considered for your hybrid cloud strategy.

Stage 5: Plan for implementation

Now you're ready for action. However, it's not practical to try to do everything at once. Most companies will need a staged implementation of a hybrid cloud strategy in which they deploy parts of the overall plan in phases. For example, the first phase might be to support all of the existing public cloud workloads by working in collaboration with business units so they have resources for management and security, for example. You will want to determine, for example, how many departments and individuals are using various cloud services so that you can negotiate better financial terms.

If your company is new to the cloud you may want to begin by selecting a few key projects that are well suited to the cloud. For example, select a SaaS application that is useful across various departments that has visibility. Begin experimenting with creating microservices and managing them within containers. You can also select a software development project that has a short deadline and build and deploy it in the public cloud.

Whatever you do, think of your hybrid cloud strategy as a multi-year effort that will include everything from a set of private cloud services to support emerging internal development and deployment needs to a way to leverage public services in conjunction with your data center.

Stages of Strategy Planning: An Overview

Consider the five stages of the overall cloud computing strategy, described in the preceding section. Think about the process in terms of the impact each stage will have on your business, as well as the value each stage will bring, as shown in Table 17-1.

You need to think holistically — not just about the most straightforward services such as infrastructure but also about data integration and integrity and cloud management issues. The way you stage these efforts will be directly tied to both the current state of IT and the business strategy for the next several years.

TABLE 17-1   **Evaluating the Impact and Value of the Strategy Planning Stages**

Stage	Rationale	Impact	Value
Assess IT's current state.	You need to understand your level of maturity.	You will better understand how much work is ahead.	You will set the stage for business and IT collaboration.
Map the future.	You need to understand where the business is headed.	You can be better prepared to map your cloud strategy to business change.	It will allow you to make strategy choices based on a different worldview.

Stage	Rationale	Impact	Value
Know your cloud computing options.	Understand the choices you have.	Without this knowledge, you will overlook emerging options.	You want to select both tried-and-true and brand-new technologies.
Create the plan.	A road map to plan over time.	This will help you stage your implementation based on business strategy.	You will be ready to execute in an organized way.
Plan for implementation.	Get ready for action.	A coordinated process of implementation and experimentation.	A dynamic approach to moving forward.

Focusing the Plan on Providing Services to Your Constituents

Once you have a concrete understanding of the technical and business considerations, it's time to put the strategy into a technical architectural plan. This technical plan must mirror the requirements and changes in the business strategy. It is helpful to think about what type of customers or consumers you are supporting. It is also important to understand where those services will come from. Your organization may provide some services directly while you will contract with commercial service providers for other services. And you also have to determine how you will create or select those providers who will create services. You need to plan for three different types of services, as we discuss in this section.

Cloud service consumer services

These are the services that touch your employees, your partners, and customers. Although there are sophisticated services underlying these services — for example, business process, SaaS applications, data services, and infrastructure services — they are hidden from the consumer. The consumer doesn't care where a service runs or what the infrastructure behind it may be. The consumer demands predictability.

Comprehensive cloud provider services

Cloud providers typically offer public cloud services to a range of constituents. In some cases, the services are designed to create a high level of service and security for corporations. Therefore, these companies will offer support for cloud applications ranging from PaaS, SaaS, as well as infrastructure services. They will also create their own service management platform and integration services. These service providers often offer a range of services depending on the level of service required by your company.

Cloud service creation services

Cloud creation services are offered by service provides as a way to create new, innovative business services from a variety of platforms and IP from your industry or company. These run-time services can be designed to create new innovative services that sit on top of a service delivery platform either from a cloud provider or within your private environment. It's common for these creation services to leverage both public and private offerings based on business strategy.

Supporting a Successful Customer Experience

Now that you have a road map for creating a strategy, take a step back and think about how a hybrid approach to cloud computing can transform the customer experience. Everything that you do with this new approach to linking IT and business through the cloud should focus on expanding opportunities. So, think about how you can expand the ability to innovate, satisfy customers, and optimize your environment to efficiently deliver those services. In this section, we focus on the elements that lead to an effective customer experience.

Supporting innovation

Most of the exciting innovations in industries come from creating change that transforms the customer experience. In the days before the Internet became the backbone of business services, companies might have innovated by simply calling customers more frequently or packaging products differently. But in the age where business is conducted online and where communities collaborate and online commerce are the norm, companies are discovering that they must use Internet-driven technologies to support innovation.

Cloud computing offers a much richer set of options to companies. For example, a retailer wanting to provide real-time access to images and videos of products anywhere in the world can select a different public cloud provider in each market it serves, thus reducing latency and improving the customer experience. Likewise, another company may combine these public services with the same type of services behind the firewall that ensures that intellectual property and highly secure data to be managed safely. Other companies are discovering for privacy reasons and cultural reasons, the private cloud is their preferred model. Now that the same standardized services are available both inside and outside the firewall, the private cloud is becoming another deployment model based on organizational preferences.

Defining the optimal customer experience

Although most companies will first think about the technology and business model options offered by cloud computing vendors, it's important to put the customer first. The greatest benefit of the hybrid cloud strategy is the way it helps to transform and optimize the customer experience. More and more companies are interacting with their customers online. Customers will judge your company by how well your entire cloud environment performs. Abundant statistics demonstrate that customers who have a poor online experience rarely come back for a second try. Therefore, a hybrid cloud implemented with a strong strategic foundation can help enhance the customer experience.

Optimizing for workloads

Thinking about the depth and breadth of cloud computing offerings can be overwhelming. There are different business models, different platforms, and many different types of services. But at the end of the day, one of the most important considerations is how you handle and manage workloads across your various computing environments. Remember, a workload is a unit of work that you execute to complete a task.

So, from a business-strategy perspective, think about every business activity being supported by a computing workload. Using this perspective helps you get a firmer handle on the right cloud service to support each problem. For example, if you're managing a workload that has stringent security requirements, a private cloud environment may be more appropriate. There are also some public clouds that will offer security warranties that you will be able to consider to support security requirements. On the other hand, a temporary workload such as extra storage capacity needed for a day or a month can be supported by a commodity public service. By focusing on the nature of workloads, you're in a better position to create a strategy that matches business requirements.

Supporting a Dynamic Life Cycle

As your cloud computing strategy emerges, you will begin to understand some important differences between the old way of operating and the cloud computing style. In traditional computing environments, it's assumed that different organizations inside and outside of IT will select numerous different tools and technologies to support any given IT initiative. IT then has to do a lot of the hard work of making sure all these disconnected components can communicate or connect to each other so that they act as though they were a single unified environment.

Accomplishing this task has never been easy, but the consequences of failures have become more extreme. For example, several different systems may depend on database configurations, and IT must make sure all of the correct changes are made across the IT operations. If someone forgets to make a change based on the implementation of a new version of a database or tool, the consequences can be serious. Systems can stop working, and customers can be seriously affected.

Abstracting Complexity in the Cloud

In the emerging world of cloud computing, platforms will be much more abstracted. The level of complexity will not be reduced, but the complexity will be managed at an infrastructure level rather than at a tool level. This means that there will be a central way to manage configurations and versions. There will be more centralization of core functions that are leveraged across hybrid environments. Fewer moving parts that are subject to human error will help transform IT into a smoother computing utility in a much more dynamic fashion. These changes will not happen overnight, but looking forward, IT must adopt goals and strategies that promote the automation of the complexity that leads to unintended consequences and errors.

Balancing Costs and Benefits

How you plan your hybrid cloud environment will be driven by economics. You, therefore, need to think in terms of the total costs and whether those expenditures will be worthwhile in the long run. Achieving this balance isn't simple. Many cloud services, including IaaS and SaaS, are offered based on a per-user, per-month, or per-year contract. Some other services are designed for occasional use. Balancing costs may require you to negotiate volume discounts with your providers. Emerging private cloud models are designed as appliances that are preconfigured with the same cloud services found in the public cloud. With the appliance model, the cloud vendor may provide all of the support and management needed behind your firewall. No simple formula will give you the most optimal way to define the total cost of ownership or whether a cloud service will accomplish your long-term goals.

Defining the purpose of your cloud services

Because of the economic impact, you have to look at cost-benefit issues though a different lens than in a traditional data center environment. You need to think about the purpose of each service you are considering and how it will affect the business. For example, a SaaS environment may be more expensive in yearly license fees, but save the company money in terms of hardware, software, maintenance, and support requirements. SaaS also may better support the internal needs of the business. Perhaps the SaaS environment means that your company can be more proactive in addressing customer or employee needs. This SaaS service could result in better internal productivity.

On the other hand, in other situations, a public cloud service won't make economic sense, such as when your company's actual business is a set of cloud services. In this situation, your company is, in reality, a cloud service provider. Therefore, bring these services in-house, because a well-architected cloud service model will provide the most economically viable solution to support the business. If big enough, the company might be able to use its buying power to purchase in a less expensive way than a third-party company could. Likewise, this company can be in a good position to support innovation and optimize the private cloud model so that it produces the right workloads in the right way.

In yet other situations, companies will find that splitting services between public and private is the most optimal financial approach. The company that needs extra storage capacity three times a year will be best served by leveraging a public storage service than by purchasing extra storage capacity.

The bottom line is that there is no one approach to determining total cost of ownership or your return on investment in a hybrid cloud environment. So, part of your planning process is to take into account the financial measures you'll need when moving to the hybrid cloud. What issues will most directly affect your ability to compete? What type of innovation is likely to be important for your long-term strategy for success? Simply looking at all expenses in the same way will not be the best method for determining your strategy. Establishing a set of guidelines for the economics of your cloud strategy will help your decision-making process.

Taking a holistic approach

When you are planning for your movement to a hybrid cloud environment, make sure that you aren't looking though only one lens. Instead, view the hybrid cloud from the perspective of flexibility and agility for your business needs. The hybrid cloud also needs to be understood from a technical implementation strategy so that plans can be put into action in a staged and well-thought-out fashion. Your success with the hybrid cloud will depend not just on how you can justify what you spend and what you save, but also how you affect the bottom line of the business.

6

The Part of Tens

Explore ten cloud resources.

Discover ten cloud do's and don'ts.

Chapter **18**

Ten Cloud Resources

You can find many resources that will help you find out more about cloud computing. There are standards organizations that enjoy wide participation from the most important companies in the cloud market. There are organizations benefiting from the participation of companies on the leading edge of implementing hybrid cloud services within their companies and that are eager to help guide your way. In addition, you can find open-source offerings that are helpful in moving the market forward. Of course, all the vendors in the market have research, papers, and best practices that they're happy to share. In this chapter, we offer you some practical ideas on where to go for resources that can really help.

Standards Organizations

For cloud computing to meet requirements and stability of enterprises across industries, it needs standards. Luckily, a number of important organizations are working hard at bringing vendors together to help the process evolve. Here are two you should play attention to.

» **National Institute of Standards and Technology:** The National Institute of Standards and Technology (NIST) is a U.S. government agency that focuses on emerging standards efforts. This organization has done a considerable amount of work defining and providing good information on cloud computing. Check out its website at www.nist.gov/itl/cloud.

>> **OASIS:** OASIS, the Organization for the Advancement of Structured Information Standards, is a global consortium focused on the creation and adoption of standards for electronic business. The consortium is a nonprofit organization that relies on contributions from its member organizations. OASIS creates topic-specific committees that are beginning to focus on cloud computing. Check out its site at www.oasis-open.org.

Creating standards takes a lot of work — often volunteer, financially uncompensated work by dedicated people determined to get things right. People who sit on standards committees deserve the undying gratitude of the rest of us. We thank you, standards committee members.

Consortiums and Councils

There are important organizations that are not strictly standards bodies. These organizations work closely with vendors and standards groups to move requirements along.

>> **Cloud Standards Customer Council:** The Cloud Standards Customer Council (CSCC) is a combination of vendor and large corporate customers. It was established to focus on cloud best practices. Today, the organization includes more than 100 of the world's leading organizations, including Lockheed Martin, Citigroup, State Street, and North Carolina State University. It is operated by the Object Management Group (OMG). Check out its website at www.cloud-council.org.

>> **OMG Cloud Workin Group:** The OMG Cloud Working Group (CWG) takes over the mission of the CSCC, an OMG-managed program that launched in 2011 and published 28 deliverables over the course of its operation. It publishes vendor-neutral guidance on important considerations for cloud computing adoption, highlighting standards, opportunities for standardization, cloud customer requirements, and best practices to foster an ecosystem of open, standards-based cloud computing technologies.

CWG will maintain and update these papers. For more information, watch the webinar, Introducing the OMG Cloud Working Group.

>> **The Open Group:** The Open Group is a global consortium that enables the achievement of business objectives through IT standards. With more than 400 member organizations, it has a diverse membership that spans all sectors of the IT community — customers, systems and solutions suppliers, tool vendors, integrators, and consultants, as well as academics and researchers. The group has a cloud working group and has lots of good source material available. Check out its website at www3.opengroup.org.

Open-Source Offerings

Open source has become incredibly important, especially as a foundation for cloud computing. There is consistent support, for example, for Linux as the foundation for most of the cloud platforms. Therefore, open-source offerings, such as the following, are playing an increasingly important role.

» **The Apache Foundation (ASF):** This nonprofit corporation was founded in 1999 to support a variety of projects for the open-source developer community. The group offers software that is distributed as free under an Apache License. All projects are managed by active technical experts.

» **The Linux Foundation:** The Linux Foundation is the nonprofit consortium dedicated to fostering the growth of Linux. Founded in 2000, the Linux Foundation sponsors the work of Linux creator Linus Torvalds and is supported by leading technology companies and developers from around the world. The Linux Foundation promotes the platform and works with those vendors and customers that leverage Linux. Check out the Linux Foundation at www.linuxfoundation.org.

» **The Eclipse Foundation:** The Eclipse Foundation is an open-source community focused on providing a vendor-neutral open development platform and application frameworks for building software. It's a nonprofit organization and has widespread participation from developers and corporations around the globe. The Eclipse platform is written in Java and runs on most popular operating systems, including Linux, HP-UX, AIX, Solaris, QNX, Mac OS X, and Windows. Check out the Eclipse Foundation at www.eclipse.org.

» **Open Cloud Computing Interface:** The Open Cloud Computing Interface (OCCI; http://occi-wg.org) is made up of a set of open community-led specifications delivered through the Open Grid Forum. The group is based on its development of a protocol and API for all types of management tasks.

OCCI was originally initiated to create a remote management API for IaaS-based services, allowing for the development of interoperable tools for common tasks including deployment, autonomic scaling, and monitoring. It has since evolved into a flexible API with a strong focus on integration, portability, interoperability, and innovation, while still offering a high degree of extensibility.

The current release of the Open Cloud Computing Interface is compatible with many other models in addition to IaaS, including, for example, PaaS and SaaS.

» **OpenStack:** OpenStack is an open-source platform originated by Rackspace and NASA for building both public and private clouds. It is supported by more than 150 companies. The organization has hundreds of different initiatives underway. Check out its website at http://openstack.org. The group also has a Wiki which can be found at http://wiki.openstack.org/.

The Cloud Security Alliance

The Cloud Security Alliance (CSA) was established to promote the use of best practices for providing and ensuring security within cloud computing, and to educate people about the uses of cloud computing to help secure all other forms of computing. Check out its website at https://cloudsecurityalliance.org.

The Cloud Storage Initiative

The Storage Networking Industry Association (SNIA) is a trade organization focused on the networked storage industry. The cloud storage initiative focuses on the needs for cloud storage standards. Its strategic goal is to lead the storage industry worldwide in developing and promoting standards, technologies, and educational services to empower organizations in the management of information. Check out its website at www.snia.org.

Vendor Sites

All the major cloud computing vendors provide great resources online. We recommend checking out vendors such as Google, VMware, Dell, Amazon, IBM, Microsoft, HP, Cisco, Salesforce.com, ServiceNow, and Oracle. Consulting firms and systems integrators, such as Accenture, Wipro, Cognizant, and Deloitte, also offer content that will help provide perspective about cloud computing services and industry best practices.

This is only a partial list. Hundreds of vendors are in the space, so don't stop with this list; check sites of all the vendors we mention throughout the book. You can find great resources on systems integrators' sites. Take advantage.

Cloud Computing Conferences

One of the best ways to learn about what is happening in cloud computing is to go to one of the conferences. Since cloud computing has become so ubiquitous almost all conferences provide lots of meaningful sessions about cloud computing. There are local meet-ups that allow you to get together with other interested parties to exchange ideas.

CIO.gov

CIO.gov is the website of the U.S. CIO (chief information officer) and the Federal CIO Council, serving as a central resource for information on federal IT. By showcasing examples of innovation, identifying best practices, and providing a forum for federal IT leaders, CIO.gov keeps the public informed about how our government is working to close the technology gap between the private and public sectors. Check out its website at www.cio.gov.

Open Data Center Alliance

The Open Data Center Alliance (ODCA) is an independent organization that is developing a unified vision for cloud requirements — particularly focused on open, interoperable solutions for secure cloud federation, automation of cloud infrastructure, common management, and transparency of cloud service delivery. Check out its website at www.opendatacenteralliance.org.

Chapter **19**

Ten Cloud Do's and Don'ts

M any companies that have begun to move into the cloud don't do a lot of planning. Executives in different business units began to use public cloud services out of frustration because of inefficiencies in the IT organization. Over time, the cloud has taken a front seat in the way the overall business is approaching its future of computing platforms.

It is increasingly clear that it is no longer good practice to simply move ahead with cloud services without a plan. Without careful planning things will invariably go wrong. In this chapter, we give you some ideas about what you should do and what you should avoid as you begin your journey to the cloud.

Do Plan for Cloud Native

As your cloud strategy matures, you should begin to think about building services based on a cloud native architecture. One of the benefits of cloud native is that you are building services that are designed specifically to operate in the cloud. A key benefit of cloud native services are modular and are therefore built with microservices and packaged in containers.

You will want to focus on a continuous development and deployment approach so that your applications and services are constantly evolving based on changing customer needs.

Do Plan for Data Consistency and Manageability

Ironically, one of the reasons companies look to cloud computing is to move away from the silos of data. In the highly distributed model of the cloud, data is stored across a wide variety of applications and services. There are many issues confronting businesses as they look for ways to manage data so that it can be effectively used to help the business understand results and plan for the future.

Although many tools allow data to be integrated across silos, it is more difficult than it may appear. To be successful, it is important that there be a common catalog where data elements are defined and managed. It is important that the organization understands the nature of stored data — for example, can data be readily shared or are there restrictions based on privacy requirements?

You also need to understand how the data can be used and who is allowed to access and change that data. You also have to consider where data needs to be located. For example, certain countries have rules that restrict where personal data can reside. When you need a fast response, you may want to place data near the source where queries are taking place. Security, governance, and manageability are top issues for managing data in the cloud.

Do Decide and Plan for Cloud Services

Public cloud services offer incredible ease of use and flexibility to add and subtract services as needs change. Increasingly, businesses are finding that they're using more than one public cloud across the organization. For example, one set of developers may have standardized on a specific public cloud while another business unit may rely on a different platform. It is not uncommon for one company to use as many as five public clouds. In addition, these same businesses may be using hundreds of different SaaS applications. It can be difficult to keep track of all of the cloud services that are being used. It is therefore important to use tools that can discover what services are being used and by which departments.

In some cases, you'll be in a good position to negotiate advantageous financial terms with cloud providers. When selecting public clouds, it will be important to focus on those that are using standards such as Kubernetes, Istio, and Dockers so that you have a better chance of having some level of portability across cloud services. When you determine that you need private cloud services, review the offerings that use the same standards as those available on the public cloud. Consistency will make planning and execution much easier in the long term.

Do Have a Service Management Plan

As the hybrid cloud that consists of many different services in many different deployment models, you need to prepare for multicloud and hybrid cloud management. You do need to start thinking about all your public cloud services, platform services, SaaS applications, private clouds, and data center services and applications as a unified computing environment. There are many different levels of management that you need to consider and plan for. Do decide what is practical to do right away and what you'll do over time as technology matures.

Initially, for example, you need to be able to monitor each service that you use for performance and security. Test new service management products and services as they become available so you're ready when these services are mature enough to support your long-term plan. Begin evaluating management platforms that provide you with visibility across your entire computing environment. In the long run, you'll want to understand performance across all services as though they were one computer.

REMEMBER

The bottom line is that you want to demonstrate to your internal customers, external customers, and partners that you can provide them with a well-managed computing experience.

Do Plan for Portability

Many companies that are using SaaS don't make plans for the future, including what happens if their SaaS vendor goes out of business or becomes too expensive. Another issue to consider for the future is what you'll do if you discover a different SaaS vendor who is better able to meet your needs.

TIP

You do need a plan for how you can move your data from one cloud environment to another. Make sure that your selected vendors provide a simple and inexpensive way to move your data. You don't want to be surprised. With the advent of microservices and containers, it's becoming more likely that you'll be able to focus on portability. It may not be as easy as you would like, but it's an important practice to get ready for the future.

Do Plan for Security

Security can't be ignored in a cloud environment. In fact, fear of security breaches is one of the primary reasons that management is hesitant to move key services to the cloud.

REMEMBER

Security is more than simply putting workloads behind the firewall. Organizations have to make sure that they have security across all their assets across all the cloud services they're using. One of the biggest risks is to make sure that sensitive data is protected through encryption techniques. Do make sure that you have a well-constructed plan to protect your data no matter where it lives.

Do Execute on an Overall Hybrid Cloud Plan

When you're creating a cloud strategy, it's important to think about an overall plan for the services that will live across the public and private clouds and the data center. Many cloud services will be shared by developers in your company and with contractors. These same services may become product offerings that you provide to partners and customers. It's therefore important that services are well tested, monitored, and catalogued.

At the same time, you have to know what your company's IT assets are so that you can create a hybrid environment that's accurate and efficient. Unless you control the quality of your overall environment, your company will be at risk. If you're using a public cloud or a SaaS application, does your management care whether your application and data reside in a multi-tenant environment?

In most cases, multi-tenant is a secure and well-managed environment. However, you may have circumstances where your management team wants to isolate your company's intellectual property from those belonging to other businesses. While it may not be technically necessary, it may be a governance requirement demanded by the business.

Don't Rely on only a Single Vendor

WARNING

It's tempting to find a cloud vendor you like and stop. However, that can be a mistake. Do plan to work with more than one cloud vendor so that you're not stuck if something happens. Anything can happen. A vendor can have a catastrophic failure and be out of commission for a few hours or a few days. For example, if you're developing and deploying an important application, you may want to have it replicated in several regions or on several different clouds.

You won't understand these distinctions until you have some experience with cloud computing. This is especially important when you're working in a hybrid cloud environment. You may find that certain cloud services require the capabilities of a high-performance network. Other services may not require this type of sophisticated performance. You need to plan for all the different requirements.

Don't Over-Invest in Licenses

WARNING

Many cloud vendors create packages to make it attractive for their customers to buy in bulk. So, it's tempting to buy more licenses for more years because of price. However, this can be a trap if you over-buy.

For example, a vendor might offer you half the list price per user per month if you sign up for 100 users over three years. The price is so attractive that you take the plunge, only to discover that you really are supporting only 25 users. No vendor is going to let you scale down those licenses once you have signed your contract.

At the same time, keep track of the tools you use to enhance your SaaS applications. Are these tools provided by independent vendors with well-defined APIs? Are the tools proprietary to that application? You need to determine which approach is going to service you best in the long term.

Don't Overlook the Need to Manage Infrastructure

One of the reasons companies are attracted to the cloud is that they don't have to worry about the details of managing software and infrastructure. However, don't be fooled. Even if you're using only a couple of public cloud services, you need to keep track of the performance of these vendors. If you're using a customer relationship management SaaS platform and it's unavailable for a couple of days, who is to blame? It's quite likely that the sales and marketing team will blame the IT department, not the vendor. Increasingly, IT will have to provide performance, governance, and security oversight of cloud services.

Don't Leave Your Data Center Alone

It might be a relief to use cloud services to get around some of the inconsistencies and complexities of the existing data center. However, it's dangerous to assume that the data center should wither and die. The data center will remain viable for many years to come. However, you need to continue to transform it so that it can work in collaboration with cloud services. So, don't leave your data center in the dark. Begin to plan a strategy to optimize the data center so that it handles the applications and tasks it's best suited for.

Don't Ignore the Service Level Agreement

All public cloud vendors, including IaaS, PaaS, and SaaS providers, will offer some sort of service level agreement that explains what obligation the vendor assumes and what risks you have to assume.

REMEMBER

No vendor will take on obligations it doesn't have to. So, it's up to you to read the fine print and understand exactly what reality looks like. For example, no cloud vendor will reimburse you if you lose business because the service is not operational. The vendor may indeed give you the money back that you spent on a service, but that will be small comfort if you've lost an important customer.

So, you must decide how much risk is acceptable. This information will help you determine which services can reside with a commodity cloud service provider, which ones need to be with a provider that offers a higher level of service, and which services should remain in your private cloud.

Do Move Forward and Don't Look Back

We think that the movement to the cloud is inevitable. However, it's not a strategy that you should adopt without careful planning. You must deal with issues in the cloud that are very different than those you encounter in a traditional data center. Software license models are different. Vendors take some responsibility for protecting your data and the performance of your services. However, the responsibility will land with your own company. Therefore, you need to move forward armed with the right information and with the right level of caution. However, if you take the right steps, we think that the future can be quite exciting.

Glossary

abstraction: The idea of minimizing the complexity of something by hiding the details and just providing the relevant information. It's about providing a high-level specification rather than going into lots of detail about how something works. In the cloud, for example, in an IaaS delivery model, the infrastructure is abstracted from the user.

access control: Determining who or what can go where, when, and how.

ACID: An acronym for *atomicity, consistency, isolation,* and *durability,* which are the main requirements for proper transaction processing.

Alibaba Cloud: A set of public and private cloud service operated by Chinese cloud vendor, Alibaba Group.

API (application programming interface): A collection of subroutine calls that allows computer programs to use a software system.

application life cycle: The process of maintaining a piece of code so that it's consistent and predictable as it's changed to support business requirements.

architecture: In information technology, the design approach taken in developing a program or system.

archiving: The process by which database or file data that's seldom used or outdated but that's required for historical or audit reasons is copied to a cheaper form of storage. The storage medium may be online, tape, or optical disc.

asset management: Software that allows organizations to record all information about their hardware and software. Most such applications capture cost information, license information, and so on. Such information belongs in the configuration management database. See also *CMDB.*

audit: A check on the effectiveness of a task or set of tasks, and how the tasks are managed and documented.

audit trail: A trace of a sequence of events in a clerical or computer system. This audit usually identifies the creation or modification of any element in the system, who did it, and (possibly) why it was done.

authentication: The process by which the identity of a person or computer process is verified.

AWS (Amazon Web Services): The set of web services that Amazon offers to help web developers build web applications and use Amazon's cloud computing environment.

Azure: An operating system for cloud computing from Microsoft. The hosting and management environment are maintained at Microsoft data centers, so there's no need to use internal data center resources when developing applications in Azure.

backup: A utility that copies databases, files, or subsets of databases and files to a storage medium. This copy can be used to restore the data in case of serious failure.

bandwidth: Technically, the range of frequencies over which a device can send or receive signals. The term is also used to denote the maximum data transfer rate, measured in bits per second, that a communications channel can handle.

batch: A non-interactive process that runs in a queue, usually when the system load is lowest, generally used for processing batches of information in a serial and usually efficient manner. Batch process can't be used if you want insights from real-time data. Early computers were capable of only batch processing. Today, batch is frequently used to process large data sets for Hadoop.

best practice: A proven and effective way to execute a process. It can relate to anything from writing program code to IT governance.

binding: Making the necessary connections among software components so that they can interact.

biometrics: Using a person's unique physical characteristics to prove his identity to a computer — by employing a fingerprint scanner or voice analyzer, for example.

black box: A component or device with an input and an output whose inner workings need not be understood by or accessible to the user.

BPaaS: See *Business Process as a Service*.

BPEL (Business Process Execution Language): A computer language based on WSDL (Web Services Description Language, an XML format for describing web services) and designed for programming business services. See also *XML*.

BPM (business process management): A technology and methodology for controlling the activities — both automated and manual — needed to make a business function.

broker: In computer programming, a program that accepts requests from one software layer or component and translates them into a form that can be understood by another layer or component.

browser: A program that lets you access information on the Internet. Originally browsers could only operate on a person computer. However, now there are browsers that support mobile devices and sensors.

bus: A technology that connects multiple components so they can communicate with one another. In essence, a bus is a connection capability. A bus can be software (such as an enterprise service bus) or hardware (such as a memory bus). See also *ESB*.

business process: The codification of rules and practices that constitute a business.

Business Process as a Service (BPaaS): A whole business process is provided as a service involving little more than a software interface, such as a parcel delivery service.

business process modeling: A technique for transforming how business operates into a codified source in code so that it can be translated into software.

business rules: Constraints or actions that refer to the actual commercial world but may need to be encapsulated in service management or business applications.

business service: An individual function or activity that is directly useful to the business.

cache: The storage of data so that future requests for that data can be achieved more quickly.

center of excellence: A group of key people from all areas of the business and operations that focuses on best practices. A center of excellence provides guidance across the business to help organizations take advantage of proven methods to achieve predictable results. This group also becomes a force for change, because it can leverage its growing knowledge to help business units benefit from experience.

change management: The management of change in operational processes and applications.

cloud computing: A computing model that makes IT resources and applications available as services to business organizations in a self-service manner.

cloud ecosystem: Independent software and hardware vendors that partner with cloud providers to create a partnership for selling to customers.

CMDB (configuration management database): In general, a repository of service management data.

COBIT (Control Objectives for Information and Related Technology): An IT framework with a focus on governance and managing technical and business risks.

component: A piece of computer software that can be used as a building block in larger systems. Components can be parts of business applications that have been made accessible through web service–related standards and technologies, such as restful APIs See also *microservices* and *web service*.

compute unit: A measure of the cost and capacity of a cloud workload. For example, within its EC2 service, Amazon uses computer units to measure the infrastructure used by virtual server instances. Currently, one EC2 Compute Unit provides the equivalent CPU capacity of a 1.0–1.2 GHz 2007 Opteron or 2007 Xeon processor. Other IaaS providers also have units for measuring resource usage.

configuration: The complete description of the way in which the constituent elements of a software product or system interrelate, both in functional and physical terms.

configuration management: The management of configurations, normally involving holding configuration data in a database so that the data can be managed and changed where necessary.

container: In computer programming, a data structure or object used to manage collections of other objects in an organized way. Often microservices are stored inside a container. There are a number of emerging container open-source offerings, including Dockers, CRI-O, Containerd, and frakti. Kubernetes has become the de facto standard for container orchestration.

container orchestration: A typical application may include a number of containers that are integrated together through container orchestration — or a process for managing how containers are intended to be used to execute a process.

CRM (customer relationship management): Software intended to help you run your sales force and customer support operations.

data cleansing: Software used to identify potential data-quality problems. If a customer is listed multiple times in a customer database because of variations in the spelling of her name, the data-cleansing software makes corrections to help standardize the data.

data fabric: The part of the computer network devoted to transmissions.

data federation: Data access to a variety of data stores, using consistent rules and definitions that enable all the data stores to be treated as a single resource.

data profiling: A technique or process that helps you understand the content, structure, and relationships of your data. This process also helps you validate your data against technical and business rules.

data quality: Characteristics of data such as consistency, accuracy, reliability, completeness, timeliness, reasonableness, and validity. Data-quality software ensures that data elements are represented in a consistent way across different data stores or systems, making the data more trustworthy across the enterprise.

data transformation: A process by which the format of data is changed so it can be used by different applications.

data warehouse: A large data store containing the organization's historical data, which is used primarily for data analysis and data mining.

database: A computer system intended to store large amounts of information reliably and in an organized fashion. Most databases provide users convenient access to the data, along with helpful search capabilities.

dedicated hosting: Dedicated hosting is where the customer is given full control over the server that's hosted in the cloud. This contrasts with managed hosting, where management is the responsibility of the hosting company.

dedicated server: A dedicated server is one the customer doesn't share with other users of the hosting cloud service.

directory: The word is used in both computing and telephony to indicate an organized map of devices, files, or people.

distributed processing: Spreading the work of an information-processing application among several computers.

early binding: Making necessary connections among software components when the software system is first put together or built.

EC2 (Elastic Compute Cloud from Amazon): Amazon's commercial Infrastructure as a Service (IaaS) web service that pioneered cloud computing.

elasticity: The ability to expand or shrink a computing resource in real time, based on need.

emulation: When hardware or software, or a combination of both, duplicates the functionality of a computer system in a different, second system. The behavior of the second system will closely resemble the original functionality of the first system. See also *virtualization*.

ERP (enterprise resource planning): A packaged set of business applications that combine business rules, process, and data management into a single integrated environment to support a business.

ESB (enterprise service bus): A distributed middleware software system that allows computer applications to communicate in a standardized way.

eSCM (eSourcing Capability Model): A framework developed at Carnegie Mellon University to provide a best-practices model for improving relationships between customers and suppliers in outsourcing agreements.

ETL (Extract, Transform, Load): Tools for locating and accessing data from a data store (data extraction), changing the structure or format of the data so it can be used by the business application (data transformation), and sending the data to the business application (data load).

eTOM (enhanced Telecom Operations Map): A framework that provides a business process model for the telecommunications industry.

fault tolerance: The ability of a system to provide uninterrupted service despite the failure of one or more of the system's components.

federation: The combination of disparate things so that they can act as one — as in federated states, data, or identity management — and to make sure that all the right rules apply.

framework: A support structure for developing software products.

Google Cloud Platform (GCP): Google's public cloud service offering.

governance: The ability to ensure that corporate or governmental rules and regulations are conformed with. Governance is combined with compliance and security issues across computing environments.

granularity: An important software design concept, especially in relation to components, referring to the amount of detail or functionality — from fine to coarse — provided in a service component. One software component can do something quite simple, such as calculate a square root; another has a great deal of detail and functionality to represent a complex business rule or workflow. The first component is fine grained, and the second is coarse grained. Developers often aggregate fine-grained services into coarse-grained services to create a business service.

grid computing: A step beyond distributed processing, involving large numbers of networked computers (often geographically dispersed and possibly of different types and capabilities) that are harnessed to solve a common problem. A grid computing model can be used instead of virtualization in situations that require real time where latency is unacceptable.

hardware partitioning: The act of subdividing and isolating elements of a physical server into fractions, each of which can run an operating system or an application.

HTML (Hypertext Markup Language): A data-encoding scheme invented by Tim Berners-Lee in 1991 and the basic way that information is encoded over the World Wide Web.

HTTP (Hypertext Transport Protocol): The basic way that information is linked and transmitted over the World Wide Web. HTTPS is a version of HTTP with encryption for security.

hybrid cloud: A computing environment that includes the use of public and private clouds as well as data center resources in a coordinated fashion.

hypervisor: Hardware that allows multiple operating systems to share a single host. The hypervisor sits at the lowest levels of the hardware environment and uses a thin layer of code in software to enable dynamic resource sharing. The hypervisor makes it seem like each operating system has the resources all to itself.

IaaS: See *Infrastructure as a Service.*

IBM Cloud: IBM's public and private cloud service.

identity management: Keeping track of a single user's (or asset's) identity throughout an engagement with a system or set of systems.

information integration: A process using software to link data sources in various departments or regions of the organization with an overall goal of creating more reliable, consistent, and trusted information.

infrastructure: The fundamental systems necessary for the ordinary operation of anything, be it a country or an IT department. The physical infrastructure that people rely on includes roads, electrical wiring, and water systems. In IT, infrastructure includes basic computer hardware, networks, operating systems, and other software that applications run on top of.

Infrastructure as a Service (Iaas): Infrastructure, including a management interface and associated software, provided to companies from the cloud as a service.

infrastructure services: Services provided by the infrastructure. In IT, these services include all the software needed to make devices talk to one another, for starters.

Internet: A huge computer network linking almost all the computers in the world and enabling them to communicate via standard protocols (TCP/IP) and data formats. See also *SMTP, TCP/IP,* and *XML*.

interoperability: The ability of a product to interface with many other products; usually used in the context of software.

IP (Internet Protocol): A codified technique for communicating data across a packet-switched network. IP can also mean intellectual property such as patents, trademarks, copyrights, and trade secrets. See also *TCP/IP*.

ISO (International Organization for Standardization): An organization that has developed more than 17,000 international standards, including standards for IT service management and corporate governance of information technology.

ITIL (Information Technology Infrastructure Library): A framework and set of standards for IT governance based on best practices.

JCA (J2EE Connector Architecture): A technology that enables Java programs to talk to other software, such as databases and legacy applications.

KPI (key performance indicator): An indicator used to measure the effectiveness of a process.

Kubernetes: Kubernetes is an open-source container-orchestration system for automating application deployment, scaling, and management. It was originally designed by Google, and is now maintained by the Cloud Native Computing Foundation.

LAMP (Linux, Apache, MySQL, PHP, Perl, or Python): An increasingly popular open source approach to building web applications. LAMP is a software bundle made up of the *L*inux operating system; the *A*pache web server; a *M*ySQL database; and a scripting language, such as PHP, Perl, or Python.

late binding: Deferring the necessary connections among applications to when the connection is first needed. Late binding allows more flexibility for changes than early binding does, but it imposes some cost in processing time.

latency: The amount of time lag that enables a service to execute in an environment. Some applications require less latency and need to respond in near real time, whereas other applications are less time-sensitive.

legacy application: Any application more than a few years old. When applications can't be disposed of and replaced easily, they become legacy applications. The good news is that they're still doing something useful when selected pieces of code can be turned into business services with new standardized interfaces.

Linux: An open source operating system based upon and similar to Unix. In cloud computing, Linux is the dominant operating system, primarily because it is supported by a large number of vendors and is the predominate cloud operating system.

Linux web hosting: The vast majority of websites run on the Linux operating system managed by a Linux web hosting service using the LAMP (Linux, Apache, MySQL, PHP) software stack.

loose coupling: An approach to distributed software applications in which components interact by passing data and requests to other components in a standardized way that minimizes dependencies among components. The emphasis is on simplicity and autonomy. Each component offers a small range of simple services to other components.

malware: The general term for computer software that intentionally does ill, such as viruses, Trojans, worms, and spyware.

markup language: A way of encoding information that uses plain text containing special tags often delimited by angle brackets (< and >). Specific markup languages are often created, based on XML, to standardize the interchange of information between different computer systems and services. See also *XML*.

mashup: A program (possibly installed on a web page) that combines content from more than one source, such as Google Maps and a real estate listing service.

master-slave: An arrangement in which one system or process is designated as a controller and other participating systems or processes respond to this controller. Should a master fail, the slaves are unable to continue.

metadata: The definitions, mappings, and other characteristics used to describe how to find, access, and use the company's data and software components.

metadata repository: A container of consistent definitions of business data and rules for mapping data to its actual physical locations in the system.

microservices: An architectural style that decomposes an application into a collection of services that are loosely coupled and independently deployable.

middleware: Multipurpose software that lives at a layer between the operating system and application in distributed computing environments.

mission critical: An application that a business cannot afford to be without at any time.

MOM (Message Oriented Middleware): A precursor to the enterprise service bus. See also *ESB*.

multi-tenancy: The situation where a single instance of an application runs on a SaaS vendor's servers, but serves multiple client organizations (tenants), keeping all their data separate. In a multi-tenant architecture, a software application partitions its data and configuration so that each customer has a customized virtual application instance.

MySQL: An open-source option to SQL.

NAS (Networked Attached Storage): A disk that includes its own network address rather than being tied to a server.

.NET: Pronounced *dot-net;* a Microsoft programming framework, with heavy emphasis on web services. See also *web service*.

network: The connection of computer systems (nodes) by communications channels and appropriate software.

NoSQL: A set of technologies that created a broad array of database management systems that are distinct from relational database systems. One major difference is that SQL is not used as the primary query language. These database management systems are also designed for distributed data stores.

OASIS (Organization for the Advancement of Structured Information Standards): A consortium promoting e-business and web services standards.

Oracle Cloud Platform: Oracle's public and private cloud services.

open source: A movement in the software industry that makes programs available along with the source code used to create them so that others can inspect and modify how programs work.

P2P (peer to peer): A networking system in which nodes in a network exchange data directly instead of going through a central server.

PaaS: See *Platform as a Service.*

Perl (Practical Extraction and Report Language): A powerful scripting language in widespread use in system administration, web development, and other activities.

PHP (PHP Hypertext Processor): An open-source scripting language (originally designed in Perl) used especially for producing dynamic web pages.

Platform as a Service (PaaS): A cloud service that abstracts the computing services including the operating software and the development and deployment and management life cycle. It sits on top of Infrastructure as a Service.

portal: In computing, a window that contains a means of access, often a menu, to all the applications throughout the whole network that the user is able to run. Often, the window is segmented into smaller windows, or *portlets,* that provide direct access to applications such as stock-market price feeds or email.

private cloud: A single tenant cloud service that operates within a company's data center.

programming in the large: An approach to developing business software that focuses on the various tasks or business processes needed to make the business function — processing an order, for example, or checking product availability — as opposed to more low-level technical tasks such as opening a file.

protocol: A set of rules that computers use to establish and maintain communication among themselves.

provisioning: Making resources available to users and software. A provisioning system makes applications available to users and makes server resources available to applications.

public cloud: A multi-tenant cloud service available to any consumer either on a fee per transaction service or as a free service.

real time: A form of processing in which a computer system accepts and updates data at the same time, feeding back immediate results that influence the data source.

real-time event processing: A class of applications that demand timely response to actions that take place out in the world. Typical examples include automated stock trading and RFID. See also *RFID*.

registry: A single source for all the metadata needed to gain access to a web service or software component.

repository: A database for software and components, with an emphasis on revision control and configuration management (where they keep the good stuff, in other words).

resource pool: A set of compute, storage, or data services that are combined to be used across hybrid environments.

response time: The time from the moment at which a transaction is submitted by a user or an application to the moment at which the final result of that transaction is made known to the user or application.

REST (representational state transfer): A software architecture style interface that is commonly used to provide flexible interaction and often stateless interaction in highly distributed environments, including the cloud. REST and SOAP are used in Amazon's S3. See also *SOAP*.

RFID (radio frequency identification): A technology that uses small, inexpensive chips attached to products (or even animals) that then transmit a unique identification number over a short distance to a special radio transmitter/receiver.

RPC (remote procedure call): A way for a program running on one computer to run a subprogram on another computer.

S3 (Simple Storage Service): A distributed storage service, from Amazon, that constitutes part of AWS. Amazon provides the capability to read, write, and delete objects (of data) that are up to 5GB in size. This isn't a database capability — just a place to store and access files. See also *AWS*.

SaaS: See *Software as a Service.*

SAML (Security Assertion Markup Language): A standard framework for exchanging authentication and authorization information (that is, credentials) in an XML format called *assertions.*

SAN (storage area network): A high-speed network of interconnected storage devices. These storage devices might be servers, optical disk drives, or other storage media. The difference between a SAN and a NAS is that a SAN runs at a higher speed than a NAS, while a NAS is generally easier to install and provides a file system.

Sarbanes-Oxley: The Public Company Accounting Reform and Investor Protection Act of 2002, a U.S. law enhancing standards for all U.S. public companies' boards of directors, resulting in substantial new requirements for corporate IT.

scalability: As regards to hardware, the ability to go from small to large amounts of processing power with the same architecture. It also applies to software products such as databases, in which case it refers to the consistency of performance per unit of power as hardware resources increase.

scripting language: A computer programming language that is interpreted and has access to all or most operating-system facilities. Common examples include Perl, Python, Ruby, and JavaScript. It is often easier to program in a scripting language, but the resulting programs generally run more slowly than those created in compiled languages such as C and C++.

semantics: In computer programming, what the data means as opposed to formatting rules (syntax).

server farm: A room filled with computer servers, often needed to run large Internet sites.

serverless: A cloud execution model that dynamically manages a machine resource. It is intended to simplify the way code is deployed into production in a cloud environment.

service: A purposeful activity carried out for the benefit of a known target. Services are often made up of a group of component services, some of which may also have component services. Services always transform something, and they complete by delivering an output.

service catalog: A directory of IT services provided across the enterprise, including information such as service description, access rights, and ownership.

service desk: A single point of contact for IT users and customers to report any issues they may have with the IT service (or, in some cases, with IT's customer service).

SLA (service level agreement): A document that captures the understanding between a service user and a service provider as to quality and timeliness.

service management: Monitoring and optimizing a service to ensure that it meets the critical outcomes that the customer values and the stakeholders want to provide.

servlet: A program that runs on a web server in response to an action taken by the user via a browser.

silo: In IT, an application with a single narrow focus, such as human resources management or inventory control, with no intention or preparation for use by others.

Six Sigma: A statistical term meaning six standard deviations from the norm and the name of a quality-improvement program that aims at reducing errors to one in a million.

SMTP (Simple Mail Transfer Protocol): The basic method used to transmit electronic mail (email) over the Internet.

SOA (service oriented architecture): An approach to building applications that implements business processes or services by using a set of loosely coupled black-box components orchestrated to deliver a well-defined level of service.

SOAP (Simple Object Access Protocol): A protocol specification for exchanging data. Along with REST, it is used for storing and retrieving data in the Amazon storage cloud. See also *REST*.

Software as a Service (SaaS): The delivery of computer applications over the Internet.

SQL (Structured Query Language): The most popular computer language for accessing and manipulating databases.

SSL (Secure Sockets Layer): A popular method for making secure connections over the Internet, first introduced by Netscape.

standards: A core set of common, repeatable best practices and protocols that have been agreed on by a business or industry group. Typically, vendors, industry user groups, and end users collaborate to develop standards based on the broad expertise of a large number of stakeholders. Organizations can leverage these standards as a common foundation and innovate on top of them.

subroutine: A piece of computer code that can easily be used (called) by many other programs, as long as they are on the same computer and (usually) are written in the same programming language.

TCP/IP (Transmission Control Protocol/Internet Protocol): The complex stack of communications protocols that underlies the Internet. All data is broken into small packets that are sent independently over the network and reassembled at the final destination.

thin client: Client hardware in the client/server environment that is dependent on the server for loading applications. Most hardware designed for this purpose is similar to a cut-down PC, with no floppy disk drive or hard drive.

throughput: The rate at which transactions are completed in a system.

tiered storage: The assignment of data to different types of media, generally to reduce storage costs. Data is placed into tiers 1, 2, or 3, depending on how often it must be accessed or how critical it is.

TLS (Transport Layer Security): A newer name for SSL. See also *SSL*.

TQM (Total Quality Management): A popular quality-improvement program.

transaction: A computer action that represents a business event, such as debiting an account. When a transaction starts, it must either complete or not happen at all.

UDDI (Universal Description, Discovery, and Integration): A platform-independent, XML-based services registry sponsored by OASIS. See also *OASIS* and *XML*.

utility computing: A metered service that acts like a public service based on payment for use of a measured amount of a component or asset.

virtual memory: The use of a disk to store active areas of memory to make the available memory appear larger.

virtualization: When one computer runs software that allows it to emulate another machine. This kind of emulation is commonly known as virtualization. See also *emulation*.

VPN (virtual private network): A VPN uses a public telecommunications infrastructure to provide secure access. This is a virtual network dedicated to providing a customer with more security within a cloud environment. Each VPN runs its own operating system, bandwidth, and disk space, and can be individually booted.

W3C: A handy way of referring to the World Wide Web Consortium, an organization that coordinates standards for the World Wide Web.

web service: A software component created with an interface consisting of a WSDL definition, an XML schema definition, and a WS-Policy definition. Collectively, components could be called a service contract — or, alternatively, an API. See also *API, WSDL, WS-Policy,* and *XML*.

workflow: A sequence of steps needed to carry out a business process. Workflow technology automates the passage of information between the steps.

World Wide Web: A system built on top of the Internet that displays hyperlinked pages of information that can contain a wide variety of data formats, including multimedia.

WSCI (Web Services Choreography Interface): An XML-based interface description language that describes the flow of messages exchanged by a web service when it participates in choreographed interactions with other services.

WSDL (Web Services Description Language): An XML format for describing web services.

WS-Policy (Web Services Policy): The Web Services Policy Framework, which provides a means of expressing the capabilities, requirements, and characteristics of software components in a web services system.

WSRP (Web Services for Remote Portlets): A protocol that allows portlets to communicate by using standard web services interfaces.

XML (eXtensible Markup Language): A way of presenting data as plain-text files that has become the lingua franca of SOA. In XML, as in HTML, data is delimited in tags that are enclosed in angle brackets (< and >), although the tags in XML can have many more meanings. See also *SOA*.

XML Schema: A language for defining and describing the structure of XML documents.

XSD (XML Schema Definition): The description of what can be in an XML document.

XSLT (eXtensible Stylesheet Language Transformations): A computer language, based on XML, that specifies how to change one XML document into another. See also *XML*.

Index

About the Authors

Daniel D. Kirsch is a consultant, analyst, and thought leader focused on how emerging technologies such as cloud, AI, machine learning, and advanced analytics are impacting businesses. Dan is particularly interested in how businesses use these emerging technologies to alter their approaches to data management, information security, governance, and risk. Dan has consulted directly with executive leadership teams at technology firms who must make strategic changes to their businesses. In addition, he provides advisory services to technology vendors. He assists these vendors in aligning their solutions with enterprise requirements. Dan is viewed as an expert in understanding cloud, AI, and security solutions and mapping them to the complex needs of business across industries. He developed the Hurwitz & Associates security audit and assessment tools. These tools help customers determine how well they are achieving compliance, and outline practical next steps.

Dan earned his B.A. in Political Science from Union College in New York and a J.D. from Boston College Law School, where he focused on emerging corporate strategies and intellectual property. As an attorney, Dan represented start-ups, cloud computing ventures, and young companies seeking financing. Dan has co-authored two other business technology books: *Augmented Intelligence: The Business Power of Human–Machine Collaboration* (CRC Press, 2020) and *Hybrid Cloud For Dummies* (John Wiley & Sons, 2012) as well as reports and custom publications in the areas of security, mobility, and analytics.

Judith S. Hurwitz is president and CEO of Hurwitz & Associates, LLC, a research and consulting firm focused on emerging technology including cloud computing, artificial intelligence, cognitive computing, service management, software development, and security and governance. She is a technology strategist, thought leader and author. A pioneer in anticipating technology innovation and adoption, she has served as a trusted advisor to many industry leaders over the years. Judith has consulted for senior management teams for some of the largest technology companies in the market as well as start-ups. In addition, Judith has served on several advisory boards. Prior to starting Hurwitz & Associates, she founded two other companies. She was the founder of CycleBridge, a life sciences software consulting firm and Hurwitz Group, a research and consulting firm. She has worked in various corporations, including Apollo Computer and John Hancock. Judith has written extensively about all aspects of enterprise and distributed software. Judith is a co-author on *Augmented Intelligence: The Business Power of Human-Machine Collaboration* (CRC Press, 2019) and *Cognitive Computing and Big Data Analytics* (Wiley, 2015). In 2011, she authored *Smart or Lucky? How Technology Leaders Turn Chance into Success.* (Jossey Bass, 2011).

She also co-authored seven retail For Dummies books including: *Big Data For Dummies, Hybrid Cloud For Dummies, Cloud Computing For Dummies, Service Management For Dummies,* and *Service Oriented Architecture For Dummies,* 1st and 2nd Editions (all John Wiley & Sons).

Judith holds B.S. and M.S. degrees from Boston University. She serves on several advisory boards of emerging companies. She is on the board of Boston University's College of Arts and Sciences and the Alumni Council.

Dedications

Dan:

To my wonderful wife, Sara, and my sons, Jack and Sam, who always keep us on our toes.

Judith:

I dedicate this book to my family — my husband and life partner, Warren; my children, Sara and David, and my two grandsons, Jack and Sammy.

Acknowledgment

We'd like to thank Fred Dalrymple for his help in completing this book.

Publisher's Acknowledgments

Executive Editor: Steve Hayes

Project Editor: Kelly Ewing

Technical Editor: Scott Proctor

Sr. Editorial Assistant: Cherie Case

Proofreader: Debbye Butler

Production Editor: Mohammed Zafar Ali

Cover Image: © Ivcandy/DigitalVision Vectors/ Getty Images

Leverage the power

Dummies is the global leader in the reference category and one of the most trusted and highly regarded brands in the world. No longer just focused on books, customers now have access to the dummies content they need in the format they want. Together we'll craft a solution that engages your customers, stands out from the competition, and helps you meet your goals.

Advertising & Sponsorships

Connect with an engaged audience on a powerful multimedia site, and position your message alongside expert how-to content. Dummies.com is a one-stop shop for free, online information and know-how curated by a team of experts.

- Targeted ads
- Video
- Email Marketing
- Microsites
- Sweepstakes sponsorship

20 **MILLION** PAGE VIEWS **EVERY SINGLE MONTH**

15 MILLION **UNIQUE** VISITORS PER MONTH

43% OF ALL VISITORS ACCESS THE SITE **VIA THEIR MOBILE DEVICES**

700,000 NEWSLETTER SUBSCRIPTION **TO THE INBOXES OF**

300,000 UNIQUE **INDIVIDUALS EVERY WEEK**

# of dummies

Custom Publishing

Reach a global audience in any language by creating a solution that will differentiate you from competitors, amplify your message, and encourage customers to make a buying decision.

- Apps
- Books
- eBooks
- Video
- Audio
- Webinars

Brand Licensing & Content

Leverage the strength of the world's most popular reference brand to reach new audiences and channels of distribution.

For more information, visit **dummies.com/biz**

PERSONAL ENRICHMENT

Staying Sharp

9781119187790
USA $26.00
CAN $31.99
UK £19.99

Facebook

9781119179030
USA $21.99
CAN $25.99
UK £16.99

Guitar

9781119293354
USA $24.99
CAN $29.99
UK £17.99

Investing

9781119293347
USA $22.99
CAN $27.99
UK £16.99

Beekeeping

9781119310068
USA $22.99
CAN $27.99
UK £16.99

Digital Photography

9781119235606
USA $24.99
CAN $29.99
UK £17.99

Meditation

9781119251163
USA $24.99
CAN $29.99
UK £17.99

Pregnancy

9781119235491
USA $26.99
CAN $31.99
UK £19.99

Samsung Galaxy S7

9781119279952
USA $24.99
CAN $29.99
UK £17.99

iPhone

9781119283133
USA $24.99
CAN $29.99
UK £17.99

Crocheting

9781119287117
USA $24.99
CAN $29.99
UK £16.99

Nutrition

9781119130246
USA $22.99
CAN $27.99
UK £16.99

PROFESSIONAL DEVELOPMENT

Windows 10

9781119311041
USA $24.99
CAN $29.99
UK £17.99

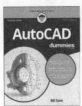

AutoCAD

9781119255796
USA $39.99
CAN $47.99
UK £27.99

Excel 2016

9781119293439
USA $26.99
CAN $31.99
UK £19.99

QuickBooks 2017

9781119281467
USA $26.99
CAN $31.99
UK £19.99

macOS Sierra

9781119280651
USA $29.99
CAN $35.99
UK £21.99

LinkedIn

9781119251132
USA $24.99
CAN $29.99
UK £17.99

Windows 10

9781119310563
USA $34.00
CAN $41.99
UK £24.99

SharePoint 2016

9781119181705
USA $29.99
CAN $35.99
UK £21.99

Fundamental Analysis

9781119263593
USA $26.99
CAN $31.99
UK £19.99

Networking

9781119257769
USA $29.99
CAN $35.99
UK £21.99

Office 2016

9781119293477
USA $26.99
CAN $31.99
UK £19.99

Office 365

9781119265313
USA $24.99
CAN $29.99
UK £17.99

Salesforce.com

9781119239314
USA $29.99
CAN $35.99
UK £21.99

Coding

9781119293323
USA $29.99
CAN $35.99
UK £21.99

dummies.com

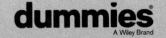